BRITISH COLUMBIA PLACE NAMES

MARK THORBURN

DRAGON
HILL

The Publisher: Dragon Hill Publishing Ltd.
Website: www.dragonhillpublishing.com

Library and Archives Canada Cataloguing in Publication

Thorburn, Mark, 1958–
      British Columbia place names / Mark Thorburn.

Includes bibliographical references.
ISBN 978-1-896124-46-9

      1. Names, Geographical—British Columbia.
2. British Columbia—History, Local. I. Title.

FC3806.T48 2010   917.11003   C2009-906390-5

Project Director: Gary Whyte
Project Editor: Nicholle Carrière
Cover Image: © S. Greg Panosian | iStockphoto

We acknowledge the support of the Alberta Foundation for the Arts for our publishing program.

PC: 5

CONTENTS

Introduction 5

British Columbia Place Names from A to Z 8

Appendix: Notes on Non-English Names and Words
and Names of British Columbia First Nations 323

Notes on Sources 323

DEDICATION

To "Grandpa" Martin Vanderhof, for knowing what's important in life and achieving it, and to Johnny Case and Tony Kirby, for having the courage to go out and seek it.

INTRODUCTION

B ritish Columbia is a land of many places. The province is over 900,000 square kilometres in size and has over 600 separate cities, district municipalities, towns, villages and unincorporated communities. And that's not including the many First Nations reserves, neighbourhoods (such as Vancouver's Kitsilano or Delta's Tsawwassen) and ghost towns. Forty percent of Canada's mountains are in British Columbia. There are thousands of islands, bays, inlets and coves off the coast and an equal number of rivers, streams, lakes and ponds throughout the province. And virtually all of these places have names. In fact, according to the third edition of the British Columbia volume of the *Gazetteer of Canada*, which was printed in 1985, there are over 42,500 officially recognized place names in the province.

These monikers come from a variety of sources. There are, of course, the First Nations. At one time, 32 distinct First Nations languages, along with a number of dialects, were spoken across British Columbia, and their legacy can be found in place names like Comox, Coquitlam, Haida Gwaii, Okanagan and Squamish. In addition, there is Chinook Jargon, a mixture of languages that was created and used to promote trade among a diverse population that otherwise could not communicate with one another. It, too, contributed to the variety of BC place names (for example, Cultus Lake).

Eighteenth-century Spanish naval explorers such as Alexandro Malaspina, Dionisio Alcalá-Galiano and Cayetano Valdés y Flores gave us such names as Texada Island. While sailing along British Columbia's coast between 1792 and 1794, British naval captain George Vancouver christened numerous places, including Burrard Inlet and Howe Sound. Other maritime explorers and fur traders such as George Dixon gave us monikers like Queen Charlotte Sound. And in the 19th century, Royal Navy surveyors such as Daniel Pender and George Richards were the first to identify Alert Bay and Mayne Island.

But that was not all. On the mainland, other explorers, fur traders and surveyors, including Alexander Mackenzie, Simon Fraser, David Thompson, George Dawson and the Hudson's Bay Company, left behind names like Fort Langley, Quesnel River and Victoria. The Fraser River and Cariboo gold rushes were responsible for such names as 100 Mile House, Barkerville and Boston Bar. The coming of the railways resulted in monikers like Revelstoke and Vanderhoof. Wartime brought British Columbia place names such as Ladysmith and Mount Bishop. Even mountaineers like Norman Collie and Arthur Wheeler christened such spots as Fleming Peak.

Locations were sometimes named for other places (for example, Richmond and Surrey), the famous and not so famous (Vancouver and Likely), geographic features (Delta), social movements (the Liberated Group), economic opportunities (Peachland) and even the whimsical (Naramata).

It is impossible to discuss the origins and history of all British Columbia's place names in a single volume. Choices had to be made. This book takes a look at the names of all the province's incorporated communities plus a number, but not all, of its unincorporated settlements, as well as the monikers of the tallest mountains, the largest lakes and islands, the longest rivers and other place names that might be considered significant, entertaining or of historical interest. Some inclusions and omissions can certainly be debated, but hopefully there is enough here to satisfy everyone's interest.

Enjoy!

1, 2, ...

70 MILE HOUSE (estimated pop. 450) This small community began when a roadhouse was built on the site in 1862. The name refers to its location, 70 miles along the Cariboo Wagon Road from Mile 0, at Lillooet.

100 MILE HOUSE (2006: pop. 1885) This district municipality began as a popular camping ground for 19th-century Hudson's Bay Company fur traders who were travelling to and from Fort Kamloops. A roadhouse was built on the site in 1861, and a settlement quickly surrounded it. The name refers to its location, 100 miles along the Cariboo Wagon Road from Mile 0, at Lillooet.

150 MILE HOUSE (2006: pop. 893) The first settler arrived in the area in 1861, and a roadhouse was built about two years later to provide accommodation for those travelling to the Cariboo gold fields. A community quickly arose around the roadhouse. The name derives from its location, 150 miles along the Cariboo Wagon Road from Mile 0, at Lillooet. It is also 15 kilometres south of Williams Lake.

A A

ABBOT PASS (2922 m) This mountain pass was named in 1896 by American alpinist Charles Fay for his friend, Philip Abbot. It is located between Mount Lefroy and Mount Victoria, along the border separating Banff and Yoho national parks. Abbot fell 330 metres to his death in 1896 while climbing Mount Lefroy; he was the first mountaineer to die in the Canadian Rockies. A stone cabin at the pass, built in 1923 and maintained for the use of hikers, is the second-highest habitable structure in Canada.

ABBOTSFORD (2006: pop. 123,864) There has been a lot of controversy over what John Charles Maclure had in mind when he named this city in 1889. The townsite was laid out on his land that year, next to the Canadian Pacific Railway's tracks. Most say that Maclure was honouring his friend, Henry Braithwaite Abbott, a prominent Vancouver businessman and CPR engineer and company executive. (Abbott was also the brother of the future prime minister of Canada, Sir John Abbott.) The community's moniker was originally spelled Abbottsford, but a *t* was officially removed in 1922. Maclure's sons claimed that year that their father named the community not after Abbott but after Sir Walter Scott's Scottish mansion, Abbotsford. Maclure himself wrote in 1924 that the city's name was "a combination of two ideas." It doesn't help that Maclure spelled the city's name with one *t* in his personal diary but with two on an 1891 map he deposited with the government.

Abbotsford was incorporated as a village in 1924, merged with the Sumas District Municipality in 1972 to form

A

the Abbotsford District Municipality, and then merged with Matsqui in 1995 to form the City of Abbotsford. Abbotsford is 75 kilometres east of Vancouver.

ABBOTT The city of Abbotsford is not the only place in British Columbia christened after Henry Braithwaite Abbott; two mountains and two lakes also bear his name. One mountain is Abbott Peak (2961 m), located northwest of Duncan Lake. Abbott staked a mineral claim in the area in 1894 and eventually established Abbott Mines Ltd. to exploit it. Originally called Mount Abbott in 1913, the name was changed in 1962 to avoid confusion with the other mountain that bears Abbott's name. The second Mount Abbott (2465 m) was christened in 1901 and is located only 40 kilometres away in Glacier National Park.

Between Kamloops and Merritt, in the Nicola Valley, is an Abbott Lake. It was officially named in 1949, but the moniker had been in use long before then. Abbott had purchased the Farr and Marpole ranches in the valley and rechristened the property Quincharden Ranch. His son, Harry Hamilton Abbott, managed the ranch for several years. The second Abbott Lake is west of Horsefly and south of Antoine Lake, where Abbott acquired property nearby in 1898. Its name dates from at least 1919.

ABERDEEN LAKE / HADDO LAKE These lakes, located southeast of Vernon, were named sometime before 1916 for John Campbell Hamilton-Gordon, the 7th Earl of Aberdeen and the Governor General of Canada from 1893 to 1898. (Lord Haddo was a courtesy title that Gordon held before he succeeded to the earldom.) Not only did the earl visit central British Columbia in 1894, but he also purchased a 13,000-acre (5260-hectare) ranch near the lakes from Forbes George Vernon (for whom Vernon was named) three years earlier.

ACTIVE PASS This seaway was named in 1855 by Lieutenant Commander James Alden for his ship, an American revenue and survey vessel called the *Active*. The vessel was the first naval ship to navigate the channel. The passage runs between Galiano and Mayne islands and connects Georgia Strait with the inner waters of the Gulf Islands. Millions of BC Ferry passengers sail through the pass each year while travelling between Tsawwassen and Swartz Bay. Three years after the *Active*'s visit, the HMS *Plumper* arrived, and its captain, George Richards, christened the passage after his ship. When Richards learned about the *Active*, he falsely claimed that the Americans had beat him to the passage by only one month (in fact, he and the *Plumper* did not even arrive in British Columbia until 1857). Richards later asked the British Admiralty to adopt the American name, instead. Local residents, however, continued to refer to the waterway as Plumper Pass for several years, and it was also the official name of Mayne Island's post office from 1880 to 1900.

ADAMANT MOUNTAIN (3345 m) Located 57 kilometres northwest of Donald, this mountain was named in 1909 by alpinist Howard Palmer for its very steep south face. The word "adamant" is synonymous with "immovable" and "unyielding." An adamant was a legendary stone that was impregnably hard.

ADAMS LAKE / ADAMS RIVER A lake, a river and a small community (Adams Lake) are all named after a local Sexqeltqin chief, Sel-howt-ken. The Sexqeltqin are a branch of the Secwepemc (Shuswap) First Nation and have lived around the lake for hundreds of years. Chief Sel-howt-ken was given the name Adam when he was baptized by Jesuit missionary Father John Nobili in 1849, and the lake has been known by his name ever since. (And, yes, the Christian name of Sel-howt-ken's wife was Eve.) The lake lies northwest of Shuswap Lake.

Adams River takes its name from the lake. Early documents record the Sexqeltqin's traditional name for the

A

lake as Shtle-al-lun (also spelled Sl-hes-tal-len), which means "many bark canoes." The Adams River flows southwest through Adams Lake and then southeast into Shuswap Lake. The 11-kilometre stretch of water between the two lakes is the site of one of North America's largest salmon runs. The community, located on the southwest side of the lake, was established in about 1913.

AENEAS LAKE Located west of Skaha Lake, this lake is named after Little Aeneas, a First Nations man who lived on the south end of the lake for many years and died in about 1946, when he was more than 100 years old. The name goes back to at least 1936.

AGAMEMNON CHANNEL This seaway was named in 1860 by Captain George H. Richards in honour of the 64-gun battleship, HMS *Agamemnon*. It was the first battleship commanded by Horatio Nelson and was later part of Nelson's fleet at the Battle of Trafalgar. The channel is located between Nelson Island and the Sechelt Peninsula.

AGASSIZ / MOUNT AGASSIZ The community of Agassiz, located south of Harrison Lake, was named after the area's first non-Aboriginal resident, Captain Lewis (or Louis) Agassiz. This former Royal Welch Fusiliers officer came to British Columbia in 1858 to strike it rich in the Cariboo Gold Rush. He settled in the Fraser Valley in 1867 and became a farmer and the postmaster of nearby Hope. Agassiz originally called his homestead Ferney Coombe and, by 1884, there was a large enough community surrounding it to warrant a post office. The Canadian Pacific Railway built a station there in 1888, and British Columbia's former lieutenant-governor, Sir Joseph Trutch, the "dominion agent" for BC with responsibility for railway matters, christened the station—and, hence, renamed the town—after the former British Army captain. Agassiz is the commercial centre of the district municipality of Kent, and the vast majority of Kent's

5208 residents live there. Nearby Mount Agassiz (962 m) was named after the village in 1955.

A

AHBAU LAKE This lake, located northwest of Quesnel, was christened after a Chinese trapper and prospector, Ah Bau (also spelled Ah Baw), who lived in a cabin on the lake for many years. The name dates back to at least 1907. The lake was previously known as Graveyard Lake.

AHNUHATI RIVER / AHNUHATI VALLEY The Ahnuhati Valley is located west of Knight Inlet. The river flows through the valley into the inlet. The valley's name is found on British Admiralty charts dating from 1865; the river's name goes back to at least 1930 and is possibly older. *Ahnuhati* is a word from the Kwak'wala language spoken by the people of the Kwakwaka'wakw (Kwakiutl) First Nation. In English, it means "where the humpback salmon go."

AHOUSAT This community on Flores Island northwest of Tofino was named for the people of the Ahousaht First Nation, who still reside here. The earliest known application of the name by a non-Aboriginal was by Captain John Kendrick of the ship *Columbia Rediviva* when he visited the local bay in 1791. He spelled the name Ahassert, and some early records refer to the Ahousaht people as the Ah-owz-arts and the Ah-ous-aht. The current spelling of the village name was adopted by Captain George Richards in 1861 when he was surveying Clayoquot Sound. The site was originally occupied by the Otsosaht, a band of the Nuu-Chan-Nulth (Nootka) First Nation. The Otsosaht were conquered and assimilated in the early 19th century by the Ahousaht (another band of the Nuu-Chan-Nulth), who were from nearby Vargas Island. One early anthropologist suggested that the name is a Nootka First Nation word that means "people living with their backs to the land and mountains." Another possible translation is "facing opposite from the ocean."

A

AINSWORTH HOT SPRINGS (2006: pop. 50) This community on the west side of Kootenay Lake was originally known as Hot Springs Camp (named for the local hot springs), until railway promoter and owner of the famous Bluebell Mine, George J. Ainsworth, bought the site in 1883. Ainsworth promptly renamed the mining camp after his father, wealthy Portland, Oregon, steamboat operator John C. Ainsworth. The community's name was changed from Ainsworth to Ainsworth Hot Springs in 1963 to promote tourism.

AIYANSH *See* New Aiyansh.

AKAMINA Akamina Pass (1799 m) is located in the southeast corner of British Columbia and is the most easterly point in the province. Akamina Creek and Akamina Ridge are close by. The name was first applied by non-Aboriginals to the Akamina Camp and Astronomical Station, built there in 1861 by the British-American Boundary Commission. *Akamina* is a word in the Ktunaxa language, spoken by the Kutenai (Kootenay) First Nation, and most authorities believe it means "mountain pass." Others, however, argue that it means "high bench land," in reference to the naturally formed benches near the summit of the pass. Still other sources say that the word means "small streams."

ALBAS Now a ghost town, this small logging community sat on the east side of Seymour Arm at Shuswap Lake. It was named after Albert Bass, a trapper and guide who lived on Seymour Arm. It is now part of Shuswap Lake Provincial Marine Park; none of the town's buildings remain.

ALBERNI INLET This narrow, 40-kilometre-long fjord on the west coast of Vancouver Island was originally named Canal de Alberni in 1791 by Spanish Navy Lieutenant Francisco de Eliza y Reventa, in honour of Pedro de Alberni. Alberni was the Spanish army officer who, with 76 soldiers, accompanied Eliza to Friendly Cove in Nootka Sound in 1791 and helped him build a fort there. It is doubtful that Alberni himself ever saw the fjord. The British Admiralty later anglicized the name to Alberni Canal. The current name was suggested in 1931 and approved 14 years later because of concerns that merchant vessels might erroneously think the inlet was an artificial canal and that levies were charged for passage. It is the longest inlet on Vancouver Island, and the city of Port Alberni lies at its head.

ALBERT Albert Canyon is 35 kilometres east of Revelstoke and stretches along the Illecillewaet River. Formerly known as Box Canyon, it was renamed in 1884 by the Reverend George Munro Grant for Albert L. Rogers, the nephew and namesake of Canadian Pacific Railway survey engineer Albert B. Rogers. In 1881–82, young Albert helped his uncle find the pass through the Selkirk Mountains that the CPR used to complete the intercontinental railway. Pastor Grant walked through the canyon with the famous engineer and inventor Sanford Fleming in 1883. A community, also named Albert Canyon, was once located there but is now essentially a ghost town. Nearby Albert Glacier and Albert Peak were both named for the young Rogers in 1906.

ALBERT HEAD This rocky promontory was named in 1846 after Queen Victoria's husband, Prince Albert. It is located just across the roadstead, southwest of the city named after the prince's wife.

ALBION The first settler arrived in the area in 1857, and the place was initially called East Haney, after a community to the northwest. However, when a post office was built in 1907, the federal postal authorities said that one locale with Haney in its name was enough. At a town meeting to choose a new moniker, a short-term resident from the United States suggested the name Albion, the ancient name for the isle of Britain. The community's other

A

residents, most of whom were of British origin, liked it and agreed. Albion is now part of the community of Maple Ridge.

ALBREDA Located southeast of Valemount, between the North Thompson River and Canoe Reach of Kinbasket Lake, are Mount Albreda (3052 m), Albreda Glacier and the Albreda River. Albreda Lake, which is now filled in, was the head of the river. About 25 kilometres south of Valemount, where the Yellowhead Highway passes over the Albreda River, lies the ghost town of Albreda. Sources disagree as to whether the lake or the mountain was named first, but all of these sites can thank William Wentworth-FitzWilliam, the Viscount Milton, for their names. When Lord Milton and others travelled through the area in 1863, on their way to the Pacific, Milton named either the lake or the mountain after his aunt, Lady Albreda Elizabeth Wentworth-Fitzwilliam.

ALDERGROVE (estimated pop. 5000) This community was named by Philip Jackman, former Royal Engineer and New Westminster's first policeman, after the area's dense alder groves. Jackman settled in Aldergrove in about 1877. The two-word form of the name, Alder Grove, was used until 1919. Aldergrove is part of the township of Langley.

ALERT BAY A bay and a village (2006: pop. 472) on Cormorant Island in Broughton Strait share this name. The community was established when the 'Namgis First Nation village at the mouth of the Nimpkish River near Port McNeill was moved here in 1880. The village took its name from the bay, which was christened in 1860 by Captain George Richards after the screw corvette HM *Alert*. The *Alert* and its crew were conducting a survey of the British Columbia coast at the time.

ALEXANDRA BRIDGE The current bridge, which crosses the Fraser River about 20 kilometres north of Yale on the Trans-Canada Highway, was built in the 1960s and is located a short distance downstream from the first Alexandra Bridge. The original bridge, which was constructed in 1863 but washed out in 1894, was named after Alexandra, the Princess of Wales, who had just married Prince Edward, the future King Edward VII.

ALEXANDRA PEAK *See* Mount King Edward.

ALEXANDRIA This community was indirectly named after explorer Alexander Mackenzie. Located on the Fraser River between Quesnel and Williams Lake, the site marks the most southerly point along the Fraser that Mackenzie reached in 1793, before he turned back and headed west to the Pacific. In 1821, the North West Company established Fort Mackenzie nearby, on the east side of the Fraser River. It was used as a trading post by the NWC and later by the Hudson's Bay Company until 1836. A year after the fort was abandoned, the HBC established the Alexandria trading post on the west side of the river, around which the community of Alexandria grew.

ALEXIS CREEK Both the village (2006: pop. 127) and the nearby creek are named after the Tsilhqot'in (Chilcotin) chief Alexis, who met with colonial governor Frederick Seymour after the Chilcotin War of 1864. The creek's name was officially adopted in 1911, though it may have been in use much longer. The community was founded in about 1917 and is located on Highway 20, about 112 kilometres west of Williams Lake.

ALEZA LAKE Both the small community and the nearby lake were named in 1913 after a woman of the Dakelh (Carrier) First Nation who lived in the area. Both are located near Hansard Lake, about 50 kilometres northeast of Prince George.

ALICE ARM A fjord and a community share this name. The 15-kilometre-long fjord, located 125 kilometres northwest of Terrace, is the eastern part of Observatory Inlet in the Coast Mountains. It was named in 1868 after Alice Mary Tomlinson, the new wife of prominent Anglican minister Robert Tomlinson, who was in charge of the mission 40 kilometres away at Kincolith, at the mouth of the Nass River. The community of Alice Arm, established in 1916 and named after the fjord, is located at the point where the Kitsault River flows into the fjord.

ALKALI LAKE (0.77 km²) Despite the name, there is no alkali in this lake. It was christened after a patch of alkali on a hillside that overlooks the lake. That spot was a landmark for miners heading north to the Cariboo gold fields. The name dates back to at least 1861, when the Alkali Lake Ranch, the oldest cattle ranch in British Columbia, was founded in the area. The lake is on the east side of the Fraser River, about 50 kilometres south of Williams Lake. Also nearby is the community of Alkali Lake (2006: pop. 363), which had been established by 1881 and was named for the lake.

ALLIFORD BAY This bay was named in 1866 by Captain Daniel Pender after Able Seaman William Alliford. Alliford was the coxswain of Pender's ship, the *Beaver*, when that vessel was being temporarily used as a naval surveying ship. The vessel and crew visited the bay that year. The bay is on the southeast side of Skidegate Inlet in Haida Gwaii (Queen Charlotte Islands).

ALLISON PASS (1340 m) This mountain pass between Hope and Princeton was named after John Fall Allison, the prospector who discovered it in 1860 while searching on behalf of the colonial government for gold along the Similkameen River and for a trail between the Similkameen and Tulameen areas. The moniker dates back to at least 1914.

ALOUETTE Alouette Lake and the Alouette River were originally called Lillooet Lake and Lillooet River until 1915, when the names were changed to avoid confusion with the identically named bodies of water north of Garibaldi Park. It is assumed that the new monikers were chosen because they sound so similar to the previous ones. In French, *alouette* means "lark." The lake and river are northeast of Haney. Nearby Alouette Mountain (1361 m), formerly known as Battery Mountain, was renamed after the lake in 1925.

ALSEK RIVER This river begins in Kluane National Park in the Yukon and flows through the St. Elias Mountains of northwest British Columbia before continuing into Alaska. It was known as Rivière du Behring, Jones River and Harrison River before the original First Nations name was adopted in 1891 by both Canada and the United States. The name is a derivation of the Southern Tutchone First Nation name A?séxh', which means "the river belonging to A?séxh'." Pre-1891, spellings of the name included Alseck, Alsekh, Altsekh and Alzech.

ALTA LAKE (1.1 km²) This lake, located just north of Whistler, was called Summit Lake until 1930, when the name was changed to avoid confusion with the other Summit Lakes in the province. The new moniker was chosen to indicate that the lake is the highest in the Cheakamus Valley. *Alta* is Spanish for "high." There was also a nearby community called Alta Lake, which was established before 1915, but it was swallowed up by Whistler in the 1970s.

AMBLESIDE This part of West Vancouver, located on the north side of Burrard Inlet, was named by Morris Williams, who settled there in 1912 and had fond memories of his earlier residence in the town of Ambleside in Westmoreland, England.

A

ANAHIM LAKE A lake and a community share this name. The lake is really an expansion of the Dean River and is located about 20 kilometres north of Charlotte Lake. On the south end of the lake is the community of the same name (2006: pop. 140), where one of the first Hudson's Bay Company trading stores in British Columbia once stood. The lake was called Lake Anawhim as far back as 1861 by non-Aboriginals visiting the area, but it was also labelled on maps as late as 1903 as Na-coont-loon and Na-coot-loon, the Tsilhqot'in (Chilcotin) First Nation name meaning "a fence built across" or "fish trap." The lake officially acquired its current name in 1911. The moniker honours Chief Anaham (also spelled Anawhim and Aunihime), a Tsilhqot'in leader who served as a guide and mediator between local First Nations people and the explorers and others who came to the area. According to one source, Anaham was originally a Nuxalk (Bella Coola) First Nation chief from the British Columbia coast who married a Tsilhqot'in woman. His wife did not like living on the coast and became homesick, so they moved to her native territory surrounding Anahim Lake. After the Chilcotin War of 1864, Chief Anaham, his wife and the Tsilhqot'in band with whom they lived were moved 160 kilometres east to the Anaham Reserve in the Chilcotin River Valley. In 1938, Stan Dowling bought the HBC property on the lake and started a store, around which the community of Anahim Lake grew. When the post office was opened there the following year, Dowling, as the first postmaster, called it (and, hence, the village) Anahim Lake, to avoid confusion between it and the Anaham Reserve. Ironically, the name of the reserve has since been changed to Anahim.

ANARCHIST MOUNTAIN (1233 m) This mountain was originally called Larch Tree Hill but was renamed after Richard G. Sidley, who ranched on its summit. The Irishman arrived in the Osoyoos area in about 1889 and became the first postmaster in 1895, as well as the justice of the peace and customs officer of the nearby community of Sidley (which, of course, was also named after him; it is now a ghost town). Because of his extreme political views, Sidley was called an anarchist, and the peak became known by locals as "the anarchist's mountain." Sidley's politics eventually cost him all three jobs, but the name Anarchist Mountain was approved by the government in 1922. The peak is nine kilometres east of Osoyoos.

ANDERSON LAKE (28.3 km²) This lake was named in 1858 by Hudson's Bay Company fur trader Alexander Caulfield Anderson. Anderson had been hired by the British Columbia colonial government to find a passable route from Harrison Lake to Lillooet, and Anderson Lake was the first lake he came across in his journey. At the request of BC colonial governor James Douglas, Anderson named the lake after himself. It is south of Carpenter Lake, between Lillooet and Pemberton. *See also* Birken/Birkenhead and Seton.

ANGLEMONT / ANGLE MOUNTAIN The community of Anglemont (2006: pop. 454), located on the north shore of Shuswap Lake, was named in 1914 by its first postmaster, W.A. Hudson, after nearby Angle Mountain. The mountain (1777 m), which is located southwest of Shuswap Lake, was in turn christened in 1877 by noted geologist George M. Dawson for the angle created by the Seymour Arm of Shuswap Lake and the main part of the lake.

ANMORE (2006: pop. 1785) This village takes its name from nearby Anmore Creek, which was originally called Annore Creek. The waterway got its moniker in 1914 from F.J. Lancaster, a Vancouver resident who was applying for water rights to the stream. His wife's name was Annie, and his daughter's name was Lenore, and Lancaster just

A

put the two together. Somehow, by 1923, the spelling had been changed to Anmore. The village is directly north of Port Moody.

ANNACIS ISLAND This island in the south arm of the Fraser River, east of Richmond and southwest of New Westminster, is named after Métis fur trader Francis Noel Annance. He was one of three clerks accompanying Hudson's Bay Company chief factor James McMillan, when McMillan travelled past the island and up the Fraser River in 1827 to establish Fort Langley. British government maps from 1849 and 1853 refer to the isle as "Annance's Island," but the 1858 edition of those charts misspelled it, and the mistake was never corrected.

ANNIEVILLE This small community in northern Delta is located on the south arm of the Fraser River, directly east of Annacis Island. There are two stories about the origin of the name. One is that the village was named after Annie Laidlaw, the wife of Fergus Laidlaw, one of the first owners of a cannery that was located there. The other story is that, in 1871, when James Symes, his wife, Annie, and others were sailing up the Fraser looking for place to build a cannery, they located a spot but could not land because the water was too shallow. Annie Symes then jumped out of the boat and waded ashore while somebody shouted "Annie will make it!" and the first cannery on the Fraser River was built on that spot.

ANVIL ISLAND This island in Howe Sound was named by Captain George Vancouver in 1792 because its shape—when viewed from the water, the isle resembles an anvil. The community of Anvil Island was established there in about 1896 and was christened after the island.

ANYOX / ANYOX CREEK Anyox Creek flows southeast into Granby Bay near the head of Observatory Inlet and takes its name from the Nisga'a First Nation word *anyoose*, which means "hidden water" or "place of hiding." The town, which was established in 1912 but abandoned 30 years later, was the site of a large copper mine and smelter and was christened after the nearby creek.

ARGENTA This community's name is a derivation of either the Latin adjective *argentea*, the Latin noun *argentum* or the word *argent*, all of which refer to silver. The community was christened by the Argenta Mining Company and refers to the silver mining that took place in the area when this community was established in about 1892. It's not known whether the company or nearby Argenta Creek was named first. Argenta is located on the northeast end of Kootenay Lake.

ARISTAZABAL ISLAND (420 km²) This island in Hecate Strait was named in 1792 by Spanish Navy Lieutenant Commander Jacinto Caamaño Moraleja for Gabriel de Aristazábal, the famous Spanish naval officer under whom Caamaño had previously served.

ARMSTRONG (2006: pop. 4241) The general area in which this city is located was originally called Aberdeen. The site was renamed in honour of William C. Heaton-Armstrong, an English banker who helped finance the building of the Shuswap and Okanagan Railway, when the railway built a station there in 1892. Armstrong is located in the North Okanagan Valley, just north of Vernon. Encircled by Spallumcheen, it is the only municipality in British Columbia entirely surrounded by another muncipality.

ARRAS (2006: pop. 166) This village, about 20 kilometres west of Dawson Creek, was named in 1923 by its first postmaster, R. Soutes. He was a veteran of the Battle of Arras, which was fought in 1917 in France during World War I.

ARROW LAKES (499 km²) This name once referred to both Upper Arrow Lake and Lower Arrow Lake. The

A

lakes were merged in 1969 when the Keenleyside Dam was built near Castlegar, and the moniker (in the plural) now refers to the giant lake that was created as a result. The name comes from Arrow Rock, a steep, perpendicular cliff on the east side of Lower Arrow Lake. High above the waterline were three large crevices into which hundreds of First Nation arrows were embedded. There are different stories as to why the arrows were shot. One is that it was to determine a person's luck; if an arrow was shot and lodged into the cliff, the person would have good luck, but if the arrow fell into the water, he'd have bad. Another story is that First Nations warriors used the cliff for target practice before going to war. A third is that the local First Nations people, after defeating a large war party from another tribe, shot off all the arrows they captured into the cliff as a celebration of their victory. And yet a fourth tale says that the local First Nations came to Arrow Lakes to fight off an attacking war party but discovered, once they got there, that a giant storm had killed all of the enemy warriors. As a token of respect, the defenders shot all their arrows into Arrow Rock. With the construction of Keenleyside Dam, Arrow Rock is now submerged.

ARTHUR SEAT (1672 m) According to Inga Teit Perkin in 1979, her great uncle, Spences Bridge pioneer John Murray, named this mountain because it reminded him of an 882-foot hill near Edinburgh, Scotland, that was also named Arthur's Seat. That Scottish hill, in turn, is named after the legendary king. The name has been applied to both the mountain (the back of the "seat") and the flat area below the summit (the "seat" itself) since at least 1895. Arthur Seat is also commonly known as Art's Ass and is located six kilometres west of Spences Bridge.

ASHCROFT (2006: pop. 1664) This village is located on the east side of the Thompson River, eight kilometres south of Cache Creek. Two brothers, Clement and Henry Cornwall, from Ashcroft, Gloucestershire, England, arrived at the site in 1862. Members of the English upper class, both were graduates of Cambridge University, and their father was an Anglican vicar. The Cornwalls originally came to Canada to make their fortune in the Cariboo Gold Rush but instead acquired a large parcel of land on which they farmed, ranched, operated a gristmill and sawmill and sold flour to passing miners and packers. The Cornwalls' home, which they called Ashcroft, became a major stopping point for travellers. Living like English country gentlemen, the brothers also raised racehorses and foxhounds and held coyote hunts (no foxes were around). Their annual horserace attracted hundreds of visitors. Clement entered politics and became the lieutenant-governor of British Columbia in 1881. In 1884, the Canadian Pacific Railway built a station just east of the Cornwalls' home and named it Ashcroft in honour of the brothers. The name was soon applied to the nearby village, which had previously been known by several names. This forced the Cornwalls to rename their home Ashcroft Manor (it is now know as Ashcroft Ranch), to avoid confusion between the community and their home.

ASPEN GROVE Located 22 kilometres southeast of Merritt, this small community had been established by 1900 and was named for the large number of cottonwood—also known as wild aspen—trees in the area.

ATCHELITZ / ATCHELITZ CREEK The small community of Atchelitz, located six kilometres southwest of Chilliwack, was established by 1892 and took its name from nearby Atchelitz Creek. The creek, in turn, was at one time called the Atchelitch River. The name was also spelled as Atchelits and Atchletch in early records and is a derivation of Áthelets, the Halq'eméylem (Halkomelem) First Nation place name for the small valley in which

A

the community and the creek are located. The word is most commonly translated as "bottom" and is believed to refer to the fact that the creek flows along the base or bottom of Chilliwack Mountain. Áthelets has also been interpreted to mean "inlet" or "bay."

ATHABASCA PASS (1753 m) This mountain pass was named after the Athabasca River, which begins nearby and flows eastward across Alberta. *Athabasca* is a Cree First Nation word meaning "where there are reeds" and refers to the delta where the river flows into Lake Athabasca in northern Alberta. The pass is on the Continental Divide, which separates Alberta and British Columbia, and is located in the southwest corner of Jasper National Park.

ATHALMER This small community is located on the north end of Windermere Lake where the lake's waters flow into the Columbia River. Once an independent municipality, it is now a suburb of Invermere. The area was originally called Salmon Beds because the local First Nations people caught salmon there as they travelled up the Columbia. The current name was chosen by a civil engineer, Frederick W. Aylmer, of Golden, British Columbia, when he laid out the townsite in the 1880s. Aylmer could trace his ancestry back to Athalmer (or Athelmer), the son of the ninth-century Anglo-Saxon king, Ethelred of Wessex, from whom Aylmer's surname was derived. Aylmer also knew that, in Old English, the word *athol* meant "most noble" and the word *mere* meant "lake." So, by naming the site Athalmer, he was both referring to Windermere Lake and honouring himself and his family.

ATHLONE ISLAND Originally called Smyth Island, the name of this island was changed in 1944 in honour of Major-General Alexander Augustus Frederick William Alfred George Cambridge, 1st Earl of Athlone and the Governor General of Canada. The island is near Milbanke

Sound on the south side of Seaforth Channel, west of Bella Bella.

A

ATKINSON POINT *See* Point Atkinson.

ATLIN A lake, a community, a mountain and a river all share this name. Atlin Lake is the largest natural lake (556 km² in British Columbia) in the province, though part of it lies in the Yukon. It is located between Tagish and Teslin lakes. Michael Byrnes (of Burns Lake fame) might have been the first non-Aboriginal to see the lake when he was searching for a route to lay telegraph lines for the Western Union Telegraph Company in 1867. An early map labels the body of water as Tako Lake (probably after the nearby Taku River). The lake was given its current name by explorer George Dawson in 1887. Dawson never saw Atlin Lake, but when he visited nearby Tagish Lake, he was told about the other lake by his Tagish First Nation guides, who suggested three possible names for it. A-tlin, or Aht-lah, was the one Dawson picked. The Tlingit First Nation name for the lake is Ahklen, Aht'lan or Atlah. All these names mean "big water" or "stormy water." The modern Tlingit spelling is A Tlen.

The community of Atlin (estimated pop. 400) was established on the eastern shore of the lake in 1898 and was originally called Atlin City. The moniker was shortened to Atlin the following year.

Atlin Mountain (2046 m), 11 kilometres west of the community, was named in 1900. The Atlin River was christened the Atlinto River in 1897. It was rechristened the following year, but for decades, many people continued to refer to it by its old label.

ATNARKO / ATNARKO RIVER The Atnarko River flows westward 100 kilometres from Charlotte Lake, through Tweedsmuir Provincial Park and into the Bella Coola River. It was first called Driver River and then Stillwater

A

River. The current name was officially adopted in 1947, though it had been used as early as 1905. There is a difference of opinion as to what *atnarko* means. Some say it's a Tsilhqot'in (Chilcotin) First Nation or Dakelh (Carrier) First Nation word meaning "river of strangers." Others say it's a Nuxalk (Bella Coola) First Nation word meaning "river of the coast people." All agree that the name refers to the time when the Nuxalk lived near the Atnarko River and were forced out by the Dakelh. The community of Atnarko, which sits on the river, was established in about 1907 but was originally called Anahim. The name was changed in 1913.

AUSTRALIAN This unincorporated community was originally settled in the early 1860s by three or four men from Down Under who maintained a ranch in the area until 1901. The community was first called the Australians' Place and then Australian Ranch, before its current name was officially adopted in 1923. It is on the east side of the Fraser River south of Quesnel.

AVALANCHE MOUNTAIN (2861 m) This mountain was named in 1881 by Major Albert Rogers, after four of his Secwepemc (Shuswap) First Nation assistants encountered an avalanche and took an unintentional trip down the peak's west slope. The peak is just southeast of Rogers Pass in Glacier National Park.

AVOLA (estimated pop. 160) This community was first called Stillwater Flats in 1863 but was forced to change its name 50 years later, when it was discovered that another community called Stillwater already existed in the province. The current name, taken from the Sicilian town, was then adopted. Why this particular moniker was chosen is not known. The village is on the west side of the North Thompson River on the Yellowhead Highway, about 185 kilometres north of Kamloops.

B

BABINE A lake, a river, a mountain range and a community share this name. The French word *babine*, which means "large lip," was first used by North West Company voyageurs in the early 1800s to refer to the Nat'oot'en people, who still live around Babine Lake. The Nat'oot'en are a part of the Dakelh (Carrier) First Nation. The name refers to the Nat'oot'en's practice of inserting concave pieces of wood or bone about a centimetre in diameter between the teeth and lower lips of their women once they reached puberty. Over time, the plates distended the shape of the women's lips. The voyageurs came across the lake, located just west of Stuart Lake, in 1812. Babine Lake (497 km2) is the largest and longest natural lake located entirely within British Columbia. The traditional Dakelh name for the lake is Nado Bun.

The Babine River flows west from the north end of the lake into the Skeena River.

The mountain range (originally called the Babine Mountains but renamed the Babine Range in 1951) is located between the lake and the river and the Bulkley and Skeena rivers to the south. The community of Fort Babine (estimated pop. 135) lies at the north end of the lake. *See* Fort Babine.

BADEN-POWELL TRAIL This trail through the lower slopes of the North Shore Mountains north of Vancouver was built in 1971 by Boy Scouts and Girl Guides and was named for Robert Stephenson Smyth Baden-Powell, the 1st Baron Baden-Powell and the founder of the worldwide Scouting movement. The trail is 48 kilometres long and runs from Deep Cove to Horseshoe Bay.

B

BAKER / MOUNT BAKER The small community of Baker, located 15 kilometres east of Cranbrook, was named after James Baker in 1904. Nearby Mount Baker (2206 m) was also christened after him, and the peak has been known by that moniker since at least 1915. Baker owned a large ranch, where Cranbrook was later built. He was also the president of a local coal company, was active in local railway development and served in government as a long-time member of the British Columbia Legislative Assembly and as a provincial cabinet minister.

BALDONNEL (estimated pop. 132) J.W. Abbot, who arrived in the area in 1923 and later became the local justice of the peace, named this small community. He christened the town sometime before 1929 after his hometown in Ireland. Although there are no communities called Baldonnel on the Emerald Isle, there are several Ballydonnels.

BALDY HUGHES / MOUNT BALDY HUGHES Mount Baldy Hughes (1128 m) was officially named in 1963, even though the moniker was in common usage at least 50 years before. It was previously called Tsa Whuz Mountain by geologist George Dawson in 1875. The peak is 35 kilometres south of Prince George and was named in honour of 19th-century stagecoach driver and trapper "Baldy" Hughes, who lived in a cabin at the mountain's base. Hughes also ran a remount station for a stage line that used the old Cariboo Wagon Road between Barkerville and Yale. Both the station and the mountain later fell within the boundaries of an early warning, long-range radar facility operated first by the American military as USAF Baldy Hughes Air Station and, later, from 1955 to 1988, by the Canadian military as RCAF Station Baldy Hughes. The small community of Baldy Hughes grew up around the base.

BALFOUR About 25 kilometres northeast of Nelson, on Kootenay Lake, is the community of Balfour (2006: pop. 479).

It was founded and named in 1889 by Charles Wesley Busk, a wealthy Englishman who settled in Nelson in the late 1880s. Some sources say the town was christened for Arthur James Balfour, a British politician who became prime minister in 1902. Balfour's family had mining interests in the region. Others say it was named after D.B. Balfour, a local resident whose home was on the west shore of Kootenay Lake and who was in charge of bridge construction for the Canadian Pacific Railway during the building of the CPR's Crowsnest Line.

B

BALFOUR PASS / MOUNT BALFOUR This col and mountain (3284 m) were both christened in 1859 by Dr. James Hector, a Scottish geologist, naturalist and physician who explored British Columbia in the late 1850s. Hector named them after his old instructor at Edinburgh University, John Hutton Balfour, who taught botany, geology, medicine and natural history. The mountain pass and mountain are on the Alberta border near Banff.

BALLENAS ISLANDS / BALLENAS CHANNEL The Ballenas Islands were discovered and named in 1791 by Spanish mariner José Maria Narvaez, the first European to explore Georgia Strait. Narvaez called them Islas de las Ballenas, or "islands of the whales," because of the large number of whales that swim by the islands. Located in Georgia Strait, just east of Parksville, the isles were mistakenly called the Ballinac Islands on British Admiralty charts from 1864 to 1905. Nearby is the Ballenas Channel, which was similarly mislabelled for many years on the Admiralty's maps.

BAMBERTON This ghost town was named after H.K.G. Bamber. A cement manufacturer from Gravesend, England, he was the managing director of British Portland Cement Manufacturers. Bamber came to Vancouver Island in 1912, established the B.C. Cement Company and recommended the construction of a cement plant on

B

the southwest side of Saanich Inlet, about 37 kilometres north of Victoria. The community of Bamberton arose around the plant. The cement plant closed in 1980, and the company town was soon abandoned.

BAMFIELD / BAMFIELD INLET Bamfield Inlet, on the east side of Barkley Sound, was named after William Eddy Banfield, a seaman who first arrived in British Columbia in 1846 aboard the HMS *Constance*. He established his home on the inlet when he left the Royal Navy three years later. Banfield lived there for 13 years, while trading with the First Nation peoples on the west coast of Vancouver Island. He also established a trading post and became an Indian Agent for the colonial government. An amateur ethnologist, Banfield collected a large amount of information about the local First Nations peoples. While he was living there, the inlet became known as Banfield Creek. (In 19th-century naval terminology, narrow tidal inlets were called creeks.) It was renamed Banfield Inlet in 1944.

The community of Bamfield (2006: pop. 251) is on the inlet's south shore. Its first settler arrived in 1900. However, when the local post office was built in 1903, the postal authorities got the name wrong and misspelled it as Bamfield. Although they quickly acknowledged the error, it was never corrected. For a while, maps showed the community of Bamfield located on Banfield Creek (or Inlet). The mapmakers finally yielded to the overwhelming public use of the misspelled name, and the inlet became Bamfield Inlet in 1951.

BANKS ISLAND (845 km2) This island was named in 1788 by Charles Duncan, captain of the King George's Sound Company ship *Princess Royal*, for Sir Joseph Banks. Banks was a prominent British botanist and naturalist, who was, at the time, the president of the Royal Society. He also, at his own expense, accompanied Captain James Cook during Cook's worldwide voyage of 1768–71. The island is on the east side of Hecate Strait, 80 kilometres south of Prince Rupert.

B

BARKERVILLE Located 88 kilometres east of Quesnel, this ghost town was originally called Williams Creek (1864) and then Cariboo (1871), before it was finally named in 1872 after gold prospector William "Billy" Barker. In 1862, Barker and his partners found and took out more than $600,000 in gold (worth several millions today) from a nearby stream known as Williams Creek. Ironically, Barker quickly spent his fortune and died in poverty. After Barker's discovery, Barkerville sprang into existence virtually overnight and, for a short time, was the largest city in British Columbia. It was declared a heritage site in 1958 and is now a popular tourist destination.

BARKLEY SOUND This 24-kilometre-wide collection of bays, inlets and two major island groups was discovered in 1787 by Captain Charles William Barkley of the trading ship *Imperial Eagle*, and he named it after himself. At the time, Barkley was trading with First Nations peoples up and down the west coast of Vancouver Island for sea otter pelts, which he later sold in China.

BARNARD There is a Barnard Creek located south of Ashcroft that flows west into the Thompson River. It was officially named in 1956 after Francis Jones Barnard, who operated the largest stagecoach line in North America. The line ran from Barkerville to Victoria and all points in between from 1861 until 1913. Barnard was also a prominent provincial and federal politician. Another creek by the same name, christened in 1926, flows into Barnard Harbour north of Bella Bella on Princess Royal Island. This creek is named after Francis Barnard's son, George Henry Barnard, who was a member

B

of the Canadian Senate. Barnard Harbour, like the first Barnard Creek, is named after the father. It was first called Barnard Cove in 1867 and was given its current moniker in 1926. Barnard Island, located near Princess Royal Island, is named after Francis Barnard's other son, Francis Stillman Barnard. The younger Frank Barnard was one of the wealthiest men in British Columbia's history. He was a member of the House of Commons and, during World War I, was the lieutenant-governor of British Columbia. The island was formerly known as West Island but was rechristened in 1950.

BARNET James MacLaren, a wealthy lumberman from Québec, and his partner, James Ross, established the North Pacific Lumber Company in 1889 and built a sawmill on the south side of Burrard Inlet, opposite the mouth of Indian Arm. MacLaren's mother was Elizabeth (née Barnet) MacLaren, and he gave her maiden name to the community of millworkers and their families that soon surrounded the site. Barnet is now a ghost town and the site of Barnet Marine Park, which is immediately north of Simon Fraser University. Highway 7A, which is popularly known as the Barnet Highway, connects Vancouver to Port Moody and passes between SFU and the park.

BARNHARTVALE This community was named after Peter Barnhart, the conductor on the first transcontinental Canadian Pacific Railway train that entered Kamloops in 1886. Barnhart later settled in Kamloops and then, in 1905, moved to the community of Campbell Creek, 14 kilometres to the southeast. Four years later, as Campbell Creek's postmaster, Barnhart had the community renamed after himself, much to the displeasure of his neighbours. The name, however, was never changed back.

BARNSTON ISLAND Both the island and the community on it were named after Hudson's Bay Company fur trader George Barnston. He was one of the three clerks who accompanied HBC chief factor James McMillan when McMillan sailed past the island and up the Fraser River in 1827 to establish Fort Langley. The island lies in the Fraser River south of Pitt Meadows. The community was established before 1911; the island was named long before that.

BARRETT LAKE Both the lake and the nearby community were named for Charles Barrett. Beginning about 1900, Barrett and two partners packed supply trains from Ashcroft to the Yukon and from Hazelton to Telegraph Creek. They also owned the famous Diamond D Ranch near Houston. By 1911, Barrett was the sole owner of the ranch. He later acquired a second ranch to the west, and the two ranches were among the largest in the Smithers area. Barrett was also the first postmaster of Barrett Lake and named the post office (and, hence, the village) after the lake in 1915. The lake and the village are about 10 kilometres northwest of Houston.

BARRIERE Barriere River, which flows southwest into the North Thompson River between Clearwater and Kamloops, was named sometime before 1828 by French Canadian fur traders who tried to sail down it. Some sources say the name derives from the difficulty the traders had in going down the mouth of the river in the spring, because of rocks that blocked navigation. Others say the *barrière* was the two weirs, or fences, the local First Nations people placed across the river to catch fish. Both the community of Barriere (2006: pop. 1209), located where the river flows into the North Thompson, and nearby Barrière Mountain (1283 m) are named after the river. The accent in the names of the river and the town were officially deleted by the provincial government in 2007, but the accent mark above the first *e* in the mountain's name still remains.

B

BATCHELOR Batchelor Hill, at the north junction of the North Thompson and Thompson rivers in Kamloops, was named for Owen Salisbury Batchelor in 1926. Batchelor was a farmer, prospector and rancher, who came to Kamloops in 1895. He became the town jailer but later left to prospect in the Klondike Gold Rush. Batchelor returned to Kamloops and entered into various mining ventures, including the building and operation of a stamp mill just below the hill that bears his name. He also went to France with his sons to fight in World War I and was said to have been the "biggest man in the British Army." The nearby Kamloops neighbourhood of Batchelor Hills (officially named in 1977) and the body of water called Batchelor Lake (officially named in 1966), just northwest of Kamloops, are also named after Owen Batchelor.

BATTLE BLUFF An 1871 survey party named this large, 50-metre-high basalt rock on the north side of Kamloops Lake. The surveyors were told that, about 100 years earlier, a great battle between two First Nations bands was fought at the foot of the rock. It was apparently a massacre. At the end of the fight, the victors painted or stained the rock with some kind of red material to commemorate the location. Because the survey party knew of no other name for the rock, they called it Battle Bluff. Some historians, however, dispute this tale. They argue that the Secwepemc (Shuswap) First Nation word for a loud noise is the same as that for a battle and claim that the whole story is the result of a misunderstanding that took place when blasting was done near the rock for the construction of a railway line.

BATTLE MOUNTAIN There are three Battle Mountains in British Columbia. The origin of the name of the first, located between the Incompleux River and Revelstoke, is apparently unknown. The name of the second, located on the southeast side of Wells Gray Provincial Park, recalls a battle that was fought nearby in 1875, between the Tsilhqot'in (Chilcotin) and Secwepemc (Shuswap) First Nations over the right to hunt caribou on the mountain. The name of the third, located west of Alexis Creek, is for the boulders on the mountain, which are said to be the transformed bodies of warriors from the Alexandria band of the Dakelh (Carrier) First Nation who died when they strayed over a cliff at night while on their way to attack a camp of Tsilhqot'in.

BATTLE OF BRITAIN RANGE This mountain range on the west side of Northern Rocky Mountains Provincial Park commemorates the Royal Air Force's victory over the German Luftwaffe during the Battle of Britain in World War II. Located within the range are mountains named after Allied leaders (Mount Churchill and Mount Roosevelt), the places where they met (Tehran Mountain and Yalta Peak) and the names of World War II battles fought by Canadian troops (Arnhem Mountain, Campobasso Mountain, Dieppe Mountain, Falaise Mountain, Normandy Mountain, Ortona Mountain and others). The range and its mountains were christened in 1967.

BAYNES CHANNEL / BAYNES SOUND The sea channel is located between Cadboro Point (five kilometres northeast of Victoria) and the Chatham Islands. The sound separates Denman Island from Vancouver Island and extends from Comox to Deep Bay. Both were named in 1859 by Captain George Richards to honour Rear Admiral Robert Lambert Baynes, the commander-in-chief of the Royal Navy's Pacific Station from 1857 to 1860. Although the station was based in Chile, Baynes was sent to British Columbia with his flagship, HMS *Ganges*, in 1858, during the Fraser River Gold Rush, to help maintain law and order and to uphold British sovereignty. He also played a key role in 1859 in keeping the Anglo-American dispute over the San Juan Islands (the "Pig War") from becoming a full-scale conflict.

B

BAYNES LAKE The eight-kilometre-long lake and the community on its shores are both named after Andrew Bain, who established his home by the lake in 1896. It is not known how the misspelling took place, but the damage was done before the first post office was located in the community in 1904. The lake and town lie above the mouth of the Elk River, southwest of Fernie.

BAYNES PEAK / MOUNT BAYNES Captain George Richards named the mountain on the west side of Saltspring Island after Rear Admiral Robert Lambert Baynes in 1859. Within a few years, however, the island's residents started to call it Mount Maxwell, after the Maxwell family, who had lived on the island since the 1860s. The name was officially changed to reflect local usage in 1911. When a park was created on the mountain in 1939, it was agreed that the highest point on Mount Maxwell would be named Baynes Peak.

BEACON HILL Originally called Mount Beacon, the hill was named by Hudson's Bay Company officials for the two tall beacons the company erected in 1843. One beacon stood on top of the hill; the other was to the southwest, on the shore. Together, they helped ships safely navigate around the dangerous submerged offshore reef known as Brotchie Ledge as the vessels entered and left Victoria Harbour. The hill overlooks Juan de Fuca Strait and is now part of Victoria's largest urban park. The traditional Lekwungen or Lekwammen (Songhees) First Nation name for the hill has been variously spelled, including Meeacan, Mee-a-can, Meegan and Meeqan. There are two interpretations of the word. One is that it means "belly" because, from a distance, the hill looks like the belly of a fat man lying on his back. Others say it means "warmed by the sun," because the hill was where the Lekwungens came to sit and warm themselves.

BEATON This ghost town was first named Thomson's Landing, after James William Thomson, a local businessman and notary public. However, after he left in 1902 or 1907, the community was renamed after his partner, Malcolm (or possibly Thomas) Beaton, who was also the publisher of the *Nelson Miner*. The site was flooded upon the completion of the High Arrow Dam in 1969 and has been underwater ever since. The town was located at the head of the Beaton Arm of Upper Arrow Lake. Beaton Creek, which flows into Beaton Arm, was also named after the early newspaper publisher.

BEAVER COVE A cove and a community share this name. The cove, located east of Port McNeill at the south junction of the Boughton and Johnstone straits, was named in 1860 by Captain George Richards of the Royal Navy after the *Beaver*, the first steamboat to sail up and down British Columbia's coastline. The vessel was 31 metres long, with an engine-powered paddlewheel on each side. It arrived in the Pacific Northwest from England in 1836 and was used as a coastal freighter, naval survey ship and towboat until it sank off Stanley Park's Prospect Point more than 50 years later. In 1858, the steamboat carried colonial governor James Douglas and other officials from Victoria to Fort Langley so they could proclaim the creation of the mainland colony of British Columbia. The community was established in 1917 and originally called Englewood. The town's name was changed in 1958.

BEAVER HARBOUR Another location named after the steamboat *Beaver,* this bay was given its moniker in 1837 by officials of the Hudson's Bay Company, which, at that time, owned the ship. In 1792, Spanish naval officers and explorers Dionisio Alacala-Galiano and Cayetano

B

Valdes y de Flores named the harbour Puerto de Güemes (Harbour of Güemes), after their boss, Juan Vicente de Güemes Padilla Horcasitas y Aguayo, the 2nd Count of Revillagigedo and the Spanish viceroy of Mexico. The bay is located on the northeast side of Vancouver Island, just east of Port Hardy.

BEAVERDELL This village (2006: pop. 213) and its name are both the result of the amalgamation, sometime before 1901, of two earlier settlements, Beaverton and Rendell, which were about two kilometres apart. The community is about 35 kilometres west of Penticton.

BEAVERMOUTH Located at the mouth of the Beaver River where it flows into the Columbia River, this town was established before 1890 and was first called Beaver. However, it was frequently labelled Beavermouth on maps and other documents, so the settlement was officially renamed in 1954. The town was submerged under Kinbasket Lake with the completion of the Mica Dam in 1973.

BEDNESTI LAKE The name of this lake is found on a 1916 map, but the moniker is much older. Bednesti is a derivation of the Dakelh (Carrier) First Nation name for the lake, Bet Unesdai, which means "overfed char." This refers to the fact that the trout in the lake are quite large and fat. The lake is east of Cluculz Lake.

BECKER LAKE (0.43 km²) This lake, which lies west of Canim Lake, was originally named Loon Lake in 1916 by Émile Becker when he applied for water rights on the lake. According to Becker, the name was a translation of the traditional Secwepemc (Shuswap) First Nation name, Psill-ish-will. However, his handwriting was so bad that government officials recorded the name as Love Lake. When a survey party arrived, Becker asked that the name be changed, and it was—to Becker Lake.

B

BEDAUX PASS / MOUNT BEDAUX The mountain (2303 m) lies on the southeast side of Kwadacha Wilderness Provincial Park, and the pass is on the peak's northern side. The mountain was climbed by the flamboyant French American millionaire, Charles Bedaux, in 1934, during his attempt to cross northern British Columbia with five Citroën half-track trucks as well as his wife, his mistress, a maid, a group of cowboys, crates of caviar and champagne, limousines and a tonne of luggage. Needless to say, the expedition was a failure. The mountain and the pass were both named in 1934 or 1935 by surveyor Frank Swannell, who was appointed by the Canadian government to accompany Bedaux on his ill-fated expedition.

BEGBIE LAKE Two lakes in British Columbia share this name. The first (0.13 km²), located on Vancouver Island near Bamberton, was originally called Darlington Lake but was renamed in 1934 after Matthew Begbie, the famous judge who played a key role in maintaining law and order throughout British Columbia from 1858 until his death in 1894. Nearby is Judge Creek, which was also christened in 1934 after the jurist. The second Begbie Lake lies just southwest of Revelstoke. It acquired its moniker in 1982 and is named after nearby Mount Begbie.

BELCARRA (2006: pop. 676) This village is located on the southeast side of the entrance to Indian Arm in Burrard Inlet. It was named in the 1870s by William Norman Bole, a young New Westminster attorney, who was originally from the County Mayo in Ireland and owned 260 acres (105 hectares) in the area. The name comes from two ancient Irish Gaelic words—*bal* or *ball*, which means "the sun," and *carra*, which means "a fair or lovely land." Put together, they mean "fair land on which the sun shines." Nearby is Belcarra Bay.

BELIZE INLET *See* Seymour Inlet.

B

BELLA BELLA (estimated pop. 1400) This community is located on Campbell Island east of Milbanke Sound. The name refers to both the people of the Heiltsuk (Bella Bella) First Nation, who reside in the area, and the Native settlement that grew around the Hudson's Bay Company's Fort McLoughlin, which was established on nearby Denny Island in 1833. Bella Bella was originally on Denny Island, but most of the community's residents moved to Campbell Island after the Hudson's Bay Company opened a trading store there in 1868. The community that remains on Denny Island is known today as Old Bella Bella. The site on Campbell Island was called for a while by the one-word name Bellabella and then New Bella Bella, though none of the local residents ever used the word "new." New Bella Bella's name was changed in 1991 to Waglisla, a Heiltsuk name meaning "river on the beach," but the moniker was changed to simply Bella Bella four years later. The name was spelled a variety of ways by non-Aboriginals during the early 19th century, including Bel-Bellahs, Bilbilla, Bil-Billa and Billbillahs. The current spelling was not used until the last half of that century.

There are at least five theories as to the origin of the name. One is that it is a derivation of the name that a local First Nation band called themselves. The second is that it comes from the Natives mispronunciation of Milbanke Sound. A third suggestion is that the name is actually Spanish in origin, possibly an abbreviation of the names Arabella and Isabella, even though 18th-century Spanish naval explorers did not travel this far north. Fourth, it may be an adaptation of a Heiltsuk place name. On Campbell and Denny islands are spots known in Heiltsuk as Pe'blah ("flat, tapering point"), Pelbala ("point north of Waglisla village") and Pelbalaila ("point between 'Qelc and Waglisla"). Finally, the name has been interpreted by some to mean "flat, point(ed)" and is thought by some to be descriptive of the village's original location on Denny Island.

BELLA COOLA / BELLA COOLA RIVER The Bella Coola River flows west into the North Bentinck Arm, where the Atnarko and Talchako rivers meet. At the mouth of the river is the community of Bella Coola (2006: pop. 135). Alexander Mackenzie passed through the area on his way to the Pacific in 1793 and saw a Nuxalk First Nation village where Burnt Bridge Park is today. He called it Rascal's Village, and some old maps list it as Mackenzie's Outlet. In the mid-1860s, the Natives started to refer to the village as Nuxalk ("the place where fish were trapped") and to themselves as the Nuxalkmc. (The suffix *mc* is Nuxalk for "people.") They also began to call the river Bella Coola, a name that non-Aboriginals also applied to the village. Several different spellings were used by non-Aboriginals during the 19th century, including Balla Koula, Bell-houla, Bellaghchoolas, Bill Whoalla and Billa Whulha. The waterway was once also called the Nookhalk River. The name Bela Kula was officially adopted by the British Admiralty in 1867, and the river was called the Bellakula River by the Geographic Board of Canada from 1914 to 1924. The current spelling, Bella Coola, dates back to George Dawson's 1875 map. The name refers to the people of the Nuxalk (Bella Coola) First Nation and is a derivation of a Heiltsuk (Bella Bella) First Nation word. The original word could be *plxwlaq's*, which means "foreigner" or "stranger" and is pronounced *bill-qwa-lux* or *bell-coo-la*. Other sources say that it is an adaption of *bəlxwəla*, which means "person from Bella Coola," though it refers to the Nuxalk's entire traditional territory and not just to any one specific village or band.

BELL-IRVING The Bell-Irving River, which flows southeast into the Nass River above Meziadin Lake, was named in 1917 for Duncan Peter Bell-Irving of Vancouver.

B

The young surveyor was exploring the upper part of the Nass—including the part that now bears his name—and was cut off from the rest of the world when World War I began in 1914. One month later, he sent the following telegram: "Hear there is war. Who is fighting who?" He quickly offered his services and was off to Europe. Bell-Irving, who was shot by a sniper in February 1915, was the first Canadian Army officer from British Columbia to be killed in the conflict. Nearby Mount Bell-Irving (1570 m) was named after the river 30 years later. In contrast, Bell-Irving Lake, north of Vancouver, was named in 1996 for RCNVR Lieutenant Engineer Richard Morris Bell-Irving of West Vancouver, who died of his injuries shortly after his ship, the minesweeper HMCS *Guysborough*, was torpedoed in the North Atlantic in 1945.

BELLY UP CANYON This wash got its unusual name in 1961, when Eugene Foisy's horse fell over the ledge and down into the canyon. Foisy went after it and discovered that the horse was still alive but "belly up." The canyon is located between Peters and Spectrum lakes on the east side of the Shuswap River.

BEN-MY-CHREE This once-popular tourist destination at the southwest end of Taku Arm in Tagish Lake was the site of a mid-20th-century resort owned and operated by Otto and Kate Partridge. Mr. Partridge was from the Isle of Man, where the Manx language is spoken, and *ben-my-chree* is Manx for "girl of my heart."

BENNETT BAY This bay on the east side of Mayne Island was named for a couple from Scotland, whose home overlooked it. In the late 19th and early 20th centuries, Thomas Bennett was the proprietor of a bar on the island and his wife, Alice, was a local midwife. It's said that, when they arrived in about 1879, Mrs. Bennett complained that they had reached "the arse end of the world."

BENNETT DAM *See* W.A.C. Bennett Dam.

BENNETT LAKE This lake sits on the BC-Yukon border west of Atlin Lake. It was originally called Boat Lake, until American army officer and explorer Frederick Schwatka stopped by in 1883 and renamed it after James Gordon Bennett. Bennett was the editor of the *New York Herald* and, a few years earlier, had financed Schwatka's expedition to find the remains of the Franklin Expedition. The ghost town of Bennett was located at the south end of the lake. The range of mountains on the west side of the lake is the Bennett Range.

BENTINCK The two eastern extensions of the Burke Channel, the North and South Bentinck Arms, were both named in 1793 by Captain George Vancouver for William Henry Cavendish Bentinck, the 3rd Duke of Portland, a prominent British politician who briefly served as prime minister in 1783 and became Home Secretary in 1794. The community of South Bentinck was established much later on the eastern side of South Bentinck Arm. *See also* Portland Channel/Portland Inlet.

BENTINCK ISLAND This island, located between the southern tip of Vancouver Island and Race Rocks, was named sometime before 1860. The origin of its name is uncertain, but one source suggests it might be in honour of Lord George Bentinck, a prominent British politician in the late 1840s, who was the grandson of the 3rd Duke of Portland. In 1924, the island became one of only two leper colonies in Canada and replaced the colony on D'Arcy Island. Over the years, 22 patients, mostly of Asian descent, lived in the colony. The hospital was closed in 1956 (though some sources say 1958), when the last patient died. The navy began using the island as a demolition training area in 1962.

B

BENVOULIN This neighbourhood in Kelowna was named in 1891 by George Grant MacKay after his home in Scotland. Mackay invested heavily in real estate in both Vancouver and the Okanagan and had purchased land in the area.

BERNARD CREEK This creek's name recalls an incident right out of the stories of Robin Hood. At this creek in 1828, Sir George Simpson of the Hudson's Bay Company was being carried from a canoe to shore on the back of his French Canadian guide. The guide slipped, and both men fell into the water. Simpson later named the creek to honour the guide. Unfortunately, the guide's first name is apparently lost to history. The creek flows southeast into Peace Reach, the east arm of Williston Lake.

BESSBOROUGH This community, located 18 kilometres west of Dawson Creek, was named for Vere Brabazon Ponsonby, the 9th Earl of Bessborough. He was the Governor General of Canada when the town's first post office was opened in 1935.

Bessborough Bay is hundreds of kilometres away, on Hardwicke Island between Johnstone Strait and Sunderland Channel. The bay was named in 1865 by the British Admiralty for the ennobled Bessborough family. At this time, Edward Ponsonby, the future 8th Earl of Bessborough and the father of the future Governor General, was a young midshipman in the Royal Navy serving on the BC coast.

BIG BAR CREEK This creek, north of Lillooet, flows southwest into the Fraser River. It got its name during the Cariboo Gold Rush because of the large amounts of the yellow metal found on the banks of the Fraser at the creek's mouth. The community of Big Bar Creek lies at the junction of the creek and the Fraser River and dates back to when a roadhouse was built there in 1862.

In addition, the entire area surrounding the creek is ranch country, which is also known as Big Bar Creek.

BIG EDDY This name originally referred to a giant whirlpool in the Columbia River about three kilometres west of Revelstoke. The moniker is found on maps dating back to 1915, but it is much older. When a community was established nearby in the 1890s, the residents took the name as their own.

BILLY WHISKERS GLACIER This glacier was named by mountaineer Norman Brewster for a wild mountain goat. Late in the 1940s, Brewster and others spent a night on a nearby mountain while a violent storm raged around them. When they got up the next morning, they discovered the tracks of a mountain goat that had stood in the lee of their tent the previous night. The glacier is just south of Glacier National Park.

BIRKEN / BIRKENHEAD Birkenhead River was named in 1858 by fur trader Alexander Caulfield Anderson, who came across it while searching for a passable route between Harrison Lake and Lillooet. The river was named for the HMS *Birkenhead*, a British troopship that sank near the Cape of Good Hope in 1852. A number of the soldiers had their families with them, and because the ship had only a few lifeboats, the men famously lined up at attention and met their fate while their wives and children were put into the boats and survived. A relative of Anderson's, Lieutenant-Colonel Alexander Seton, commanded the soldiers on the *Birkenhead* and drowned along with 453 of his men. The river flows into Lillooet Lake east of Pemberton. Sources vary as to whether Anderson also named nearby Birkenhead Lake or if the lake was later named by the government to match the name of the river. The community of Birken, as well as Birken Glacier and Birkenhead Peak, all within five kilometres of Birkenhead River, were also named after the river. *See also* Seton.

B

BISHOP RIVER This river was named in 1923 for Richard P. Bishop, a land surveyor who spent most of his career, beginning in 1911, surveying all across British Columbia. Bishop River, which may have been surveyed and named by Bishop himself, flows west into Southgate River, southwest of Chilko Lake.

BLACK CAT MOUNTAIN (1605 m) This mountain's moniker honours a nameless feline. In the 1920s, a man named Geoff Capes and a group of hikers were on their way to Comox Glacier. It was raining and conditions seemed hopeless for a climb, but as the party started out, a black cat ran in front of their vehicle. Shortly afterward, the weather cleared and the group had a successful hike, which they attributed to having crossed paths with the cat. The mountain is southwest of Comox Lake.

BLACK DIAMOND MOUNTAIN (2956 m) This mountain is named after the Black Diamond Mining Company, which mined the mountain in the 1910s, not for diamonds, but for coal. The mountain is west of Invermere.

THE BLACK TUSK (2319 m) Located on the north side of Garibaldi Lake, this mountain was named in 1912 by members of the BC Mountaineering Club because the colour and shape of the towering bare rock at its peak reminded them of a black tusk.

BLACKFRIARS PEAKS (3226 m) This mountain was named in 1913 at the suggestion of mountaineer Howard Palmer, who thought the two peaks looked like a pair of black-robed monks. There was some confusion in the early days about whether the moniker should be singular or plural; the Geographic Board of Canada settled on the plural in 1914. Blackfriars Peaks is 57 kilometres northwest of Donald.

BLAEBERRY / BLAEBERRY RIVER Named in 1859 by naturalist James Hector, the Blaeberry River flows into the Columbia River at a spot between Donald and Golden. *Blae* is the old form of the word "blue," and it is believed that Hector named the river for the abundance of huckleberries along its banks. Northeast of the junction of the Blaeberry and Columbia rivers is the small community of Blaeberry, which dates from at least 1915.

BLAKEBURN The moniker of this ghost town is an amalgamation of the names of William John "Blake" Wilson, a Vancouver meatpacker, and his boss, the famous Alberta businessman Patrick Burns. The two also owned a large coal mine at Blakeburn in the early part of the 20th century. The town was located near the junction of Granite Creek and the Tulameen River, northwest of Princeton.

BLESSING'S GRAVE This resting place of Charles Morgan Blessing's remains was once British Columbia's smallest provincial park. Blessing was an American who came to the Cariboo during the gold rush and was murdered in 1866 by fellow prospector, James Barry. The grave is still an official BC Historic Site and is located 44 kilometres east of Quesnel.

BLIGH ISLAND This island in Nootka Sound was named in honour of William Bligh, whose crew famously mutinied while he was captain of the HMS *Bounty* in 1789. Eleven years earlier, as the master of the HMS *Resolution*, he had visited Nootka Sound with Captain James Cook. Captain George Richards of the British Navy named the island after Bligh in 1860.

BOB QUINN LAKE A lake and a community share this name. The lake, located north of Bowser Lake, was named after Robert Quinn, a long-time resident and trapper who operated a relay cabin there for the Yukon Telegraph Line. It was called Quinn Lake by 1928 but was rechristened Bobquinn Lake in 1945 and Bob Quinn Lake in 1954.

B

The nearby community was named for the lake. Not far away is another body of water called Broken Leg Lake, where Quinn broke his leg in the winter of 1911. Quinn had to set the leg and walk back to Stewart, about 160 kilometres south, on his own.

BOSTON BAR (2006: pop. 188) This community in the Fraser Canyon, 42 kilometres north of Yale, is named for the gold-laden sandbar on the river below, where numerous Americans tried to make their fortune during the Fraser River Gold Rush. At this time, many First Nations peoples referred to Americans as "Boston men" because most of the ships that brought them to British Columbia were from Boston.

BOSWELL Located on the east short of Kootenay Lake, this community was originally called McGregor. However, in 1906, Albert Grey, the 4th Earl Grey and Governor General of Canada, paid Kootenay Lake a visit and bought some land here for his son, Lord Howick. The surveyor employed by the earl during the transaction was Elias John Boswell. Earl Grey was so impressed with Boswell that he named the property Boswell Ranch. The community of McGregor was renamed Boswell the following year.

BOWEN ISLAND An island (50 km²) and a municipality located on it share this name. The island is at the mouth of Howe Sound and was christened in 1860 by Captain George Richards for British naval officer James Bowen. Bowen was master of Admiral Earl Howe's flagship, the HMS *Queen Charlotte*, at the battle of the Glorious First of June in 1794. For his exceptional services, Bowen was quickly promoted to lieutenant, commander and then post captain. Lord Howe himself told Bowen "you... deserve to be a prince!" He later became a rear admiral. The community was established in the early 1890s, and the entire isle was incorporated in 1999 as British

Columbia's first Island Municipality. In 2006, the island's population was 3362.

BOWSER (estimated pop. 131) The community of Bowser, located 66 kilometres northwest of Nanaimo, was established in 1914 during the construction of the Esquimalt and Nanaimo Railway. It was named for William John Bowser, the provincial attorney general and the most influential member of Premier Richard McBride's cabinet. Bowser would later become premier in 1915. The combined population of Bowser and nearby Deep Bay in 2006 was 1485. Hundreds of kilometres away, north of Stewart, are Bowser Lake and Bowser River. The lake was christened after the provincial attorney general by Charles P. Hickman, who became the first non-Aboriginal to see it in 1912. The river was named after the lake in 1945.

BRAS CROCHE (3286 m) This mountain was first called Mount Bras Croche in 1924 and was then rechristened Bras Croche Mountain in 1981. Today, it is simply called Bras Croche. The name is French for "crooked arm," and there are at least four theories as to its origin. One is that Bras Croche was a First Nations guide who led a party of immigrants over the Rocky Mountains in 1841. The other is that Bras Croche was an early Métis trapper whose arm had a peculiar set, caused by his having broken it when he was young. The third candidate for the moniker is John Macdonald of Garth, a partner of the North West Company, who was known by the French Canadian voyageurs as "Monsieur Macdonald le bras croche" because of his slightly withered right arm, the result of an accident at birth. Finally, some believe that Bras Croche refers to the Cree First Nation leader Maskipiton, whose name means "broken arm." Bras Croche is on the Alberta border, 63 kilometres south of Jasper.

BRITANNIA BEACH / BRITANNIA RANGE The community of Britannia Beach (estimated pop. 300) is located

B

on Howe Sound's eastern shore, 11 kilometres south of Squamish. It was established in 1905 as a company town by the Britannia Mining and Smelting Company, which operated a copper mine in the area that was the largest in the British Commonwealth for much of the early 20th century. The company and the Britannia Mine took their names from the nearby Britannia Range, which, in turn, was christened in about 1859 by Captain George Richards in honour of the HMS *Britannia*, a 100-gun warship that was at both the Battle of St. Vincent in 1797 and the Battle of Trafalgar in 1805.

BRITISH COLUMBIA New Caledonia was the name that explorer Simon Fraser gave to the British Columbia Interior between the Coast and the Rocky Mountain ranges in 1805. The moniker means "New Scotland" and was chosen because of the Interior's resemblance to the Scottish Highlands. The new mainland colony, which was established in 1858, was to be called New Caledonia as well, until it was pointed out at the last moment that the French already had a colony by that name in the Pacific. Other monikers were considered, including Albertoria, Borelia, New Cornwall, New Georgia, New Hanover, Nigrentia, Pacifica and West Britannia. The name British Columbia was finally chosen by Queen Victoria herself. The Queen Charlotte Islands (now Haida Gwaii) and the Stikine Territory, which were separate colonies, were merged with BC in 1863, as was the colony of Vancouver Island three years later.

BROKEN LEG LAKE *See* Bob Quinn Lake.

BROUGHTON An archipelago, an island and a strait were all named in 1792 by Captain George Vancouver after one of his officers, Lieutenant Commander William Robert Broughton. Broughton was the commander of the HMS *Chatham*, an armed tender that accompanied Vancouver and the HMS *Discovery*, during the latter's exploration of the British Columbia coast, until Vancouver sent Broughton back to England in 1793 with dispatches. The archipelago is the group of islands between Drury and Knight inlets. Broughton Island (125 km²) is one of the largest islands in the archipelago. Broughton Strait is on the south side of Cormorant and Malcolm islands, near Port McNeill.

B

BROWN PASSAGE This sea channel just south of Melville Island at Chatham Strait was named in 1793 by Captain George Vancouver for Captain William Brown of the ship *Butterworth*. Brown was sailing on his own off the coast of northern British Columbia and met with Vancouver in July 1793 at Stephens Island. At that meeting, Brown provided Vancouver with valuable information about the waters near present-day Prince Rupert, including the existence of Observatory and Portland inlets.

BULKLEY A small community, a lake and a river share this name. The 257-kilometre-long river starts at Bulkley Lake, 40 kilometres west of Burns Lake, and flows north and west to join the Skeena River at Hazelton. The traditional Wet'suwet'en First Nation name for the river was Wa Dzun Kwuh. The current moniker dates from at least 1871, when a map labelled it the "Bulkley or Wastonquah River." (Wastonquah is a derivation of Wa Dzun Kwuh. In addition, Wet'suwet'en means "people of the Wa Dzun Kwuh River.") The name Bulkley River was officially adopted in 1917 and honours Colonel Charles S. Bulkley of the U.S. Army, the chief engineer of the Western Union Extension Company from 1864 to 1866 and the man in charge of that company's construction of the Collins Overland Telegraph, which was strung through the valley during those years. Maps from 1919 label the river's headwaters as Bulkley Lake.

B

The community of Bulkley House is on the site of an old Hudson's Bay Company trading post that was built at the north end of Takla Lake and was identified as Bulkley House on an 1871 map. The name was shortened to Bulkley in 1975, but the original moniker was reinstated eight years later. It, too, honours Colonel Bulkley.

BURKE CHANNEL This channel was named in 1793 by Captain George Vancouver in honour of Edmund Burke. Burke was a philosopher, political theorist and long-time member of the British House of Commons. Burke Channel is 35 kilometres southwest of Bella Coola.

BURKEVILLE This small community, now part of Richmond, lies near the entrance to the Vancouver International Airport. It was established during World War II, when the federal government built more than 300 homes for the people who worked at a nearby Boeing plant. The community was named after the president of Boeing, Stanley Burke.

BURNABY A lake, a city (2006: pop. 202,799), a small mountain, an island, a strait and two mountain ranges are named after Robert Burnaby. Burnaby Lake was named in 1859 by Colonel Richard Moody of the Royal Engineers; Burnaby was, at the time, Moody's private secretary. That year, Moody was surveying land for the construction of New Westminster, and he heard from the local First Nations people about a large freshwater lake to the north. Burnaby led the party sent by Moody to find and survey it. The small settlement that grew around the lake was incorporated as Burnaby in 1892. The peak (370 m) at the northeast end of the city was named Mount Burnaby in 1948; it is frequently called Burnaby Mountain in error.

Burnaby Island (56 km²) and Burnaby Strait, both near Moresby Island in Haida Gwaii (Queen Charlotte Islands), were named in 1862 by Francis Poole, a geologist sent by the Queen Charlotte Mining Company to explore the potential riches of Burnaby Island. Burnaby himself was, by this time, a prominent Victoria merchant and a member of the Vancouver Island colonial legislature. The mountain range on Pitt Island was called the Burnaby Mountains at least as far back as 1870 and was renamed the Burnaby Range in 1950. The second Burnaby Range, located on the south side of Mackenzie Sound and west of Kingcome Inlet, was named by Captain Daniel Pender in 1865.

BURNS LAKE A lake and a village share this name. The lake, which is a widening of the Endako River, was christened in 1866 for Michael Byrnes, a surveyor and explorer for the Collins Overland Telegraph, who passed through the area a short time before. A settlement (2006: pop. 2107) soon became established on the west side of the lake. It's not clear how or why the spelling was changed, though it was done sometime before 1876.

BURRARD INLET This inlet, which reaches from Point Atkinson to Port Moody and is the harbour of the city of Vancouver, was named in 1792 by Captain George Vancouver for his good friend, Royal Navy Commander Sir Harry Burrard. Burrard and Vancouver were acting lieutenants together on the HMS *Europa* in the West Indies in 1785.

BUTCHART GARDENS Located 21 kilometres north of Victoria, this exceptional 22-hectare garden was established in 1904. Robert Butchart, a wealthy cement manufacturer, and his wife Jeanette ("Jennie") arrived in British Columbia that year and built their home near a limestone quarry. As more and more of the quarry was excavated by Butchart's company, Jennie beautified what was left behind by laying down topsoil and planting gardens. The site was opened to the public in the 1920s and became a major tourist attraction.

BUTE INLET This 65-kilometre-long fjord on the British Columbia mainland between Loughborough and Toba inlets was named in 1792 by Captain George Vancouver for John Stuart, the 3rd Earl of Bute. The earl died earlier that year, but Vancouver probably had not yet heard of his passing. Bute was a former British prime minister and the "dearest friend" of King George III. His 16-year-old grandson, Charles Stuart (and not his son Charles, as is often misstated), was that year a midshipman on Vancouver's ship, the HMS *Discovery*. Vancouver also named Stuart Island, at the mouth of the inlet, after the earl. Mount Bute (2810 m) and Bute Glacier, both at the head of the inlet, were named for the inlet in 1928 and 1930, respectively.

BUTTLE LAKE (28 km²)This lake in Strathcona Provincial Park on Vancouver Island was named in 1864 for John James Buttle. It is identified as Buttles Lake on many early maps. Buttle was a botanist and naturalist who, as a member of the 1864 Vancouver Island Exploring Expedition, helped explore the island's interior. It was said for many years that, in 1864, he was the first non-Aboriginal to see the lake, but this is now disputed by some. Nearby Mount Buttle (1379 m) was also named for the explorer in 1864.

C

CACHE CREEK (2006: pop. 1037) This village just north of Ashcroft was established in the 1860s as a stopping point along the Cariboo Wagon Road for prospectors heading north to the Cariboo Gold Rush. The community was named after a small nearby creek, called Rivière de la Cache by French Canadian fur traders in the early and mid-19th century. The earliest known reference to the stream as Cache Creek appears on an 1833 map. In French, *cache* means "a hiding place," but for the voyageurs, the word had a more specific meaning. To them, a cache was a hiding spot in the ground that was created by removing a circle of turf about 50 centimetres across and laying dry branches at the bottom of the hole. Then they placed their possessions in the hole and covered their goods with the removed turf. It is likely that someone before 1833 hid (or cached) something along or near the stream of Cache Creek.

CADBORO BAY This bay, just east of Victoria and southeast of Saanich, was named in 1842 by Hudson's Bay Company officers for the HBC brigantine *Cadboro* shortly after she became the first vessel to anchor there. She was also the first vessel brought by the HBC to the Pacific Coast, the first to enter the Fraser River and the first to sail into Victoria Harbour.

CALVERT ISLAND (320 km²) Located just north of Smith Sound, this island was named in 1788 by Captain Charles Duncan, the commanding officer of the King George's Sound Company sloop *Princess Royal*, while he was trading for furs in the area. No one really knows who Duncan named the island for, but Calvert was the family name of the Barons Baltimore, who were closely connected to the state of Maryland during its colonial days.

C

CAMPANIA ISLAND / CAMPANIA SOUND Campania Island (166 km²) was originally christened Compañia Island in 1792 by Lieutenant Commander Jacinto Caamaño, the commanding officer of the Spanish Navy corvette *Aránzaza*, while he was exploring the British Columbia coast around Dixon Entrance. Captain George Vancouver retained the name when he visited the area the following year. Sometime between 1886 and 1926, the spelling was changed to Campania. The isle is just west of Princess Royal Island. Campania Sound, which separates Campania and Princess Royal islands, was named in 1926. *Compañia* is Spanish for "company," as in either the company of friends or people or as in a business or society. It is no longer known to which "company" Caamaño was referring, but it might have been the Primera Compañía franca de Voluntarios de Cataluña (or "First Independent Company of Catalonian Volunteers"), a Spanish colonial military force that garrisoned the Spanish outpost at Nootka in 1790.

CAMPBELL A bay, two communities, an island, a lake and a river all share this name. Campbell Bay, on the east side of Mayne Island, was named in 1859 by Captain George Richards for Dr. Samuel Campbell, the assistant surgeon on Richards' ship, HM survey vessel *Plumper*. Campbell River, on the east coast of Vancouver Island, near the top of the Strait of Georgia, was also christened for Dr. Campbell, probably by Richards in 1860, though one source suggests that it was named by Captain Daniel Pender between 1866 and 1869 during one of his surveys of the area.

The city of Campbell River (2006: pop. 29,572), located just south of where the river flows into Georgia Strait, was established by 1889. Most historians think Campbell Island (133 km²), located near Milbanke Sound, was probably named (possibly also by Pender) after the good doctor. In any case, the island was known by that name by 1872. The lake was christened in about 1887 after the river. The small community of Campbell Island, located on the northeast side of the island, was known by its current name by 1936.

CANAL FLATS (2006: pop. 700) The site where this village is located, one kilometre from Columbia Lake, was originally named McGillivray's Portage by explorer David Thompson when he visited the area in 1807 or 1808. It's not known whether Thompson was honouring his friend and fellow explorer, Duncan McGillivray, or one of Duncan's brothers, Simon and William, both of whom were officers in the North West Company, which employed Thompson. Land developer and big-game hunter William Adolphe Baillie-Grohman built a canal there in 1887–89 that connected Columbia Lake to the nearby Kootenay River. A settlement arose during construction, and a post office was opened in 1888. Baillie-Groham was the first postmaster, and he named the post office (and, hence, the community) Groham. The name was changed to Canal Flat sometime after 1890, probably after Baille-Groham left Canada in 1893. The *s* was added later; according to local tradition, it was because of a spelling error on a highway sign. In any case, a 1909 gazetteer lists the village's moniker as Canal Flats.

CANFORD This small community's first settlers were Theophilis Hardiman and his family, who arrived in 1903. A settlement was soon established, which Hardiman named after Canford Manor near Bournemouth, England. Depending on the source, the manor was either his wife's home or the place where Hardiman and his family vacationed when he was a boy. (Who knows? It could have been both.) Canford is 15 kilometres west of Merritt.

C

CANIM LAKE A lake and a community share this name. The lake (54 km²) takes its name from *canim*, the Secwepemc (Shuswap) First Nation version of the Chinook Jargon word *can-aim* or *kaním*, which, in turn, is a derivation of the Chinook First Nation word *ekaním* or *ikaním*. The word means "canoe" or "dugout." Canim Lake is 35 kilometres northeast of 100 Mile House. It is not certain when the name was first applied to the lake, but it is found on a 1916 map. The community of Canim Lake (2006: pop. 243) is located on the lake's southwest shore. The village sits on land that was set aside for the people of the Canim Lake (Tsq'escenemc) First Nation in 1887, and it has been known by its current name since at least 1914.

CANOE This small, unincorporated community on Shuswap Lake, just northeast of Salmon Arm, was founded in about 1909. First Nation dugout canoes were once often seen going up and down the lake, and the beach at nearby Canoe Creek was frequently used as a landing spot. It's also been said that it was here that the First Nations people found excellent logs from which to make their canoes.

CAPE BEALE This entrance to Barkley Sound was named in 1787 by Captain Charles Barkley of the *Imperial Eagle* for his ship's purser, John Beale. Beale and several other members of Barkley's crew were killed by First Nations people that same year in a small river near Destruction Island off the coast of Washington State. Their deaths led Barkley to give that island its name.

CAPILANO This name applies to a lake, a mountain and a river. The Capilano River flows southward 35 kilometres from the mountains north of Vancouver into Burrard Inlet. The waterway was officially christened Capilano Creek in 1917, though the name was in use before then. The river was given its current moniker 30 years later. Capilano Mountain (1692 m), located at the headwaters of the river, was named in 1923. Capilano Lake was christened in 1956, after it was created by the completion of the Cleveland Dam on the Capilano River two years earlier. Capilano is a derivation of the Squamish First Nation personal name, Kiapila'noq, the hereditary moniker of the S̲k̲w̲x̲wú7mesh (Squamish) chiefs who lived at the mouth of the Capilano River. Chief George Capilano met explorers Captain James Cook in 1782 and Captain George Vancouver 10 years later, and his descendant, Chief Joe Capilano, travelled to London, England, to meet King Edward VII in 1906. One source indicates that the name's meaning is no longer known, whereas another says that it translates into "people of Kiap."

CAPITAL GROUP This group of mountains is located just west of Chilko Lake and was named in 1976 after the song "A Capital Ship" by Charles Edward Carryl. The mountains within the group were individually christened with names from the tune: Anagazander Mountain, Boatswain Mountain and Tickletoeteaser Tower. The mountains are surrounded on two sides by Chilko Lake, which inspired the nautical monikers.

CARIBOO This name applies to an entire region as well as to a mountain, a mountain range, a lake and a river. "The Cariboo" originally referred to the area surrounding the gold mines of Barkerville and Quesnel. The name dates from 1860, when a group of prospectors shot a caribou and, to celebrate, applied the name of the animal's species to the area. In the 19th century, cariboo was a commonly used alternate spelling of caribou. Over time, the phrase "the Cariboo" eventually came to include the entire plateau between Kamloops and Prince George, from the Fraser River to the Cariboo Mountains, though the spelling is no longer used to refer to the animal. The Cariboo Mountains, a northern range of the Columbia Mountains, are immediately to the east of the Cariboo. They were christened the Cariboo Range in 1887 but were

C

renamed in 1918. The range includes Cariboo Mountain (1938 m), which was also named in 1887.

Cariboo Lake and the Cariboo River lie north of Quesnel Lake. The lake's name goes back to an 1871 map. However, that same map labelled the part of the Cariboo River that flows south into the lake as Swamp River and the part that flows southwest from the lake as North Fork Quesnel River. (The river later merges with the Quesnel River.) It was not until 1936 that the Cariboo River officially received its current name.

CASSIAR This name applies to a mountain range and a river as well as to a ghost town and a mining district. The name was first applied to the Cassiar Land District, which is centred around Dease Lake, when a gold rush occurred there in the 1870s. Geologist George Dawson called the nearby mountains the Cassiar Ranges in 1887; they were officially renamed the Cassiar Mountains in 1917. The Cassiar River was so christened in 1944 because of its proximity to the Cassiar Land District. The settlement, which used to exist between Dease Lake and the Yukon border, was named after the Cassiar Asbestos Corporation. The company opened a mine there in 1952, but the mine and the townsite were abandoned 40 years later.

Cassiar is a derivation of the name Kaska, which is both the name of the Kaska First Nation and the name given by the Kaska Dene to a local creek where they went in the summer to fish and trade. The word *kaska* means either "creek" or "small river" or was a term of derision meaning "old moccasins," given to the Kaska Dene by the neighbouring Tahltan First Nation.

CASSIDY (2006: pop. 976) This community, along with a local coal mine, was built in 1918 by the Granby Consolidated Mining, Smelting & Power Company to provide homes for the company's employees who worked at the mine. The mine closed in 1932, but the settlement has survived. It was named after Thomas Cassidy, a farmer who arrived in the area from Iowa in 1878. By the time of his death in 1912, the locale was already variously known as Cassidy's, Tom Cassidy's and Cassidy Siding. Cassidy is 13 kilometres south of Nanaimo.

CASTLEGAR (2006: pop. 7259) This city was named by Edward Mahon when the townsite was laid out on his ranch in 1897. The moniker was that of the Mahon family manor in Ahascragh, County Galway, Ireland, and is believed to derive from the Gaelic name Caislean Gearr, which means "short castle." The community lies at the junction of the Columbia and Kootenay rivers. In 1898, Mahon sold the townsite to the Canadian Pacific Railway and moved to North Vancouver, and, until recently, his connection to the city was forgotten. As a result, several erroneous theories arose about the origin of the name. One of these was that the name was derived from the city of Castlebar in County Mayo, Ireland. Another is that Castlegar refers to a prominent rock formation that overlooks the nearby Columbia River. It was also incorrectly suggested that the city was named after the Castle Garden immigration centre in New York City.

CAWSTON (2006: pop. 973) Located five kilometres southeast of Keremeos, this community dates from 1860, when the Hudson's Bay Company opened a store on the site. By the time the townsite was laid out and a post office opened in 1917, the place had already been named after its first permanent non-Aboriginal settler, Richard Lowe Cawston, who was a cattle rancher in the area from 1884 to 1911.

CEDAR (2006: pop. 3043) This community was established in the 1880s and named for the great abundance of cedar trees in the area. Cedar is 12 kilometres southeast of Nanaimo.

C

CEEPEECEE / CEEPEECEE LAKE Ceepeecee is a small community just southwest of Tahsis. It was founded when the Canadian Packing Corporation, a subsidiary of the California Packing Corporation, built a fish-packing plant there in 1926. The name is a phonetic rendering of the initials CPC. The nearby lake was officially named in 1946 after the settlement that grew around the plant.

CHALK ISLAND Formerly known as Price Island, it was renamed (probably to avoid confusion with the other Price Island in British Columbia) in 1945 after William Max Chalk, a native of New Westminster, who was a clerk and stenographer with the Pacific Coast Hydrographic Service. The island is located off Barkley Sound.

CHARLIE LAKE A lake and a community just northwest of Fort St. John share this name. The settlement (2006: pop. 1884) dates from at least 1933; the name of the lake goes back to at least 1911. The body of water was previously known as Old Charlie's Lake and was christened after Charlie Chok (also known as Big Charlie), a Dunne-za chief, who was the only person who lived along the lake year round. It was also once known as Fish Lake, though it has been said that there were no fish "worthy of the name" in it. The Sekani First Nation name for the lake is Tahkahje Dat'ona Manè. Animal remains and 11,500-year-old stone artifacts found in a nearby cave make it the oldest site of human occupation in the province.

CHASE / MOUNT CHASE The village of Chase (2006: pop. 2409) was named for Whitfield Chase, the first settler in the area, who started a large farm and ranch there in 1865. The Adams River Lumber Company laid out the townsite in 1908 and offered to name it after the company's secretary, James Magee. Magee declined and insisted that it be named after Chase. The community is on the west end of Little Shuswap Lake. Nearby Mount Chase (1666 m) was named in 1932 after the community.

CHASE RIVER Both a river that flows into Nanaimo Harbour and a community in Nanaimo share this name. The name dates to November 1852, when two Aboriginal youths murdered a young Scotsman who was employed as a shepherd in the Saanich area. One of the assailants was soon captured, but the other escaped and was tracked to his village near present-day Nanaimo. Once he heard that an armed party was after him, the murderer fled into the forest and was chased through the snow to the river, where he was caught. The river officially received its name in 1915, though the moniker was commonly used long before then. A community called Chase had been established along the river by 1914. Its name was changed to Chase River in 1951, probably to avoid confusion with the village along Little Shuswap Lake, and it is now a part of Nanaimo. Gallows Point, on the shores of Protection Island in Nanaimo Harbour, was named by Captain George Richards in 1860 to mark the place where the two killers paid for their crime.

CHATHAM A point on Vancouver Island north of Campbell River, a group of islands in Baynes Channel and a channel in Knight Inlet are all named after the HMS *Chatham*. The vessel accompanied Captain George Vancouver and the HMS *Discovery* from 1791 to 1795. The *Chatham* was named after John Pitt, the 2nd Earl of Chatham, who was the First Lord of the British Admiralty when it and the *Discovery* left London in 1791. Chatham Point was named by Vancouver the following year. The Chatham Islands were probably christened by either Captain Kellett or Lieutenant Commander Wood of the HMS *Herald* in 1846, at the same time that nearby Discovery Island was named after Vancouver's ship. Chatham Channel was named by Captain Daniel Pender in about 1866.

CHATHAM SOUND According to Captain George Vancouver in 1793, this sound between Portland Inlet and Porcher Island was christened by an earlier visitor,

C

possibly Captain Charles Duncan of the trading ship *Princess Royal*, who sailed through the area in 1788. All agree that the sound was christened after John Pitt, the 2nd Earl of Chatham and the First Lord of the British Admiralty from 1788 to 1794. The sound marks the north end of Pitt Archipelago, which was named after the earl's younger brother, British Prime Minister William Pitt.

CHEAKAMUS A community, a glacier, a lake, a mountain and a river, all just north of Squamish, share this name. The first to be christened was the Cheakamus River. It was initially labelled as such on a 1914 map, though it was named the Chikamus River in a 1908 survey. The community is located on the east side of the river and dates back to at least 1914. The lake, an expansion of the river inside Garibaldi Provincial Park, had been named by 1920. The glacier and the mountain (2588 m), which are also located in the park, were named after the river in 1930. Cheakamus is a derivation of *Tseearkamisht*, a Sḵwx̱wú7mesh (Squamish) First Nation word that means "people who use the cedar-rope fishing net." (The Sḵwx̱wú7mesh people used to live along the banks of the Cheakamus River.)

CHEAM Two small communities, Cheam and Cheam View, as well as a mountain and a former lake, all a few kilometres east of Chilliwack, share this name. Cheam is a derivation of the Halq'emeylem (Halkomelem) word *xwchi:ya:m*, which means "strawberry place" and refers to the wild strawberries that grow on Cheam Peak and nearby Lady Peak. (Halq'emeylem is the language of the local Stó:lô First Nation, and *shchi:ye* means "strawberry.") The community of Cheam was founded in about 1870; Cheam Village was established approximately 40 years later. The mountain (2104 m) has been known as Cheam Peak since at least 1914. Its traditional Halq'emeylem name is Theeth-uhl-kay, which translates as "the source" or "the place from which the waters spring (or slide)." There was once a Cheam Lake, but it was drained in the 1950s.

CHEHALIS LAKE / CHEHALIS RIVER Maps have identified both the lake and river by the current spelling of their
names since at least 1914. The river flows south into the
Harrison River; the lake is an expansion of the river west
of Harrison Lake. The two were named after the Sts'ailes
people of the Chehalis First Nation, who live in the upper
Fraser Valley. Previous spellings include Chahales, Saelis
and StsEe'lis. There are a number of interpretations of
what *sts'ailes* means. The two most probable include "the
place one reaches after ascending the rapids" and "where
the 'chest' of a canoe grounds on a sandbar." ("Chest" in
this case refers to the widest part of a dugout canoe.)

CHEMAINUS A bay, a community, a lake and a river, all
located between Duncan and Ladysmith, share this name.
The community of Chemainus (estimated pop. 5000)
was named by Thomas George Askew, one of the first
settlers to arrive in the area in 1856, and is part of the
municipality of North Cowichan. Chemainus River is
found on British Admiralty charts dating from 1865, and
Chemainus Lake appears on an 1871 map. The bay was
originally christened Horseshoe Bay by Captain George
Richards in 1859 because of its shape but was renamed
by the British Hydrographic Office in 1895. According
to the Hul'qumi'num First Nation, the moniker is
a derivation of the name of the Chemainus First Nation
village, Shts'emines, which is located less than five
kilometres away at Kulleet Bay. Early settlers and other
non-Aboriginals also spelled Shts'emines as Tsa-mee-mis
and Tsiminnis, and it is the source of the name of the
Chemainus people, who are a part of the Hul'qumi'num
(Island Halkomelem) First Nation. Most sources agree that
the Hul'qumi'num word means "bitten breast," and many
say it refers to Chemainus Bay, whose shape resembles the

C

bite that an extremely excited shaman would take from a spectator during a First Nations ceremony. One source, however, contends that Chemainus is actually the anglicized spelling of the Chinook Jargon word *sménəs*, which, in turn, is a derivation of either the Puyallup First Nation word *sma'nch* ("hill") or the Cowlitz First Nation word *smant*. If correct, then Chemainus means "hill" or "hilly." Furthermore, another source says that Chemainus is a derivation of the name of a great First Nation prophet and shaman, Tso-meeun-is, who willingly received a massive wound to his chest to become a chief. When translated, his name means "broken chest."

CHERRYVILLE (2006: pop. 614) This community, located 37 kilometres east of Vernon, was established in the 1860s during the Big Bend Gold Rush. It was called Camagna when the post office opened there in 1909, after the first postmaster, E. Camagna, who settled there that year and held the job until 1919. He must not have been too popular, because a short time after Camagna retired, the town was renamed Cherryville, for all the wild cherries that grow in the area.

CHETWYND (2006: pop. 2633) This district municipality was originally called Little Prairie by the first settlers who arrived in the area in 1912. The community received an economic boost in the 1950s, when the Pacific Great Eastern Railway (PGE) came to town. In 1959, the settlement was renamed in honour of Ralph L.T. Chetwynd, the recently deceased provincial Minister of Railways and a former PGE director.

CHILCOTIN The Chilcotin Plateau (also known as the Chilcotin or Chilcotin Country) is in central British Columbia and extends 300 kilometres from the Fraser River to the Coast Mountains. Chilcotin is the anglicized version of tsiłqoxt'in, the name of the people of the Tsilhqot'in First Nation that live in the area. The explorer

Simon Fraser called them the "Chilk-hodins," when he travelled through the plateau in 1808. One translation of the name is "ochre river people," which refers to the naturally occurring orange, red and yellow ochre found in the soil. The iron-oxide substance was valued by the Tsilhqot'in as a base for paint and dye. Another translation is "people of the young man's river."

Within the Chilcotin Plateau and to the west of Williams Lake is the 235-kilometre-long Chilcotin River, which has been known by its current name since at least 1871. Chilcotin Lake (officially named in 1917) lies near the north end of the river. East of Chilko Lake is a mountain range called the Chilcotin Ranges, whose name was adopted in 1968.

CHILKAT PASS / CHILKAT RIVER The Chilkat Pass is in the Coast Mountains of northwestern British Columbia, between Haines, Alaska, and Haines Junction, Yukon. It was used by the people of the Chilkat (a Tlingit First Nation) as a trade route between the coast and the interior. The Haines Junction Highway now goes through the mountain pass, and it has been labelled on maps as the Chilkat Pass as far back as 1899.

The Chilkat River, which begins east of the pass and flows south across the Alaska border and then west into the Klehini River, was named by the Russians sometime before 1867, while they occupied Alaska. Late 19th-century anthropologists identified *tschilkathin,* which means "salmon storehouse," as the original Tlingit word. The name has been spelled many ways over the years, including Chilcat, Tchillkat, Tschilkat, Tschilkathin, Tsilkat and Tsl-kaht, but the current spelling has been used since it first appeared on American maps in 1880. The moniker was the name of a Tlingit village on the Chilkat Peninsula, about three kilometres south of Haines, Alaska, which was later abandoned in about 1910. The name also refers to the Chilkat people.

C

CHILKO A glacier, a lake, a mountain and a river all share this name. Chilko Lake (192 km²) and Chilko River have both been known by their current monikers since at least 1871, though the current spelling was not adopted until 1911. Early maps spelled the name as Chilco and Chilcote. The lake is 150 kilometres southwest of Williams Lake. The river flows northeast from the north end of the lake and into the Chilcotin River. Nearby Chilko Glacier and Chilko Mountain (2709 m) were named in 1913 and 1924, respectively, after the lake and river. Chilko is a derivation of the Tsilhqot'in (Chilcotin) First Nation word *tsiɬhqox*, which means "ochre river" or "young man's river." (The "ochre" does not refer to the colour but to the naturally occurring orange, red and yellow iron-oxide substance found in the soil, which was valued by the Tsilhqot'in as a base for paint and dye.)

CHILKOOT PASS This mountain pass (1067 m) on the northwest tip of British Columbia, along the Alaska border, was known by a number of other names, including Dejah, Perrier Pass and Shasheki Pass, before the locally popular Chilkoot Portage won out in 1890. The current name was adopted eight years later. The name is frequently spelled Chilcoot and Chilkat. Chilkoot is taken from the name of the Chilkat (or Chilkoot) band of the Tlingit First Nation, whose main village was near the mouth of Chilkoot River about 20 kilometres southwest of Skagway, Alaska. The Chilkat used the pass to trade with other First Nations peoples in British Columbia. The name is a Tlingit word meaning "salmon storehouse." The Chilkoot Pass was the arduous route used by thousands of gold-seekers to get to the gold fields in the Yukon during the Klondike Gold Rush. *See* Chilkat Pass.

CHILLIWACK (2006: pop. 69,217) The city of Chilliwack lies south of the Fraser River, between Abbotsford and Hope. It was named after the Chilliwack River, which flows just south of it. The river was labelled as the Chilwayhook in an 1859 newspaper article, the Chiakweyuk on 1860 British Admiralty charts and the Chilukweyuk on an 1871 map. The river's current name dates from 1914. Nearby Chilliwack Mountain was originally called Solitary Mountain in 1860 and then Chilliwak Mountain in 1913, before acquiring its current name in 1914. Surveys of the area by Captain George Richards in 1859–60 refer to an "Old Hudson Bay Co. fishing station" in the vicinity and to a "first establishment on the river" about two kilometres away.

The first non-Aboriginal settlers arrived in 1862, and two communities developed in the area. One grew at the steamboat landing on the Fraser River and was known at various times as Codville's Landing, Miller's Landing, Sumas Landing and Chilliwack Landing. The location was renamed Chilliwack (or Chilliwhack) in 1872 and incorporated as the township of Chilliwhack in 1873. To the south, at the junction of three important transportation routes (the New Westminster–Yale Wagon Road, Wellington Avenue and Young Road) was the commercial centre called Five Corners. A nearby subdivision called Centreville was established in 1881. Five Corners was renamed Centreville in 1883. The whole community of Centreville was then rechristened as Chilliwhack in 1887 and incorporated as the city of Chilliwack in 1908. For 72 years, the city of Chilliwack was surrounded by the township of Chilliwhack, but after a public vote in 1980, the two were merged and the name Chilliwack was settled upon. The first time the place name was used by non-Aboriginals was when surveys for the Yale Road were made through the Fraser Valley in 1864. Chilliwack is an adaptation of the Halq'emeylem (Halkomelem) First Nation name Ch.ihl-kway-uhk, which denotes both the local area and the people of the Ch.ihl-kway-uhk (sometimes spelled Ts'elxwiqw) tribes of the Stó:lô First Nation (an alliance of various Halq'emeylem communities along the lower Fraser River), who lived around Sumas Lake between Abbotsford and Chilliwack.

C

CHINA CLUB BAY Located on the east side of False Bay on Lasqueti Island, this "bay" is really a cove. It was once called by the now politically incorrect name of Jap Bay because a large number of Japanese Canadian families operated a cannery and small fishing fleet there in the 1920s and '30s. It was then called Mud Bay before it acquired its current name in 2003. The *China Club* was a traditional three-masted Chinese junk that was hand-built and lived in by long-time Lasqueti Island residents Allen and Sharie Farrell. The junk and the Farrells eventually became the subject of two books, various magazine articles and video documentaries.

CHRISTINA LAKE A community (2006: pop. 986) and a lake (26 km²) share this name. Both are located 21 kilometres northeast of Grand Forks. The community was settled in the late 1890s, shortly after the Canadian Pacific Railway reached the lake. The lake was christened sometime between 1865 and 1871 for Christina MacDonald McKenzie Williams, the daughter of Catherine Baptiste and J. Angus MacDonald. Her father was the Hudson's Bay Company chief trader at Fort Colville (in present-day Washington State) from 1852 until the front closed in 1870. There are two versions of the story of how the lake got its name. In one, Christina, her father and an old HBC employee named Joseph LaFleur were travelling from Fort Colville to Victoria in 1870, after the outpost had been closed. When they got to the lake, LaFleur simply said "Here is your lake, Christina." In the other, Christina was accompanying her father and a brigade to Kamloops. Christina was her father's bookkeeper and, while crossing what is now called Christina Creek, the raft she was on suddenly disintegrated, and she and the buckskin sack containing her father's valuable HBC books and papers were thrown into the rushing water. Christina was rescued some distance downstream and, when she was dragged out of the water, she was still holding the sack. The name Christina Lake appears on an 1871 map; the body of water was previously identified as Nichelaam in 1859 and as Tsaap in 1865.

CLAYOQUOT Clayoquot Sound is a collection of bays, channels and islands on the west coast of Vancouver Island and extends from Barkley Sound to Nootka Sound. Within its vicinity are Clayoquot Island, Clayoquot Lake and Clayoquot River. The sound was christened Wichaninnish's Sound by Captain Charles Barkley in 1787, in honour of the principal Nuu-chah-nulth (Nootka) First Nation chief in the area. It was called Port Cox on a 1790 map made for John Cox and Company, a merchant establishment in Canton, China, which sent two ships there three years earlier. However, neither of those names stuck. Since 1785, fur traders had called the sound Clayocuat, Clioquatt, Klahoquaht and Klaooquat. It was labelled Plano del Archipelago de Clayocuat in a chart drawn in 1791 by Juan Pantoja, Francisco de Eliza y Reventa's pilot on the *San Carlos*. It was also called Archipelago de Claucuad on Dionisio Alcalá-Galiano's 1792 map. Captain George Vancouver gave the sound its current spelling on his 1792 chart. The moniker is a derivation of the name of the people of the Tla-o-qui-aht First Nation (a branch of the Nuu-chah-nulth Clayoquot), who still live in the area. The name has been given several interpretations, including "another (i.e., different) people," "other or (strange) house," "people different from what they used to be" and "people of a place where it becomes the same even when disturbed." Because of these definitions, it is believed by some that the name was given to the Tla-o-qui-aht by the people of another First Nation.

C

CLEARWATER One of British Columbia's most recently incorporated communities, as well as a river, a lake and a mountain, share this name. The district municipality of Clearwater (estimated population: 4960) is at the junction of the Clearwater and North Thompson rivers, 122 kilometres north of Kamloops. Incorporated in 2007, the community was originally called Raft River when it was founded in 1900, after another body of water that flows nearby. The moniker was changed to Clearwater Station in 1926 after the Canadian National Railway station that was built there a few years earlier. The name was shortened to Clearwater in 1961. That CNR station was named after nearby Clearwater River. The earliest known reference to the river was in 1862 by French Canadian voyageurs who, thinking that it was a fork of the Thompson River, called it Fourche L'eau Clair. An 1865 map labelled it the Clear Water River, and an 1871 chart named it the Clearwater River. The river expands at one point in Wells Gray Provincial Park into Clearwater Lake. The lake's name is found on a 1917 map but was well established long before that. Nearby Clearwater Peak (1912 m) was also named in 1921 after the river.

CLEVELAND DAM This dam in North Vancouver was built in 1954 and named after Ernest Albert Cleveland, the first chief commissioner of the Greater Vancouver Water District from 1926 to 1952.

CLINTON (2006: pop. 578) A roadhouse was built on this site in 1861 to accommodate travellers on the Cariboo Wagon Road. The roadhouse and the village that grew up around it were called 47 Mile House because of their distance from Lillooet. However, when the Cariboo Wagon Road was completed in 1863, the community was renamed Clinton, in honour of Henry Pelham Clinton, the 5th Duke of Newcastle, who was then the British Colonial Secretary. Clinton is 40 kilometres north of Cache Creek.

CLUCULZ LAKE The name of this lake is found on a 1916 map, but the moniker is much older. Cluculz is a derivation of the Dakelh (Carrier) First Nation name for the lake, Lhooh Kuz, which has been variously translated as "carp lake," "place of big whitefish" and "where we go for whitefish." The lake is between Prince George and Vanderhoof.

C

COAL HARBOUR This harbour on the north side of Holberg Inlet was originally called Stephens Harbour in 1927, but the name was changed 20 years later to reflect the wishes of the local residents. The community of Coal Harbour (2006: pop. 176) dates from the 1880s and was founded by coal miners, who were brought in after coal deposits were discovered nearby in 1882. The name is, obviously, a descriptive one.

COAST MOUNTAINS These mountains were originally called the Cascade Range but were renamed in 1902. They get their name because they are near the Pacific Coast and run parallel to the coastline and because they are a continuation of the Coast Range in the United States. About 300 kilometres wide, the mountain range extends 1600 kilometres, from the Alaska Panhandle to the Fraser River.

COBBLE HILL A hill (331 m) and a nearby community (2006: pop. 1775), both 12 kilometres southeast of Duncan, share this name. The community was officially christened in 1887 after the hill, but the settlement existed at least a decade before that. The hill was labelled as Mount Cobble on an 1859 chart shortly after surveyors mapped the area and was known by that moniker until 1887, when a post office opened at its base. From then on, the mountain was called Cobble Hill Mountain and the surrounding settlement Cobble Hill. No one is certain of the origins of the name. A local historian says it was named after a Captain Cobble, a member of the 1859 survey party. Others say that, while the Esquimalt and

C

Nanaimo Railway (E&NR) was laying its tracks through the area in 1886, a visiting Englishwoman commented that the hill reminded her of the community of Cobble Hill in England. However, since the E&NR did not yet exist when Mount Cobble was christened, this story can probably be discounted. The E&NR's records state that the site of the community was named after some nearby gravel quarries. (Cobble is the name of one of the four types of gravel quarried there, and there is a seemingly limitless amount of it on Vancouver Island.) Finally, there is a story that Cobble was the name of a Royal Navy lieutenant, who, if he existed, was probably an officer on a gunboat that visited nearby Cowichan Bay whenever the area's settlers were afraid of trouble from the local First Nations people.

COLDSTREAM (2006: pop. 9471) This district municipality's first settler was Charles Houghton, a former colonel in the famous 20th Regiment of Foot, who acquired property there in 1863 that became the Coldstream Ranch. His estate was named after the coldwater spring found at the head of Coldstream Creek; Houghton may have named the creek as well. A town was established in the area after John Hamilton-Gordon, the 1st Marquess of Aberdeen and Temair (and the soon-to-be Governor General of Canada), bought the ranch in 1891 and subdivided parts of it for settlement. The community is five kilometres southeast of Vernon.

COLUMBIA ICEFIELD / MOUNT COLUMBIA The Columbia Icefield was originally called the Columbia Snowfield and was renamed during a 1919 survey. The icefield is the centre of the greatest accumulation of ice in the Rocky Mountains. Less than five kilometres away is Mount Columbia (3741 m). Both the icefield and the mountain were named in 1899 after the Columbia River by J. Norman Collie who, with Hermann Woolley, discovered them the year before. The icefield and the mountain are both on the Alberta-BC border, 75 kilometres north of Donald.

COLUMBIA LAKE / COLUMBIA RIVER The Columbia River was named in 1792 by Captain Robert Gray after his ship, the *Columbia Rediviva*, while he explored the mouth of the river (which is located on the Pacific Coast between Oregon and Washington). Gray's ship, in turn, was christened in honour of Christopher Columbus, though some historians believe it was named after the sixth-century Irish saint, Columba. *Rediviva* is Spanish for "revived," which has lead some to suspect that the ship had been rebuilt. More than one-third of the Columbia River's 2000-kilometre length is in British Columbia. The river originates in Columbia Lake in southeastern BC, flows north into Kinbasket Lake, then southward into Lake Revelstoke and the Arrow Lakes, continuing past Castlegar and Trail into the United States, where it eventually turns westward to the Pacific.

Columbia Lake was discovered, but apparently not named, by David Thompson in the early 1800s. It was christened Upper Columbia (Otter) Lake by George Dawson in 1886, because the Secwepemc (Shuswap) called the body of water Otter Lake in their own language. The lake received its current name in 1913.

COLUMBIA MOUNTAINS This 600-kilometre-long collection of four mountain ranges (the Cariboos, Monashees, Purcells and Selkirks) occupies most of southeastern British Columbia. This group of mountains gets its name from the fact that the meltwater from these ranges drains into the Columbia River.

COLWOOD (2006: pop. 14,687) Captain Edward Edwards Langford, a former landowner in Sussex, England, and a veteran of the 73rd Foot Regiment, arrived in Victoria in 1851 to manage a 600-acre farm established by the Puget

C

Sound Agricultural Company, a subsidiary of the Hudson's Bay Company. Langford named the farmhouse Colwood after his farm in England. A settlement started to grow around it in the 1870s and took on the name. The city is 10 kilometres west of Victoria.

COMMITTEE PUNCH BOWL This small lake at the head of Athabasca Pass on the Alberta border was named by Hudson's Bay Company governor Sir George Simpson when he and Dr. John McLoughlin viewed it in 1824. The lake particularly impressed Simpson because it drained into streams that lead to both the Atlantic and Pacific oceans. As Simpson would later write, "I thought it should be honoured by a distinguishing title, and it was forthwith named the 'Committee's Punch Bowl.'" It is assumed that Simpson meant the HBC's managing committee.

COMOX A town (2006: pop. 12,136) located four kilometres east of Courtenay on the east shore of Vancouver Island shares this name with the valley in which it lies, as well as with a nearby harbour and a lake. According to most sources, Comox is a derivation of Comuk-thway or Komuckway, a place name in a dialect of Kwakw'ala that was spoken by the Yucultas (a group of the Kwakwaka'wakw First Nation). Another states that Comox is an adaptation of the Kwakw'ala place name q'úmuXʷs (or q'ómoxws or kw'umuxws). Sources differ as to whether the moniker referred specifically to the Comox Valley or to the entire region between Kelsey Bay to the north and Denman and Hornby islands to the south. In any case, the name means "land of abundance," "land of plenty" or "land of riches" and refers to the abundance of berries and game in the area. However, explorer Robert Brown wrote in his journal in 1864 that Comox was a "ridiculously enough" misspelling of the name of the Comoucs people. "I am a Comouc they will say & this is the country of the Comoucs." Brown also maintained that the name was originally one of derision (though he did not mention what it supposedly meant) that was given by the Yucultas to the Sathloot, who were one of the groups that now comprise the K'ómoks (Comox) First Nation that still live in the area. The British Navy used the area around present-day Comox for training purposes in the 1850s and spelled the name in a variety of ways, including Komoux, Comuck and Comax. The current spelling was in use by 1860. The first settlers arrived in 1862 and named their community after the valley.

Comox Harbour was called Port Augusta on British Admiralty charts published from 1862 to 1900, but by the 1890s, it had also become known by its current name, which was formally adopted by the Geographic Board of Canada in 1902. The lake was originally christened Puntledge Lake in 1864 by Robert Brown after the people of the Pentlatch First Nation, which was later absorbed by the Comox. It was officially renamed Comox Lake in 1922, though the current name was in use before then.

CONNAUGHT TUNNEL It took the Canadian Pacific Railway three years—from 1913 to 1916—to construct this tunnel underneath Rogers Pass in Glacier National Park. The tunnel was named by the CPR for Prince Arthur, the Duke of Connaught, who was the third son of Queen Victoria as well as the Governor General of Canada from 1911 to 1916.

COOMBS (2006: pop. 1327) This community was established when 100 settlers from Leeds, England, were brought to the area in 1910 by the Salvation Army, as part of a project to relocate Britain's poor to Canada. The settlement was named after Captain Thomas Coombs, the Salvation Army's commissioner for Canada. Coombs is near Parksville.

C

COQUIHALLA A group of lakes, an historic trail, a highway, a mountain and a river share this name. The diaries and maps of early fur traders called the Coquihalla River the Kwee Kwe ah la, the Qua-que-alla and the Quequealla. It was labelled the Coquhalla River on an 1871 chart, and George Dawson gave the name its current spelling in 1877. The river flows southwest into the Fraser River at Hope.

The Coquihalla Trail was the path used by ranchers in the 19th century to take their cattle from the Nicola Valley to Hope. The present-day Coquihalla Highway, which was completed in 1987, follows the same route. The Coquihalla Lakes, which are the headwaters of the Coquihalla River, located northeast of Hope, and Coquihalla Mountain (2157 m; previously known as Black Mountain and Rocher Noir) were both named in 1910 after the river.

There are two theories about the origin of the name. One is that the river was christened after Quaqualla, the chief of the First Nations people living near Fort Hope in the mid-19th century. It is more likely that the moniker is a derivation of the Halq'emeylem (Halkomelem) First Nation word *kw'o:kw'e'kw'iya:la*, which means "stingy container [of fish]." According to the people of the Stó:lô First Nation, of whom the Halq'emeylem are a part, there were once places in the river that were home to "little water babies" called the *skw'ikw'iy*. These mythical creatures were frequently very stingy with the fish, a behaviour known as *kw'o:kw'ekw'iy*. If the *skw'ikw'iy* did not like you, they would not let you catch any fish. *A-la* or *t-ala* is Halq'emeylem for "container."

COQUITLAM Two cities, as well as a river, a lake, a mountain and two islands share this name. Port Coquitlam (2006: pop. 52,687) is north of the Fraser River, between the Pitt River and the city of Port Moody. Directly to the north and west is the city of Coquitlam (2006: pop. 114,565). The Coquitlam River divides the two communities. Port

Coquitlam's first non-Aboriginal settlers arrived in 1853. For a while, the spot was simply known as Coquitlam, but when the Canadian Pacific Railway built a branch line from New Westminster to this location in 1886, the settlement was rechristened Westminster Junction. It was incorporated as Port Coquitlam in 1913.

C

The first non-Aboriginal settlers in present-day Coquitlam arrived in the 1860s, and the community was incorporated as Coquitlam in 1891. Sources differ as to whether these communities were named after the people of the Kwikwetlem (Kwayhquitlum or Coquitlam) First Nation or after Chief Kwikwetlem William, a Kwikwetlem leader who died in 1953 at the approximate age of 110. In either case, *kwikwetlem* is a word in the Halq'eméylem First Nation language (spoken by the Kwikwetlem), which means "red fish up the river." The name specifically refers to a species of sockeye salmon found in the Coquitlam River that became extinct shortly after the completion of the second dam at Coquitlam Lake in 1913. Some sources erroneously state that Kwikwetlem means "stinking of fish slime," in reference to the Kwikwetlem, who caught and killed salmon for the people of the Kwantlen (Qw'?ntl'en) First Nation. The Kwikwetlem were first referred to by non-Aboriginals as the Coquitlam in 1861, and they still reside in the area. The Coquitlam River, as well as Coquitlam Lake (12.5 km²), Coquitlam Island (in Coquitlam Lake) and Coquitlam Mountain (1583 m) are also named after the Kwikwetlem.

Another Coquitlam Island in British Columbia is located hundreds of kilometres away, southwest of Prince Rupert. That isle was named in 1954 after a fishing vessel called the *Coquitlam*.

CORDERO CHANNEL This sea passage on the north side of East Thurlow and Sonora islands was probably named in 1792 for Josef Cordero, the draughtsman for the

Mexicana and the *Sutil* during Spanish explorer Dionisio Alcalá-Galiano's expedition through the Strait of Georgia that year.

C

CORDOVA BAY Both the bay north of Victoria and the community on its shores share this name. Spanish Navy Sub-Lieutenant Manuel Quimper of the *Princesa Real* (the captured British sloop *Princess Royal*) christened the large bay west of Victoria Puerto de Cordova in 1790. The name honours Don Antonio Maria Bucareli y Ursua Henestrosa Lasso de la Vega Villacis y Cordova, the viceroy of Mexico from 1771 to 1779. In 1842, officers of the Hudson's Bay Company took the moniker, anglicized it and applied it to the bay that bears the name today. They renamed the original site Esquimalt Harbour. Captain Henry Kellett, however, renamed Cordova Bay in 1846, calling it Cormorant Bay, after the HM steam sloop *Cormorant* towed his own vessel, the HM survey vessel *Herald*, through the Strait of Juan de Fuca to the site. Despite the name change, the local residents always referred to the bay as Cordova Bay. Finally, at the urging of historian and mariner Captain John Walbran, the British Admiralty restored the Spanish name in 1905. The community was established sometime before 1920.

CORMORANT ISLAND Commander George T. Gordon named this island in Broughton Strait in 1846 after his ship, the HM paddle sloop *Cormorant*. The vessel was the first naval steamship in British Columbia's waters.

CORONEL MOUNTAIN (2668 m) Located west of Chilko Lake, this mountain was named by members of the Alpine Club, who were climbing a nearby peak in 1953. They christened the mountain after the Battle of Coronel, which took place off the coast of Chile in 1914. Shortly after World War I began, a German fleet of five battle cruisers sailed into the Pacific. At the time, the only naval ship protecting British Columbia was a training cruiser, and there was widespread panic that the Germans would attack Victoria and Vancouver. It was in this sea battle that the British Navy first confronted the Germans, suffering a major defeat. Nine nearby mountains are named after the officers and ships that were engaged in that battle, including Good Hope Mountain and Monmouth Mountain (after the HMS *Good Hope* and the HMS *Monmouth*, which both sank at the battle), Glasgow Mountain and Otranto Mountain (after the HMS *Glasgow* and the HMS *Otranto*, the only two British ships to survive the fight), Mount Cradock (after Rear Admiral Sir Christopher Cradock, who died in the battle), and Dresden Mountain, Leipzig Mountain and Scharnhorst Mountain (after the German cruisers *Dresden, Leipzig* and *Scharnhorst*). Admiral Ridge is also named after Admiral Cradock. Also nearby is Canopus Mountain, named after the HMS *Canopus*, which fired the opening salvo at the Battle of the Falkland Islands five weeks later, a conflict that ended with the destruction of the German fleet.

CORTES ISLAND This island (123 km²) and Hernando Island, both at the north end of Georgia Strait, were named in 1792 by the Spanish naval officers, Dionisio Alcalá-Galiano and Cayetano Valdés y Flores, in honour of Hernando Cortes, the 16th-century Spanish conqueror of Mexico.

COURTENAY / COURTENAY RIVER The river is located on the east side of Vancouver Island and flows into Comox Harbour. It was named in about 1860, probably by Lieutenant Richard Charles Mayne when he visited the Comox area that year. In any case, it is certain that the river was christened in honour of George William Conway Courtenay, the captain of the HMS *Constance* when the vessel was stationed in British Columbia waters from 1846 to 1849. By 1860, Courtenay was a rear admiral. The city

(2006: pop. 21,940) was laid out in 1891 and named after the river.

COWICHAN A bay, a lake, a river, a valley, a district municipality (North Cowichan), a town (Lake Cowichan) and two unincorporated communities (Cowichan Bay and Cowichan Station) near Duncan are all named for the people of the Cowichan First Nation. The Cowichan live on the south coasts of both Vancouver Island and the British Columbia mainland and are a part of the Hul'qumi'num (Halkomelem) First Nation linguistic group. The name comes from the Hul'qumi'num word, *quw'utsum'*, which means "warmed by the sun" or "warm land." Some sources say, however, that the name comes from the Hul'qumi'num term *shkewétsen*, which means "basking in the sun." In either case, most agree that the word refers to a time when a large frog was seen basking on top of Mount Tzouhalem and to the fact that a rock formation on the side of that mountain resembles the frog. However, others say that "warm land" is only a reference to the Cowichan Valley and has nothing to do with the peak or the frog at all.

The first known reference to the Cowichan people was made by explorer Simon Fraser, who referred to them as the Ka-way-chin in 1808. The bay and river were named in about 1850 by officers of the Hudson's Bay Company, though the name went through various spellings (Cowichin and Cowitchin) before the current spelling was officially adopted in 1908. The bay was actually known as Cowichan Harbour until 1924, though some maps as far back as 1871 used the name. The name of the lake (61 km²) went through the same multiple spellings before its current moniker was adopted in 1908. The first settler arrived in North Cowichan (2006: pop. 27,557) in 1861, and the community was incorporated 12 years later. Lake Cowichan (2006: pop. 2948) was settled before 1890 and was initially known as Sutton Green, but its name was changed to Cowichan Lake in 1890 and to Lake Cowichan in 1922. The community of Cowichan Bay (2006: pop. 1361) was once called Harrisville, but its moniker had been changed by 1907. Cowichan Station was originally known as McPherson Station, after three brothers (Donald, John and William) who settled here, but was rechristened in 1897 after a nearby railway station.

CRACROFT ISLANDS The islands of West Cracroft (123 km²) and East Cracroft (110 km²) are separated by only a small gorge that disappears at low tide. Located on the north side of Johnstone Strait, they were christened Cracroft Island (singular) by Captain George Richards. The islands were named for Sophia Cracroft, the niece of Sir John Franklin, of the famously ill-fated 1847 Franklin Expedition. The islands received their name in 1861, just after Cracroft visited the British Columbia coast with her widowed aunt, Lady Jane Franklin. The nearby Sophia Islands are also named for Cracroft. Cracroft Island was officially renamed the Cracroft Islands (plural) in 1955, at the same time the names West Cracroft and East Cracroft Islands were approved for the individual isles.

CRAIGELLACHIE This small community, located 45 kilometres west of Revelstoke, is where the "Last Spike" of the Canadian Pacific Railway's transcontinental line was driven in 1885. The moniker, which is pronounced *craig el AH-kee*, was chosen by CPR financier Donald Smith, who drove the spike. The name comes from a telegraph sent to Smith the year before by his cousin and CPR president, George Stephen. Craigellachie is a prominent rock in the Spey Valley in Morayshire, Scotland. The name comes from the Gaelic word *creag-eagalach*, which means "rock of dread (or terror or alarm)." The battle cry of the Clan Grant was "Stand fast, Craigellachie!" and it was at the rock that a beacon fire was lit whenever the Clan Grant needed to be summoned to fight. Smith and Stephen grew

C

up near the rock and were aware of the war cry. In 1884, when the CPR's financial situation was desperate, Stephen was able to obtain a substantial loan that enabled the company to complete the construction of its transcontinental line. The message that Stephen sent to Smith when he got the money simply said "Stand fast, Craigellachie!"

CRANBROOK (2006: pop. 18,267) This city sits on the site of an old Ktunaxa (Kootenay) First Nation village called ?akisqukti?it. The pronunciation of the name was similar to *a-kis-kaq-thi* and was sometimes spelled by non-Aboriginals as A'Qkis ga'ktlect. The moniker means "two streams going along together." The general area where Cranbrook is located was labelled as Joseph's Prairie on an 1871 map, and that name referred to a local Ktunaxa chief. A post office was opened on the site in 1886 and was called Cranbrook for nearby Cranbrook Farm (actually a ranch), which was owned by James Baker. The city's townsite was laid out in 1897 and also given that name. Baker, a retired British lieutenant colonel, settled there in 1885 and named his property after his hometown of Cranbrook, Kent, England. In addition to running the ranch and a trading post, Baker was also the president of a coal company, was active in local railway development and served as a long-time member of the British Columbia Legislative Assembly and as a provincial cabinet minister. Cranbrook Mountain (2059 m), located 11 kilometres south, has been known by that name at least since 1915.

CRESTON The town of Creston (2006: pop. 4826), located south of Kootenay Lake, was named after Creston, Iowa, in the United States. In the 1890s, Fred Little owned the land where the community sits, and when the Canadian Pacific Railway offered to buy his property to build a railway station, Little agreed to sell only if the CPR would name the station after his hometown in America. Creston

Valley, where the community is located, and nearby Creston Mountain are both named after the town.

CROFTON (estimated pop. 2500) Now part of North Cowichan, Crofton was established in 1902 to house the 400 men who worked at the nearby copper smelter operated by the Mt. Sticker Copper Mining Company. The town was named after the company's manager, Henry Croft.

CROWSNEST PASS (1357 m) This pass on the Alberta border, 40 kilometres north of the United States, was used by members of the Ktunaxa (Kootenay) First Nation to hunt buffalo on Alberta's plains. The Cree First Nation name for the pass was Kah-ka-ioo-wut-tshis-tun, and the Blackfoot First Nation name was Ma-sto-eeas. Both monikers mean "the nest of the crow (or raven)." The first non-Aboriginal to visit the area was Captain Thomas Blakiston of the Royal Artillery in 1858, and he called it Crow-nest Pass. The pass is identified as Crow Nest Pass in an 1859 map and as Lodge des Corbeaux in an 1860 report. It was officially called Crownest Pass in 1901, and the current spelling was adopted two years later. There are two theories about the origin of the name. One is that a group from the Crow First Nation, after stealing some horses from the Blackfeet, camped there and were caught by surprise in their "nest" and massacred by the pursuing Blackfeet. The other is that the name merely reflects the nesting of crows in the area.

CULTUS LAKE Two lakes and a community share this name. The best known of the lakes is located 15 kilometres south of Chilliwack. This body of water (6.3 km²) was named Schweltza Lake as far back as 1862 but was rechristened in 1914. The new name was probably given to reflect the moniker of the popular summer resort community of Cultus Lake (2006: pop. 22) that was established on its shores in 1913. The people of the nearby Stó:lô First Nation believed that evil spirits or supernatural creatures

C

lived at the bottom of the lake. The lake's former name, Schweltza Lake, was a derivation of the Halkomelem word *swehl-tcha*, which means "unclear liquid that warns secretly." The river that drains out of Cultus Lake is still called Sweltzer River.

The second Cultus Lake is northwest of the west end of Kamloops Lake. Its moniker dates back to at least 1895. The provincial government's Water Rights Branch suggested in 1938 that it be renamed Charette Lake to avoid confusion with the first Cultus Lake, but the proposal was rejected. There was also a community called Cultus Lake on the second lake's shores that was established before 1916, but it is now a ghost town. Cultus is the anglicized spelling of the Chinook Jargon word *kʌltəs*, which, in turn, is a derivation of the Chinook First Nation word *káltas*. Cultus means "bad," "foul," "useless" or "worthless."

CUMBERLAND (2006: pop. 2762) This village was founded in 1888 by industrialists and politicians James and Robert Dunsmuir. It was originally called Union after their Union Coal Company. However, most of the miners living in this company town were from Cumberland, England, so James Dunsmuir renamed the village in 1898. Cumberland is at the east end of Comox Lake, about 18 kilometres northwest of Union Bay.

CUNNINGHAM A sea passage, a mountain and a lake are all named after missionary, fur trader and businessman Robert Cunningham. Cunningham Passage, located at the mouth of Observatory Inlet, was christened in his honour in 1868 by Captain Daniel Pender. By this time, Cunningham had already been kicked out of the Church Missionary Society because he married a First Nations woman and was in charge of the Hudson's Bay Company post at Fort Simpson. He founded Port Essington (now a ghost town) near the mouth of the Skeena River in 1871 and became a prominent businessman there and in Hazelton. Cunningham Peak (920 m), just southwest of Port Essington, was named for him in 1914 by Captain P.C. Musgrave, and Cunningham Lake, located near the peak, was named for the mountain no later than 1930. Nearby Somerville Island was also named by Captain Pender in 1868 for Cunningham's mother, Mary Somerville.

CUNNINGHAM ISLAND (113 km^2) This island was named in about 1866 by Captain Daniel Pender for Thomas Cunningham. Cunningham immigrated to Canada from Ulster in 1853 and wound up in British Columbia six years later. He bought the Vancouver Coal Company's general store in 1864 and was doing business in Nanaimo as Cunningham Brothers when he was elected to Vancouver Island's colonial legislature in 1866. The island is located just north of Denny Island.

D

D'ARCY ISLAND (0.82 km²) This island in Haro Strait was the site of a leper colony between 1891 and 1924. It was named after Lieutenant John D'Arcy by Captain George Richards in 1858. D'Arcy was the mate on the HMS *Herald* while that ship was stationed in British Columbia waters from 1852 to 1854.

DAWSON Many sites in British Columbia have been named for the famous geologist George Mercer Dawson. Dawson spent much of the 1870s and '80s exploring and surveying the central and southern Interior, as well as northern Vancouver Island, Haida Gwaii (Queen Charlotte Islands) and the Selkirk Mountains. He was also, from 1895 to 1901, the director of the Geological Survey of Canada. Among the places named after him are Mount Dawson (3377 m), at the south end of Glacier National Park in the Selkirk Mountains, and the nearby Dawson Glacier. Both were named in 1888 by the British alpinist, the Reverend William S. Green. The Dawson Range, also in that park, was named for the geologist sometime before 1911. There is also Dawson Harbour on Graham Island in Haida Gwaii, which was christened in 1897 by Dr. Charles Newcombe of Victoria, while he was taking a cruise around the islands. The Dawson Islands on the north side of Masset Inlet near Graham Island were christened in the geologist's honour during a 1910 hydrographic survey. And it is presumed that the Dawson Peaks, near the Yukon border, west of Teslin Lake, were named after Dawson when they were christened in 1898.

DAWSON CREEK (2006: pop. 10,994) This city is near the Alberta border, about 235 kilometres northeast of Prince George. Its first settler arrived in 1907, and the community was established shortly afterward. It took its name from a small nearby stream that was originally called Dawson's Brook in 1879. The creek, in turn, was named after noted geologist George Mercer Dawson, who conducted the first surveys in the area earlier that year. Sources disagree as to whether Dawson christened the creek after himself or if it was named by Henry A.F. MacLeod, an exploration engineer for the Canadian Pacific Railway who Dawson met while he was there.

DAWSON FALLS / DAWSON RIVER Dawson Falls, in Wells Gray Provincial Park, was named in 1914 by surveyor Robert Henry Lee. The Dawson River in Spatsizi Plateau Wilderness Provincial Park was christened by E.B. Hart during his surveys of the area in 1913–14. He called it Dawson Creek, but the name was changed in 1945. Both the falls and the river are named in honour of George Herbert Dawson, the surveyor general of British Columbia from 1912 to 1917.

DEAN Dean Channel, along with nearby Raphoe Point, were named in 1793 by Captain George Vancouver for the Reverend James King, who was then the dean of the city of Raphoe, County Donegal, Ireland. King's son, Captain James King, along with Vancouver, sailed with Captain James Cook on Cook's third and last voyage of 1776–79. Captain King died in 1784. Vancouver originally named the channel Dean's Canal, and the name was misspelled as Deanes Canal on British Admiralty charts in the late 19th century. The current moniker was adopted in 1910. Dean Island, which was also presumably named after the reverend, lies southwest of the entrance to the channel. The Dean River starts 241 kilometres away, in the Chilcotin. The river flows north and west through the Coast Mountains before emptying into Dean Channel, west of Tweedsmuir Provincial Park. The river was named after the channel in 1933. Nearby King Island was christened after the reverend's family.

D

DEAS ISLAND (0.72 km²) This island in the Fraser River between Delta and Richmond was named for John Sullivan Deas from South California, who built and operated a salmon cannery there from 1873 to 1877. He was one of the first black men to live in the area. Although it is not certain when the island was first called by this name, it is labelled as such on an 1880 map.

DEASE LAKE / DEASE RIVER Dease Lake (61 km²) was named by Hudson's Bay Company chief trader John McLeod when he discovered it in 1834. McLeod named the body of water after Peter Warren Dease, who was, at the time, an HBC chief factor and the HBC official in charge of New Caledonia. The lake is 50 kilometres south of Cassiar. The community of Dease Lake (2006: pop. 384) is located on the south end of the lake. It began in 1838 as the Dease Lake trading post, and the settlement that grew around it was known for a while in the early 20th century as Lake House. The Dease River, which flows northeast from the north end of the lake, was originally called Dease Creek in 1898 but was renamed three years later.

DE COURCY GROUP This group of islands was named by Captain George Richards in 1859 in honour of Captain Michael De Courcy, the commanding officer of the HMS *Pylades* while it was stationed off the British Columbia coast from 1859 to 1861. The islands lie between Gabriola and Valdes islands. In the centre of the group is De Courcy Island, and there is also a Pylades Island. The other islands in the group are named for De Courcy's officers on the *Pylades*.

DEEP BAY Five bays in British Columbia bear this name. One, located opposite Denman Island, was once known as Lymn Bay but has been known by its current moniker since at least 1900. Overlooking the bay is the community of Deep Bay. The settlement began as a logging camp, which was established on the site in 1917. In 2006, the combined population of Deep Bay and nearby Bowser was 1485.

DEEP COVE There are two communities in British Columbia called Deep Cove. One is on the northwest end of the Saanich Peninsula; the other is on the southwest shore of Indian Arm in North Vancouver. The first, along with the identically named cove on the east side of the Saanich Peninsula, have been listed on British Admiralty charts since 1858. The second community was settled in 1919 and is part of the municipal district of North Vancouver. It was called Deepwater (or Deep Water) but was rechristened in 1940 after a nearby cove that was so named by Captain George Richards in 1859 or 1860 because of the deep waters there.

DEFENCE ISLANDS These two small islands northeast of Anvil Island in Howe Sound were named in 1860 by Captain George Richards for the British warship, the HMS *Defence*, which Captain James Gambier commanded during the 1794 naval battle known as the Glorious First of June. *See* Gambier Island, Howe Sound.

DELLA FALLS / DELLA LAKE Both the waterfall and the lake were named by Port Alberni prospector and trapper Joe Drinkwater after his wife, Della, whom he married in 1899, when she was 19 years old. Drinkwater came across the falls and lake and, with his partner, Davie Nichols, staked some claims nearby that same year. The earliest known mention of Della Lake by name is in a 1906 government report that also describes, but does not name, the waterfall. The waterfall is mentioned by name in a 1916 government report. Jo Creek drains Della Lake into Drinkwater Creek. Both the falls and the lake are about 16 kilometres from the head of Great Central Lake in Strathcona Provincial Park. At 440 metres, Della Falls is the highest waterfall in Canada.

DELTA (2006: pop. 96,723) This district municipality, located south of Richmond, was first settled in 1859. The community takes its name from the fact that it sits on part of the Fraser River delta.

D

DELTAFORM MOUNTAIN (3426 m) Mountaineer Samuel Allen originally suggested calling this mountain by its First Nations name, Saknowa (which the local First Nations people still use today), but the mountain was renamed by fellow alpinist Walter Wilcox in 1897 because of the similarity of the shape of the mountain's north face to the Greek letter *delta*. This mountain is located on the Alberta border, at the north end of Kootenay National Park.

DENHAM Denham Island was named in 1862 or 1864 by Captain Daniel Pender for Rear Admiral Sir Henry Mangles Denham. The admiral was a famous surveyor, whose assignments took him from Bristol Channel to the west coast of Africa and the Fiji Islands. Denham apparently did not, however, ever visit British Columbia. Denham Island is northwest of Gilford Island. Off the north end of Sonora Island is the much smaller Denham Islet, which was also named for the admiral by Captain Pender in about 1864. On the northwest side of Moresby Island is Denham Point, which was named in 1852 for the admiral's son, Midshipman Annesley Turner Denham of the HMS *Thetis*. The point was christened by Augustus Leopold Kuper, the captain of the *Thetis*.

DENMAN ISLAND / MOUNT DENMAN Denman Island (51 km²) was named in about 1864 by Captain George Richards in honour of Rear Admiral Joseph Denman. From 1864 to 1866, Denman was commander-in-chief of the British fleet's Pacific Station, headquartered at Esquimalt. Denman Island is 12 kilometres southeast of Comox, between Hornby and Vancouver islands. The community of Denman Island (2006: pop. 1095), located on the island, was first settled in 1874 but was called Quadra from 1878 to 1892. Nearby Mount Denman (1991 m) bore the name of the admiral by 1867.

DENNY ISLAND (125 km²) This island was named in about 1866 by Captain Daniel Pender for Lieutenant D'Arcy Anthony Denny, the commanding officer of the gunboat HMS *Forward* from 1866 to 1868. Denny Island is near the mouth of the Dean Channel, just east of Bella Bella.

DEPARTURE BAY A bay and a nearby community share this name. The bay is just northwest of Nanaimo and was originally called Bocas de Winthuysen in 1791. Sources, however, disagree as to whether it was Spanish Navy Lieutenant Francisco de Eliza y Reventa or the Spanish explorer José María Narváez who did the honours. It is presumed that the bay was christened after Spanish rear admiral Francisco Xavier de Winthuysen. The bay was renamed Departure Bay in 1852 by Hudson's Bay Company surveyor Joseph Pemberton, supposedly because a group of First Nations people had recently been seen leaving the bay. In addition, the bay was recognized as a good place for ships to harbour. The community at the bay dates from at least 1947.

DESERTERS CANYON This canyon surrounds Finlay River, just north of Williston Reservoir. It was named in 1824 by Hudson's Bay Company fur trader Samuel Black. Black was exploring the river that year for the HBC, when two of his men, Jean Marie Bouche and Louis Ossin, deserted there.

DESOLATION SOUND This body of water at the north end of Georgia Strait, between Cortes and West Redonda islands, was named by Captain George Vancouver in 1792 because of the dreary appearance of the local surroundings. According to Vancouver, not a fish could be caught, the nearby soil grew only a few small onions and a "scanty crop" of berries, and there was no wildlife nearby. He even described the local forests as gloomy, with "awful silence."

DEVASTATION CHANNEL / DEVASTATION ISLAND Both the channel, which is located south of Kitimat, and the island, just northwest of Prince Rupert, were named after the HM paddle sloop *Devastation*. The vessel was a six-gun ship that sailed in British Columbia waters from 1862 to 1865. The channel was christened in 1863 by Captain Daniel Pender; the island was named the year before by Captain George Richards.

DEWDNEY / DEWDNEY PEAK The small, unincorporated community of Dewdney, located just east of Mission, was originally called Johnson's Landing after one of its first two settlers, Norman Clarke Johnson (or Johnston), who arrived there in about 1867. In 1892, the name of the local post office (and, hence, the town) was changed to Dewdney to honour Edgar Dewdney. Dewdney was, at the time, one of the most powerful politicians in British Columbia and the federal Minister of the Interior and Superintendent of Indian Affairs. He would go on to become the lieutenant-governor of British Columbia. Nearby Dewdney Peak (930 m) was named after the community in 1939. *See also* Mount Dewdney.

DEWDNEY TRAIL This 576-kilometre-long trail stretches westward from Hope to a spot near Fort Steele. It was constructed between 1860 and 1865 and was christened in honour of future politician Edgar Dewdney, the civil engineer in charge of the project. Highway 3 follows most of the route.

DISCOVERY ISLAND *See* Chatham.

DISCOVERY PASSAGE This sea passage connecting the Strait of Georgia to Johnstone Strait was named by Captain George Vancouver in 1792 after his ship, the HMS *Discovery*.

DIXON ENTRANCE This body of water, which separates Haida Gwaii (Queen Charlotte Islands) from the Alaska Panhandle, was named in 1788 by Sir Joseph Banks, the president of the Royal Society of London, for Captain George Dixon. Dixon was one of the founding partners of the King George's Sound Company, and he commanded the company's vessel, the *Queen Charlotte*, from 1786 to 1788. Dixon discovered and named the Queen Charlotte Islands in 1787.

D

DONALD (estimated pop. 100) The site of this community, located on the Columbia River, 28 kilometres west of Golden, was originally called First Crossing because it was there that the CPR's tracks first crossed the Columbia. (Revelstoke was the site of the second crossing.) The name was changed in the early 1880s to honour Donald Alexander Smith, a prominent Canadian politician and CPR railway baron. The settlement was known from 1951 to 1982 as Donald Station because postal authorities would not accept the single name Donald.

DOUGLAS CHANNEL This sea channel on the west side of Hawkesbury Island was named in 1868 by Captain Daniel Pender for Sir James Douglas, the former Hudson's Bay Company chief factor at Fort Victoria and the recently retired governor of both the Vancouver Island and mainland British Columbia colonies.

DOUGLAS ISLAND There are two islands by this name in British Columbia. One, located on the southwest side of Ballenas Channel, was named in about 1860 for Amelia (née Connolly) Douglas, the wife of colonial governor Sir James Douglas. The second island, located where the Fraser and Pitt rivers meet, was originally called Manson Island after Donald Manson, who was part of the expedition that founded Fort Langley in 1827. However, Governor James Douglas bought the island for $4.5 million at an auction in 1859 and turned it over to his daughter, Cecilia. British Admiralty charts labelled it as Manson Island as late as 1922, but other maps as far back as 1905 call it Douglas Island, and one source suggests that the name might have been changed when the governor gave the island to Cecilia.

D

DOWAGER ISLAND (236 km²) This island, located between Finlayson and Mathieson channels, northwest of Bella Bella, was lumped together with Lady Douglas and Lake islands as a single land mass in Captain Daniel Pender's 1868 map of the area. However, an 1872 chart shows the three as separate islands. Dowager Island is, by far, the largest. Both it and Lady Douglas Island were named after Amelia (née Connolly) Douglas, whose husband was colonial governor Sir James Douglas.

DUKE POINT This narrow peninsula was named in 1903 by Commander John Parry of the HMS *Egeria* to reflect the fact that it extends into the Northumberland Channel. The channel had been named 51 years earlier after Algernon Percy, the 4th Duke of Northumberland and the First Lord of the Admiralty.

DUNCAN (2006: pop. 4986) This city takes its name from one of its first settlers, William Chalmers Duncan, who arrived in 1864. Most of downtown Duncan is on land that was part of his farm, which he called Alderlea because of the large forest of alder trees in the area. The Esquimalt and Nanaimo Railway opened a railway station on Duncan's land in 1887 and christened it Duncan's Station. A townsite called Alderlea quickly appeared, but its name was soon changed to that of the station. The moniker was shortened to Duncan when the community was incorporated in 1912.

DUNCAN LAKE *See* Howser.

DUNDAS ISLANDS / DUNDAS ISLAND The Dundas Islands were named in 1793 by Captain George Vancouver to honour Henry Dundas, a prominent British politician, who was then both Home Secretary and the Treasurer of the Navy. Vancouver thought the islands were, in fact, one large, 24 kilometre-long island, and so he called them Dundas's Island. It later turned out that the "island" was actually an archipelago. Once it was all sorted out, the largest island in the group was named Dundas Island (143 km^2). Three other isles in the archipelago are also named after Dundas: Baron Island, Dunira Island and Melville Island. (Dundas was made a peer in 1802, with the titles of Viscount Melville and Baron Dunira.) The Dundas Islands are at Dixon Entrance, northwest of Prince Rupert.

DUNSMUIR (2006: pop. 1358) This community's townsite was surveyed in 1911 and named after industrialist and politician Robert Dunsmuir. The settlement is on the east side of Vancouver Island, just south of Qualicum Bay. At one time, Dunsmuir was the richest man in British Columbia and owned one-quarter of Vancouver Island.

DUNSMUIR ISLANDS These islands were named in 1904 by Commander John F. Parry of the HMS *Egeria* while he was resurveying present-day Ladysmith Harbour. Parry named the islands after industrialist and former British Columbia premier James Dunsmuir. Dunsmuir owned extensive coal mines in the area and would become BC's lieutenant-governor in 1906. The Dunsmuir Islands are located at the entrance of Ladysmith Harbour.

DUNSTER This small community on the Fraser River between McBride and Valemount dates back to when the Grand Trunk Pacific Railway built a railway station there in 1913. A GTP inspector (whose name is now lost to history) christened the station after his hometown in England. The name stuck as a settlement grew around the station.

E

ECSTALL RIVER The name of this river dates back to British Admiralty charts of the 1860s. The name has seen a variety of spellings, including Hocsall, Huckstall and Oxstall and is pronounced with an almost silent *uc* sound in front with stress on the last syllable, as if it was a long *a*. *Ecstall* is a Tsimshian First Nation word meaning "something from the side." In this case, the Ecstall is a tributary of the Skeena River and flows into the Skeena not far from its mouth. At the head of the Ecstall River is Ecstall Lake (called Upper Lake until 1946); in the middle of the mouth of the Ecstall is Ecstall Island (called Village Island until 1927).

ELK RIVER Initially, people were not too sure what to call this river. In 1811, explorer David Thompson called it the Stag River. It is called the Elk River on an 1857 map, but another map five years later played it safe by labelling it the "Stag or Elk River." The government finally settled on Elk River in 1900. This southeastern British Columbia river flows through Elkford, Fernie and Sparwood.

ELKFORD (2006: pop. 2463) This district municipality on the Elk River, 30 kilometres north of Sparwood, was founded in 1971 as a home for the miners employed at the nearby Fording Coal Limited mine. The community's name is an amalgamation of "Elk" (from the Elk River) and "Ford" (from Fording Coal Limited).

ELKO (estimated pop. 163) This community sits on the west side of the Elk River, 32 kilometres south of Fernie. Elko's first settlers arrived in the late 1880s and named their town after the river.

ELLISON / ELLISON LAKE The community of Ellison (2006: pop. 1510), just north of Kelowna, was named sometime before 1912 after Price Ellison of Manchester, England, who settled there in 1876. Ellison later owned 80 percent of the surrounding valley and raised livestock, grew wheat and became a provincial politician and cabinet minister. The nearby lake was originally called Duck Lake but was renamed in 1930.

ENDERBY (2006: pop. 2828) This city's name was taken **E** from a poem. The first settler arrived in 1862, and, over the next 25 years, the community went through five different names. Then, in 1887, during a ladies' afternoon tea party, the nearby Shuswap (then called the Spallumcheen) River began to overflow its banks. This inspired Mrs. Henry Oliver to recite Jean Ingelow's "The High Tide on the Coast of Lincolnshire," a popular poem at the time. The piece tells the story of the 1571 flood at Boston, Lincolnshire, England, and a line in the poem refers to a tune called "The Brides of Enderby." At the end of the recital, the hostess of the party, Mrs. George R. Lawes, suggested Enderby as the settlement's new name. The idea met with the instant approval of the other ladies, and their suggestion was adopted by the government. Enderby is just north of Armstrong.

ENDAKO This community got its start in 1914 as a divisional point for the Grand Trunk Pacific Railway. It was named after either Endako Marsh Lake or the Endako River, both of which are nearby. Endako is a derivation of the Dakelh (Carrier) First Nation place name Nda K'oh, which may mean either "ancient monster river" or simply "east flowing river." (The Endako River flows southeast into the Stellako River.) Endako is just west of Fraser Lake.

ENGLISH BAY This bay is on the south side of Burrard Inlet at the mouth of False Creek. The name goes back to at least the British Admiralty charts of 1860. The bay and nearby Spanish Bank were named to commemorate the meeting of Captain George Vancouver with Spanish explorers Dionisio Alcalá-Galiano and Cayetano Valdés y Flores at Spanish Bank in 1792.

ENGLISHMAN RIVER This river on Vancouver Island flows into the Strait of Georgia at Parksville. It was originally called Englishman's River in the 1850s, in honour of some poor "English gentleman"—whose name is now lost to history—who drowned there while trying to cross the river. The official name was adopted in 1945, though some people started going without the apostrophe and the *s* as far back as 1882.

EON MOUNTAIN (3305 m) The name of this mountain dates back to at least 1914. Who named it and when is uncertain, but some have suggested that it was alpinist Sir James Outram, when he climbed nearby Mount Assiniboine in 1901. It is believed that the name refers to the apparent great age of the peak and to its several layers of fossils. Eon Mountain is on the Alberta border, 34 kilometres southwest of Canmore.

ERRINGTON (2006: pop. 2549) This community was settled in 1891 and named by one of its first residents, Duncan McMillan. It is believed that McMillan got the moniker from Sir Walter Scott's ballad "Jock o' Hazeldean." The tune has a line that refers to Errington in Northumberland, England. British Columbia's Errington is 34 kilometres northwest of Nanaimo.

ESPERANZA INLET This inlet on the northwest side of Nootka Island connects the Tahsis and Zeballos inlets to the Pacific Ocean. In 1776, Captain James Cook gave the coastline between Cape Cook and Estevan Point the name Hope Bay because, until he found it, Cook was sailing along the coast in the hope of finding a harbour. Captain Alexandro Malaspina restricted the name to the inlet and translated it into Spanish when he travelled through the area in 1791.

E

ESPINOSA Espinosa Inlet was named by Spanish Navy Captain Alexandro Malaspina for one of his officers, Lieutenant Josef de Espinosa, during Malaspina's 1791 expedition along the Pacific Northwest coast. The inlet is north of Esperanza Inlet and was originally called Espinosa Arm by Malaspina because he thought it was a branch of the inlet. Two nearby mountains are named after Espinosa Inlet. One is 11 kilometres south of Zeballos between Espinosa and Zeballos inlets and is called Mount Espinosa (918 m). The other does not have an official name yet but is known locally as Espinosa Peak (898 m) and lies 10 kilometres west of Zeballos.

E

ESQUIMALT / ESQUIMALT HARBOUR The district municipality of Esquimalt (2006: pop. 16,840), just west of Victoria, takes its name from Esquimalt Harbour. The harbour, in turn, takes its moniker from the Straits Salish First Nation name Es-whoy-malth or Is-whoy-malth, for the shallow mouth of nearby Sawmill Creek. The name means "a place gradually shoaling" ("to shoal" is to become shallow). Spanish Navy Sub-Lieutenant Manuel Quimper christened the harbour Puerto de Cordova in 1790, while his ship, the *Princesa Real* (the captured British sloop *Princess Royal*), was anchored there. The name honoured a past Spanish viceroy of Mexico (*see* Cordova Bay). The Hudson's Bay Company gave the harbour its present moniker in 1842. The British Navy built a hospital at the south end of the bay in 1855, and the settlement of Esquimalt was quickly established to the east of the harbour.

ESTEVAN Estevan Point, south of Nootka Sound, was named La Punta de San Esteban in 1774 by Spanish explorer Lieutenant Commander Juan José Pérez Hernández, for his second-in-command, Esteban José Martínez. (In Spanish, the letter *v* is pronounced like the English *b*.) This was the first place in British Columbia to be christened by a non-Aboriginal. Captain George Vancouver was unaware of the moniker when he stopped there four years later and named the spot Breakers Point. Vancouver's name for the place was dropped, and the English translation of the Spanish name was adopted by the British Admiralty in 1849. Estevan Island and Estevan Sound, both in Hecate Sound, were named in 1792 by Spanish explorer Jacinto Caamaño.

E

EUTSUK LAKE / EUTSUK PEAK The lake's name has been in use since at least 1912. It might derive from Te-oots-a-bungut, which Chief Louis of the Cheslatta Carrier First Nation told government surveyor Frank Swannell in 1910 was his people's name for the lake. The name may mean "far from Ootsa Lake." (Ootsa Lake, which used to be north of Eutsuk Lake, no longer exists and is now part of the Nechako Reservoir.) Eutsuk Lake (246 km²) is located in the northern half of Tweedsmuir Provincial Park. Eutsuk Peak (1914 m) is north of the east end of Eutsuk Lake.

EXTENSION (2006: pop. 193) This community began in 1897 as the site of a coal mine owned by the Wellington Colliery Company, which was owned by the Dunsmuir family. The area was originally called Southfield because of its location vis-à-vis Nanaimo but was changed to Wellington Extension when the mine opened. (Wellington is another former Dunsmuir company town about 20 kilometres away.) The name was shortened when a post office was opened there.

EYEBROW PEAK (3362 m) While viewing some nearby peaks in 1910, mountaineer Arthur O. Wheeler saw, through poor weather, a summit with two broad rock scars that resembled giant eyebrows. He named the mountain Eyebrow Peak, but geologist Peter Robinson later proved that it was Mount Farnham (14 kilometres to the east) that Wheeler was really looking at. Once the mistake was realized, the name Eyebrow Peak was transferred to this mountain, which had earlier been named Aurora by Wheeler. Eyebrow Peak is 12 kilometres southeast of Jumbo Mountain.

F

FAIRWEATHER MOUNTAIN (4671 m) This mountain was named in 1778 by Captain James Cook for the good weather he encountered when he saw the peak after his ship had sailed through several storms. Fairweather Mountain sits on the Alaska border, southwest of Skagway. It is frequently called Mount Fairweather, and the American government actually adopted that as the mountain's official name in 1922, but the United States has since accepted the Canadian moniker. This is the highest mountain in British Columbia.

FALSE CREEK Despite the name, this is actually an inlet of English Bay on the south side of downtown Vancouver. It was named by Captain George Richards in 1859. When he started to survey it, Richards thought it was a part of a stream that led to Burrard Inlet. He soon discovered, much to his disappointment, that the "creek" ended in mudflats, hence the name.

FERNIE (2006: pop. 4217) Located in the Elk Valley, this city was founded in 1898 by Peter and William Fernie, two brothers from England, who came to British Columbia looking for gold and, instead, discovered and mined coal deposits in the valley. In a 1921 interview, when he was 74 years old, William Fernie claimed that the community had been named for him and did not mention his sibling, but a 1917 government report stated that the city was also named for his much older brother, who died in 1915.

FEUZ PEAK (3326 m) This peak and nearby Hasler Peak are located on Mount Dawson. They were both named in 1899 by alpinists Charles Fay and Herschel Parker for their Swiss guides, Edouard Feuz Jr. and Christian Hasler.

Feuz and Hasler had been brought to British Columbia by the Canadian Pacific Railway to encourage wealthy mountaineers to visit Banff, Glacier and Yoho national parks.

FINLAY RIVER This river was named after North West Company fur trader and explorer John Finlay who, in 1797, became the first non-Aboriginal to travel down it. Finlay River is the major northern tributary of the Peace River in northeast British Columbia and was, until 1928, known as Finlay's Branch (as in a branch of the Peace). The traditional Sekani First Nation name for the river is Chu Dadi Ts'elè.

FINLAYSON ARM / FINLAYSON CHANNEL Both Finlayson Arm, located at the head of Saanich Inlet, and Finlayson Channel, north of Milbanke Sound and west of Roderick Island, were named after Roderick Finlayson. A Hudson's Bay Company official, he was made second-in-command at the HBC post at Fort Victoria in 1843 and was in charge there from 1844 to 1849. Finlayson is regarded by many as the founder of Victoria.

It is not clear when Finlayson Arm first acquired its name. The channel was named in about 1845 by Captain Charles Dodd of the HBC's steamer *Beaver*. Roderick Island is, of course, also named after the fur trader. The island was christened in 1866 or 1867 by Captain Daniel Pender, who was, by coincidence, Dodd's successor as commander of the *Beaver*. In 1867, Pender also named Sarah and Jane islands, both in Finlayson Channel, after Finlayson's wife, Sarah, and his sister-in-law, Jane Tolmie.

FINLAYSON ISLAND This island on the northeast side of Chatham Sound, near Port Simpson was named not for Roderick Finlayson but for his uncle, Duncan. Duncan Finlayson was a Hudson's Bay Company chief factor who spent quite a bit of time in this part of the British Columbia coast between 1831 and 1837. The island was

F

christened in his honour in about 1836 by the Hudson's Bay Company.

FITZ HUGH SOUND Located between Calvert Island and the British Columbia mainland, this body of water was originally named Fitzhugh's Sound in 1786 by Captain James Hanna of the *Sea Otter*. Although Hanna did not specify who Fitzhugh was, he was probably William Fitzhugh, a business partner of fur trader Captain John Meares. The sound was rechristened Sir Charles Middleton's Sound in 1788 by Captain Charles Duncan of the *Princess Royal* after a rear admiral in the British Navy. George Vancouver, however, adopted the name given by Hanna when he sailed through the area in 1792 because Hanna was the "first discoverer" of the sound. Fitz Hugh Sound has been known by this moniker ever since, though it is not clear when the current spelling was adopted.

FLEMING PEAK (3150 m) This peak on Mount Rogers, 29 kilometres southwest of Donald, was named in 1901 by mountaineer Arthur O. Wheeler for railway engineer Sir Sandford Fleming. Fleming was the first engineer-in-chief of the Canadian Pacific Railway. Wheeler also named Mount Sir Sandford after Fleming that same year.

FLORES ISLAND (154 km²) Lying in Clayoquot Sound, 40 kilometres northwest of Tofino, this island was named in 1791 by Spanish Navy Lieutenant Francisco de Eliza y Reventa for Don Manuel Antonio Flores. Flores was, until two years before, the viceroy of Mexico. To assert Spain's claim to the entire west coast of North America, Flores sent a Spanish military expedition to Nootka Sound in 1789, which, in turn, almost led to war between Great Britain and Spain. Eliza commanded that expedition.

FORT BABINE (estimated pop. 135) This community is located at the entrance to the north arm of Babine Lake. In 1822, Hudson's Bay Company chief factor William

F

Brown established an HBC trading post about 40 kilometres southeast on the shores of the lake; he named it Fort Kilmaurs, after his Scottish birthplace. The location later became known as Fort Babine. Eventually, the post was moved to Fort Babine's present location, though sources disagree as to when this occurred; some say it was the 1840s, whereas others say 1872. The community that remained at the old location became known as Old Fort and had a permanent population until the 1950s. At the new Fort Babine, the HBC post was closed in the 1970s, but the Babine Lake First Nation community that grew up around it survives. See Babine.

FORT FRASER *See* Fraser.

FORT LANGLEY *See* Langley.

FORT NELSON / FORT NELSON RIVER The town of Fort Nelson (2006: pop. 4514), located in the northeast corner of the province, dates to 1805, when the North West Company established a fur-trading post nearby and named it after British naval hero Lord Horatio Nelson, who was killed in the Battle of Trafalgar that same year. The river was originally called Nelson River, after the fort, but was renamed in 1899 to avoid confusion with the Nelson River in Manitoba.

FORT RUPERT This former Hudson's Bay Company trading post on the north end of Vancouver Island (now in ruins) was built in 1849. The fort was named by the HBC after Prince Rupert, Count Palatine of the Rhine and Duke of Bavaria, who was also a cousin of England's King Charles II. The king made Rupert the first governor of the HBC in 1670.

FORT ST. JAMES (2006: pop. 1355) Located on the southeast end of Stuart Lake, this district municipality was founded as a trading post in 1806 by North West Company explorers Simon Fraser and John Stuart.

Originally called Stuart's Lake or Stuart Lake, it acquired its current name in 1822, shortly after the NWC merged with the Hudson's Bay Company. The reason behind the change and to whom the moniker refers are lost to history.

FORT ST. JOHN (2006: pop. 17,402) This city is the oldest non-Aboriginal settlement on the British Columbia mainland. It was first established in 1794 as a North West Company trading post, about 10 kilometres southeast of the community's present location, where the Moberly and Pine rivers meet. Originally called Rocky Mountain Fort, the post was abandoned, rebuilt, relocated and renamed a number of times until 1821, when the Hudson's Bay Company acquired Fort d'Épinette from the North West Company and renamed it Fort St. John. That fort was about 460 metres from the mouth of the Pine (now called the Beatton) River. In French, *épinette* means "spruce." The fort was closed two years later but was relocated and reopened near the site of the present-day city in 1860. The settlement around the fort did not begin until 1912. Nobody today knows to whom the name "St. John" refers.

FORT STEELE HERITAGE TOWN This historic site is a reconstruction of Fort Steele as the town existed during its heyday in the 1890s. The original settlement was called Galbraith's Ferry after brothers John and Robert Galbraith, who arrived during the Kottenay Gold Rush in the 1860s and ran a ferry across the Kootenay River. Years later, tension with the nearby Ktunaxa (Kootenay) First Nation brought to town a detachment of North-West Mounted Police, led by Major Sam Steele. The NWMP built a post and named it after Steele. When the Mounties left two years later, a grateful Robert Galbraith rechristened his community after the fort. Fort Steele is 16 kilometres northeast of Cranbrook.

FORT WARE (estimated pop. 266) This community was established on the Finlay River by the Hudson's Bay Company in 1927 as the Whitewater trading post. The post was later moved upstream to a place near the junction of the Fox and Finlay rivers. In 1938, it was renamed Fort Ware after William Ware, a former HBC district manager who had worked for the company since 1895. Fort Ware is northwest of the Williston Reservoir, about 570 kilometres north of Prince George.

FRANÇOIS LAKE A 98-kilometre-long lake and a settlement on its banks share this name. Because of its shape, François Lake (233 km²) is known to the people of the local Dakelh (Carrier) First Nation as Nitapeon, which means "lip lake." Early settlers in the area confused *nita* for *neto*, the Dakelh word for "white man." Most of these "white men" were French Canadian voyageurs, and they mistranslated the name of the lake into Lac des François. Oblate missionary Adrien Morice called it French Lake in 1907, and the Geographic Board of Canada adopted the current name, probably after long local usage, in 1924. The community was established in 1910 and has always been called François Lake. The lake and the community are both 20 kilometres south of Burns Lake.

FRANKLIN RANGE This mountain range on the northeast side of Vancouver Island was named by Captain George Richards for Rear Admiral Sir John Franklin of the ill-fated 1847 Franklin Expedition to the Arctic, and for Franklin's widow, Lady Jane Franklin. The range was christened for the Franklins shortly after Lady Franklin and her niece, Sophia Cracroft, visited the British Columbia coast in 1861.

FRASER LAKE / FORT FRASER A lake (51 km²), located 40 kilometres west of Vanderhoof, and two communities on its shores, the village of Fraser Lake (2006: pop. 1113) and Fort Fraser (2006: pop. 282), were all named after

North West Company explorer Simon Fraser. In 1805, the NWC assigned Fraser the job of opening the country west of the Rocky Mountains to trade. In pursuit of that task, he led a three-year expedition through the British Columbia Interior that included spending the winter of 1806–07 at Fraser Lake. The lake was named for Fraser by fellow NWC man John Stuart, who accompanied him. It was to return a compliment—Fraser had earlier named Stuart Lake after his fellow traveller. The traditional Dakelh (Carrier) First Nation name for the lake is Nat-lih or Nat-leh Bungut. (The words *bun* and *bungut* both mean "lake.")

F

The village of Fraser Lake, on the southwest side of the lake, was established sometime before 1908 as a Hudson's Bay Company trading post and telegraph station. A settlement emerged when the Grand Trunk Pacific Railway opened a station there in 1914. Fort Fraser, on the east end of the lake, was where Fraser and Stuart opened a NWC post in 1806. The small community that developed around it was originally called Fraser Lake, but its name was changed to Fort Fraser in 1913.

FRASER RIVER In 1808, explorer Simon Fraser became the first non-Aboriginal to descend the Fraser River from present-day Fort George to the Strait of Georgia, a distance of 1370 kilometres. Fraser thought it was the Columbia River, and it was not until he reached Georgia Strait that he realized his error. The Fraser River begins at Yellowhead Pass, 34 kilometres west of Jasper, and is the longest river entirely within British Columbia. Spanish explorers, who never travelled beyond the river's mouth, called it Rio Floridablanca, in honour of Don José Moñino y Redondo, Count of Floridablanca and the long-time chief minister of Spain. Early fur traders called it the New Caledonia River and the Jackanet River. Sources differ as to how the Fraser River got its present name. Most say it was christened in 1813 by David

Thompson, who explored the real Columbia River in 1811. (Fraser named the Thompson River for his fellow explorer in 1809.) However, some sources indicate that the Fraser River was named in 1808 by NWC officers shortly after Fraser's famous adventure.

FRENCH CREEK (2006: pop. 982) This community, located 37 kilometres northwest of Nanaimo, dates from the 1880s, when a number of French Canadians decided to settle there.

F

FRIENDLY COVE *See* Yuquot.

FRUITVALE (2006: pop. 1952) This village was known as Beaver Siding at the beginning of the 20th century because of the large number of the furry critters in the area. In 1906, however, a land-development company called Fruitvale Limited bought up most of the land and rechristened the town after itself, thinking that the new name would help them market the locality to settlers as the best fruit-growing area in the West Kootenays. Fruitvale is 14 kilometres west of Trail.

FULFORD HARBOUR A harbour on the southeast side of Saltspring Island and a community on the shores of the harbour share this name. The harbour was named sometime in 1859 by Captain George Richards as he was surveying the island. Richards christened the harbour after Captain John Fulford, the commanding officer of Rear Admiral Robert Baynes' flagship, the HMS *Ganges*, which sailed off the British Columbia coast from 1858 to 1860.

G

GABRIOLA ISLAND (51 km²; 2006: pop. 4050) Two theories exist as to the origin of this island's name. One is that the southeastern tip of the island was originally called Punta de Gaviota ("Cape Seagull") in 1791 by Spanish explorer José María Narváez. (In Spanish, the letter *v* is pronounced like the English *b*.) Supposedly, over time, the spelling was corrupted from Gaviota to Gaviola, and then to Gabiola, and eventually the entire island came to be known by that name. Others, however, argue that the original name of the southeast end of the island was Punta de Gaviola. They also believe it is more likely that Spanish naval officer Juan Francisco de la Bodega y Quadra named the island and that he did so in honour of Simón de Gaviola y Zabala, a Spanish aristocrat and the treasurer of the fleet that was protecting Spain's trade routes to the Americas. In either case, the additional *r* was added by a careless mid-19th-century British mapmaker. Gabriola Island is in Georgia Strait, just off Nanaimo.

GALIANO ISLAND (56 km²; 2006: pop. 1258) This island was named in 1859 by Captain George Richards after Commander Dionisio Alcalá-Galiano. The Spanish naval officer, with his ship, the *Sutil*, explored the channels and islands between Vancouver Island and the mainland in 1792. Galiano Island is located between southern Vancouver Island and the British Columbia mainland.

GAMBIER ISLAND (69 km²; 2006: pop. 313) This island in Howe Sound was named by Captain George Richards in 1860 after James Gambier. Gambier was the captain of the HMS *Defence* at the naval battle of the Glorious First of June, which was fought in 1794 against the French.

Gambier received a gold medal for his conduct and later became an admiral and a peer. The small community of Gambier Harbour (called Gambier Island between 1938 and 1941) was founded before 1937 and overlooks a bay by the same name. There are also two other villages on the island. The first, New Brighton, was established before 1919 and named, for reasons now forgotten, for New Brighton, England. The other is West Bay, which overlooks another bay by the same name west of Gambier Harbour). The island's population grows to more than 600 every summer.

G

GANGES / GANGES HARBOUR Ganges Harbour, located on the east side of Saltspring Island, was named in 1859 by Captain George Richards for what was then the flagship of the Royal Navy's Pacific Station, the HMS *Ganges*. The 84-gun battleship was stationed off the British Columbia coast from 1857 to 1860. The community of Ganges (estimated pop. 6000), the largest in the Gulf Islands, overlooks the harbour.

GARDNER CANAL This 192-kilometre-long inlet, south of Kitimat, was originally named Gardner's Channel in 1793 by Captain George Vancouver for his friend, Captain Alan Gardner. Vancouver served under Gardner as a lieutenant from 1784 to 1789, while the latter was in command of the HMS *Europa*. In addition, it was Gardner who strongly recommended that Vancouver lead the Royal Navy's expedition to the Pacific Northwest. Even though Gardner Canal is the longest inlet in British Columbia, the Geographic Board of Canada has so far rejected all suggestions that it be renamed from a canal to an inlet.

GARIBALDI / GARIBALDI PROVINCIAL PARK *See* Mount Garibaldi.

GASTOWN This historic neighbourhood and popular tourist attraction in Vancouver derives its name from

John Deighton. Because of his love for talking and tall tales, Deighton came to be known as "Gassy Jack." Deighton built the Globe Saloon on the south shore of Burrard Inlet in 1867 to help quench the thirst of those who worked at the nearby Hastings Mill. He later built the Deighton Hotel on the same spot in 1870. The community that grew around Deighton's establishments became known informally as Gastown. The town was officially renamed Granville in 1870 and, in turn, became part of Vancouver in 1886. The public, however, continued to use the name Gastown to refer to the neighbourhood where the original bar and hotel once stood.

GEORGE MASSEY TUNNEL This 3200-metre-long tunnel takes Highway 99 under the south arm of the Fraser River, between Delta and Richmond. Construction was completed in 1959, and it was originally called Deas Island Tunnel after the nearby island in the Fraser River. It was renamed after Nehemiah "George" Massey in 1967. A civic leader in Ladner and a member of the provincial legislature, Massey worked for 23 years to garner the support needed to build the tunnel. One week before he died in 1964, he was the last motorist required to pay a toll to use the tunnel.

GEORGIA STRAIT *See* Strait of Georgia.

GIBSONS (2006: pop. 4182) This town on the west coast of Howe Sound was named for George William Gibson, who arrived here in 1886. Sources vary as to whether he was intentionally seeking a place where he and his sons could settle and farm or whether he and his family arrived by accident when their boat was blown off course. Gibson later became the local magistrate and postmaster. At one time called Gibson's Landing, the name was shortened in 1947.

GIL ISLAND / MOUNT GIL Gil Island (228 km²) was christened in 1792 by Lieutenant Commander Jacinto Caamaño, the commanding officer of the Spanish corvette *Aránzazu*. It is not known for whom Caamaño named this isle, but one historian has suggested that it might have been Juan Gil, the ensign-bearer of the Duke of Medino-Sidonia's flagship, the *San Martin*, part of the Spanish Armada in 1588. Gil Island is just northwest of Princess Royal Island. On the island is Mount Gil (2601 m), which was named in 1933.

G

GILFORD ISLAND (384 km²) In 1865, Captain Daniel Pender named this island in honour of Captain Richard James Meade, the 3rd Viscount Gilford and the commanding officer of the HMS *Tribune* while that ship was stationed off British Columbia from 1862 to 1864. Tribune Channel, located just north and east of the island, was also named by Pender in 1865, as was Viscount Island, just east of Gilford Island, in about 1867.

GILLARD CREEK *See* Kelowna.

GILLIES BAY A bay and a community share this name. The moniker's origin is unknown, but local tradition says that the bay was christened after a very unpopular 19th-century sea captain, whose crew mutinied and threw him overboard here. The bay is on the west side of Texada Island. The nearby community (2006: pop. 400) was established in the 1910s and named after the bay.

GINGOLX (2006: pop. 341) The name of this village is a Nisga'a First Nation word meaning "the place of skulls" or "the place of scalps." There are three different but similar stories about the origin of the name. One is that, after a great battle in which the Nisga'a defeated warriors of the Haida First Nation, the scalps of the dead Haida were hung on poles placed on a rock bluff at this site. Another tale is that a Haida raiding party had gone up the Nass

River in search of slaves and, as the Haida approached the open sea on their way home, some of the prisoners struggled to get free. The Haidas, fearing their canoes would be overturned, landed at the mouth of the river, killed those who were resisting and left their heads on the bluff. The third story says that a notorious Tsimshian First Nation chief, High-mahsh, nailed the scalps of his victims on the trees in a nearby ravine when he returned from his raids on neighbouring bands. From 1867 to 2000, the village was called first Kincolith Mission and then Kincolith. Kincolith is the anglicized spelling of the current name. In 2000, pursuant to the Nisga'a Treaty, the village's name was reverted to its previous spelling. The community is located about 80 kilometres north of Prince Rupert, at the mouth of the Nass River.

GITLAKDAMIKS *See* New Aiyansh.

GLADYS LAKE / GLADYS RIVER The lake (72 km²) is located west of Teslin Lake, just south of the Yukon border. It was named by Aylesworth Bowen Perry for his youngest daughter, Gladys, while he was commander of the North-West Mounted Police detachment in Dawson City, Yukon, in 1899–1900. Perry was appointed head of the nation-wide NWMP in 1900. Gladys River flows north from Gladys Lake and then southeast and east into Teslin Lake.

GLENEMMA (2006: pop. 530) This community was founded in the late 19th century. When an application was submitted to the government for a post office, the name of the office (and, hence, the town) was supposed to be Kenemma, after the town's first postmaster, Kenneth Sweet, and his wife, Emma. A spelling mistake was made by somebody in Ottawa, so the post office's sign read Glenemma when it opened in 1895. The community is 24 kilometres northwest of Vernon.

GOAT Not one, but seven, Goat Mountains (as well as three Goat Peaks) exist in British Columbia. One of them (1675 m) is located just northeast of Powell River and acquired its name when hunters shot two mountain goats there in 1894. Within five kilometres to the west are Goat Island (67 km^2; located in Powell Lake) and Goat Lake. And for those who are counting, there are three other Goat Islands and one other Goat Lake in the province.

G

GOLD RIVER A river and a village share this name. The river flows into Muchalat Inlet near Nootka Sound. Chinese miners took gold from the waterway in the 1860s, and the name appears on maps dating back to 1871. The village (2006: pop. 1362) has its origins in a logging camp called Muchalat, which was established in the early 1950s at the mouth of the river. The entire community was relocated 12 kilometres upstream to its present location in 1965 so that a pulp mill could be built at the original townsite. The community was renamed Gold River at that time.

GOLDEN (2006: pop. 3811) Located at the junction of the Kicking Horse and Columbia rivers northeast of Revelstoke, this town was originally called Kicking Horse Flats. However, around 1883, a silver-mining town called Silver City sprang up overnight on nearby Castle Mountain. Not to be outdone, the men of Kicking Horse Flats (or the owner of the town's store, depending on which story you believe) promptly renamed the community Golden City. The name was shortened to Golden when the Canadian Pacific Railway built a station there in 1885.

GOLDEN HINDE (2195 m) This mountain is the highest on Vancouver Island. Located in Strathcona Provincial Park, just west of Buttle Lake, its three peaks make the summit resemble a cockscomb when viewed from the southwest and the northeast. This led Reginald Thompson in 1913 to christen the mountain Rooster's Comb—a name that is still popular today among mountaineers—while he was making a survey of the park. The mountain was given its current moniker in 1939 (notice that the words "Mount," "Mountain" or "Peak" are not part of the name) to coincide with the 360th anniversary of the journey of English sea captain Sir Francis Drake and his flagship, the *Golden Hinde*, sailing up the Pacific Coast. The anniversary was chosen because Drake's visit was part of his circumnavigation of the globe (which has 360 degrees). Drake named his vessel *Golden Hinde* in honour of his friend and patron, Sir Christopher Hatton, whose crest included a golden "hind," or female deer.

G

GOLETAS CHANNEL This sea channel, south of Hope and Nigei islands, was named Salida de las Goletas ("Schooners Exit") in 1792 by Spanish explorers Dionisio Alcalá-Galiano and Cayetano Valdés y Flores. The moniker refers to the fact that this was the route their *goletas*, or schooners, the *Mexicana* and the *Sutil*, travelled on their way out to the Pacific when Galiano and Valdés circumnavigated Vancouver Island. The anglicized spelling was adopted by the British Admiralty sometime before 1848.

GOODLOW This community was established in the late 1910s, and its name is an amalgamation of the surnames of two of its earliest settlers, J. Good and A. Low. It is located 45 kilometres east of Fort St. John.

GRAHAM ISLAND (6362 km²) In 1853, this island was named by Commander James C. Prevost, the commanding officer of the HMS *Virago*, after Sir James Robert Graham, who was the British First Lord of the Admiralty from 1852 to 1855. Graham Island is the largest island in Haida Gwaii (Queen Charlotte Islands) and the second largest island in British Columbia.

GRAND FORKS (2006: pop. 4036) This city was named in the late 19th century because of its location, at the "fork" of the Kettle and Granby rivers, west of Trail. In addition, nearby Granby River was once known as the North Fork of the Kettle River.

GRANISLE (2006: pop. 364) This village on the shores of Babine Lake was established in 1965 by Granisle Copper Limited as a residence for employees who worked at its copper mine on an island in the lake. The corporation took its name from its parent company, the Granby Mining Company, and the fact that the mine was located on an island ("isle"). The mine is now closed, but the community survives.

G

GRANVILLE ISLAND This 17-hectare industrial park, public market and tourist destination in Vancouver's False Creek was named after Granville Street. The Granville Street Bridge spans above the island. The street's name, in turn, was adopted when the small logging town of Granville became Vancouver in 1886. The community was named in 1870 after George Leveson-Gower, the 2nd Earl Granville, who was, at the time, Britain's Secretary of State for the Colonies.

GRASMERE (estimated pop. 150) Located 70 kilometres southeast of Cranbrook, this small community was originally called McGuire, after Howard McGuire, an early settler who arrived in the area in 1898. The village acquired its current moniker in 1922 as the result of a lottery. When a new school was built that year, every student was asked to submit a new name for the settlement. The one drawn was Warren Lancaster's suggestion, Grasmere.

GREAT CENTRAL LAKE (51 km2) The name of this lake derives from the fact that it is a large body of water in the centre of Vancouver Island. It is the deepest lake on the island, with a maximum depth of 334 metres. It is not known when it acquired its current name, but it might have come from Robert Brown, who called it the "great Central Lake" in 1863, when he visited the area as leader of the Vancouver Island Exploring Expedition. The lake is noted elsewhere in Brown's journal, and was known by others into the 1860s, simply as Central Lake. At the time of Brown's visit, estimates of the lake's length varied from 54 to 80 kilometres, before Alberni Inlet sawmill manager Edward Stamp determined in 1863 that it was only 29 kilometres long. The local First Nation name for the lake is Moo-hulth, which means "burned-off face."

GREENVILLE *See* Laxqalts'ap.

G

GREENWOOD (2006: pop. 625) There are three stories about the origin of this city's name. One is that it is an amalgamation of the name of Greenwood's first settler, Robert Wood, who arrived in 1895, and the fact that the original townsite was full of green timber. A variation of this tale is that Wood's partner, C. Scott Galloway, said as the two looked upon the forested hillside, "It is a nice green wood," to which Wood supposedly replied, "That is what we will call it." Finally, many of the original miners and mining companies that were in Greenwood during the late 19th century were from the United States, and it has been suggested that Greenwood was named after the gold mining camp of Greenwood, Colorado. Greenwood is located 18 kilometres northwest of Grand Forks and is the smallest incorporated city in Canada.

GREY, POINT *See* Point Grey.

GRIBBELL ISLAND / GRIBBELL ISLET Both the island and the islet were named by Captain Daniel Pender. In 1867, Gribbell Island (205 km²) was christened by Pender after his brother-in-law, the Reverend Francis Barrow Gribbell, who arrived in Victoria in 1865. An Anglican, Gribbell would be placed in charge of St. John the Divine Anglican Church in Victoria in 1868. The islet was named by Pender in 1868. Sources disagree, however, as to whom he named it after. Some say it was for his wife, the reverend's sister, Isabel. Others say it was for Father Gribbell's daughter, who was also named Isabel. Gribbell Island is at the entrance of Douglas Channel, southwest of Kitimat. Gribbell Islet is just off Metlakatla, in Venn Passage.

GRINDROD (2006: pop. 1497) This community is located between Enderby and Salmon Arm. The townsite was laid out in 1910 and was originally called North Enderby, but the settlement was renamed the following year by the Canadian Pacific Railway after Edmund H. Grindrod, who retired in 1910, after serving 24 years as the CPR's first telegraph inspector in British Columbia.

GROUSE ISLAND *See* Quathiaski Cove.

GULF ISLANDS This name refers to the archipelago at the south end of Georgia Strait, from D'Arcy and Saturna islands in the south to Gabriola Island in the north. The term was officially adopted in 1963 after long public usage and is taken from the name, the Gulphe of Georgia, which Captain George Vancouver gave to the Strait of Georgia in 1792. Since the 1990s, some people have incorrectly applied the name to all the islands in the strait. The archipelago has also been called the "Southern Gulf Islands" and the rest of the islands in Georgia Strait the "Northern Gulf Islands." Quadra Island has also been mistakenly labelled the "northernmost of the Gulf Islands."

H

HADDO LAKE *See* Aberdeen Lake.

HAGENSBORG (2006: pop. 248) This community, located on the Bella Coola River, 20 kilometres east of Bella Coola, was established in 1894 by a group of Norwegian immigrants who had come to BC from Minnesota. When a post office was opened the following year, it (and, hence, the community) was called Bella Coola. The current moniker was adopted five years later, when the postmaster, Hagen B. Christenson, rechristened the post office after himself. In Norwegian, *borg* means "a fortified place where chiefs used to live."

HAIDA GWAII This archipelago of over 150 islands off the northwest coast of British Columbia was known for two centuries by BC's European settlers and residents as the Queen Charlotte Islands (*see* Queen Charlotte). However, in 2009, an agreement was reached between the Haida First Nation, who reside on the islands, and the British Columbia government to officially rename the Queen Charlotte Islands as Haida Gwaii, which means, in the Haida language, "Islands of the People."

HARDWICKE ISLAND (77 km²) In 1792, Captain George Vancouver named this island after British politician Philip Yorke, the 3rd Earl of Hardwicke. Vancouver was not so much honouring the earl as he was his master's mate on the HMS *Discovery*, Spelman Swaine, in whose career Hardwicke had taken an interest. Hardwicke Island is between Johnstone Strait and Sunderland Channel. Yorke Island, on the western tip of Hardwicke Island, and Mount Yorke (693 m; originally called Yorke Mountain) on

Hardwicke Island were both named in 1862 by Captain George Richards to honour the Yorke family in general.

HARDY A bay, an island and a mountain were all named for Vice Admiral Sir Thomas Masterman Hardy. Admiral Hardy is perhaps best known for holding the dying Lord Horatio Nelson in his arms, after Nelson was shot at the Battle of Trafalgar in 1805. Hardy Bay is located on the north end of Vancouver Island, near the community of Port Hardy. Hardy Island is at the entrance of Jervis Inlet, just west of Nelson Island (and, yes, Nelson Island was named for the great naval hero). Hardy Peak (691 m) is located on the north side of Johnstone Strait, near Port Neville. All three were named by Captain George Richards in 1860, while he was surveying the north and west coasts of Vancouver Island.

HARO STRAIT This strait was named in 1790 by Spanish Navy Sub-Lieutenant Manuel Quimper while he was in command of the *Princesa Real* (the captured British merchant ship *Princess Royal*). Quimper named the strait, located northeast of Victoria, for his first mate, Gonzalo López de Haro.

HARRISON Harrison Lake (223 km²) and Harrison River, located north of Chilliwack, were both named in 1828 by Hudson's Bay Company governor George Simpson in honour of Benjamin Harrison, an HBC director. The traditional Lil'wat (Lillooet) First Nation name for the lake is Qwáol'sa. Harrison Mills (2006: pop. 209), located downstream, near the junction of the Fraser and Harrison rivers, is now a neighbourhood in the district municipality of Kent. It was originally the site of a Stó:lô First Nation village. A fish plant was established there by the HBC in 1847, and its first non-Aboriginal settlers arrived 15 years later. The place may have been originally called Carnarvon by colonial governor Sir James Douglas in 1859 (or he could have been referring to an adjacent location to the south).

In any case, present-day Harrison Mills was christened Harrison River in the 1860s, and the British Columbia Directory of 1882–83 referred to it as Harrison Mouth. The current name was adopted in 1910, in honour of a sawmill (since burned down) that had been on the site since 1870.

HARRISON HOT SPRINGS A natural hot springs and a village share this name. The hot springs are at the south end of Harrison Lake. An 1846 map identifies them by their current moniker, and they were certainly named for the lake. The townsite of the nearby village (2006: pop. 1573), christened after the hot springs, was filed with the government in 1888 by Joseph Armstrong, a settler who arrived here 15 years earlier and opened a hotel near the springs in 1886.

HASLER PEAK (3377 m) *See* Feuz Peak.

HAWKESBURY ISLAND (364 km²) This island was named in 1793 by Captain George Vancouver for Charles Jenkinson, the 1st Baron Hawkesbury and the president of the Board of Trade from 1786 to 1803. Hawkesbury Island is on the east end of Douglas Channel. Mount Jenkinson (1089 m; name officially adopted in 1950) and Jenkinson Point, both on Hawkesbury Island, were also christened after the baron.

HAZELTON The village of Hazelton (2006: pop. 293), also informally known as Old Hazelton, was settled in the late 1860s and named for the abundance of hazel bushes in the area. It is located at the junction of the Bulkley and Skeena rivers, about 60 kilometres west of Smithers. Six kilometres to the east is the district municipality of New Hazelton (2006: pop. 627), which was established in 1912. Not far to the south of Old Hazelton is the community of South Hazelton (2006: pop. 213).

HELMCKEN The first geographic feature in British Columbia to be named after Dr. John Sebastian Helmcken was Helmcken Island in 1850. Located in Johnstone Strait, it was christened by Captain Charles Dodd of the Hudson's Bay Company ship, the *Beaver*. The spectacular Helmcken Falls in Wells Gray Provincial Park was discovered by a government surveyor and named in the doctor's honour in 1913. Helmcken Mountain (328 m), west of Victoria, was named in 1934. There is also Helmcken Canyon, through which the Murtle River flows, and Helmcken Inlet and Helmcken Lake, both on Princess Royal Island.

H

Helmcken arrived in Victoria in 1850 and was employed by the HBC as a medical officer and surgeon until 1886. He was also a politician and served as the Speaker of Vancouver Island's, and then British Columbia's, colonial legislature from 1856 to 1871. Helmcken was elected the first president of the British Columbia Medical Society in 1885.

HECATE A number of locations along British Columbia's coast were named by Captain George Richards between 1861 and 1862 for his ship, the HMS *Hecate*. The largest of these is Hecate Strait, which separates Haida Gwaii (Queen Charlotte Islands) from the British Columbia mainland. Other locations include Hecate Bay on Meares Island; Hecate Channel, between the Tahsis and Zeballos inlets; Hecate Island, north of Calvert Island; and Hecate Passage, off the southeast tip of Vancouver Island. Also named for the *Hecate*, though not necessarily by Richards, are Hecate Lake on Nootka Island and Hecate Mountain (1057 m), southwest of Port Alberni. The *Hecate* was a navy survey vessel that arrived in Esquimalt from England in December 1860. Richards commanded the ship from 1861 to 1862.

HERNANDO ISLAND *See* Cortes Island.

HIBBEN ISLAND This island in Haida Gwaii (Queen Charlotte Islands) was originally named Kuper Island in 1852 by Captain George Richards after fellow naval officer Captain Augustus Leopold Kuper. Richards, however, also christened another island, near Saltspring Island, after Kuper in 1859. So, in 1905, the Geographic Board of Canada renamed this island in Haida Gwaii after Thomas Napier Hibben, a prominent Victoria stationer in the late 19th century, who sold British Admiralty charts.

HIGHLANDS (2006: pop. 1903) This district municipality, locally known as The Highlands, is located north of Langford. Its first permanent non-Aboriginal settler, Caleb Pike, arrived in 1878, but the name dates back to at least 1859, when an official government map of the nearby Highland Land District was made. The moniker probably refers to the local hillsides.

HILLIERS (2006: pop. 1511) Located 42 kilometres northwest of Nanaimo, this community was originally called Hillier's Crossing after Thomas Hellier (note the misspelling), an early settler who arrived sometime before 1912. Over time, the apostrophe disappeared and the name was shortened.

HOLBERG (estimated pop. 200) Danish colonists founded this community in 1895 and named it after the 18th-century Danish dramatist and historian, Baron Ludvig Holbert (note the change in spelling in the hamlet's name). The settlement is at the head of Holberg Inlet on the northwest tip of Vancouver Island. The inlet was named after the town in 1926, as was nearby Holberg Mountain (736 m) in 1982.

HOMATHKO RIVER This river flows 137 kilometres from the Chilcotin Plateau through the Coast Mountains into Bute Inlet. The current spelling was officially adopted in 1911, but it was known as the Homalco River at least as far back as 1874. The reason for the change in spelling is not known. The name refers to the people of the Xwemalhkwu (Homalco) First Nation, one of the three groups that make up the Mainland Comox. The Xwemalhkwu once lived at the mouth of the Homathko River and at other locations along Bute Inlet. In the Mainland Comox language, *homalco* means "swift" or "swift water."

HOMFRAY CHANNEL This sea channel east of the Redonda Islands had been named by 1865 for Robert Homfray, a civil engineer from Worchestershire, England, who had arrived in British Columbia six years earlier by way of California. Homfray conducted surveys for the Canadian Pacific Railway. He also travelled to Bute Inlet in 1861 to investigate for Alfred Waddington the possibility of constructing a toll road to Barkerville. *See* Mount Waddington.

HONEYMOON BAY Both the bay, located on the southeast shore of Cowichan Lake, and the community that overlooks it are named for the intentions of an early settler from England. A young man who lived there in the late 1880s or 1890s had grown tired of the bachelor life and returned to Britain to find himself a wife whom he could bring back to Canada. The groom-to-be, whose name has been lost to history, never returned, but the moniker stuck. In 2006, the combined population of Honeymoon Bay and the nearby community of Mesachie Lake was 610.

HOODOO LAKES These lakes, located northwest of Prince George, were named in 1910 by surveyor Forrin Campbell. The moniker commemorates the misfortunes suffered by Campbell while he surveyed the local area, including injuries, a lack of horses and an early snowstorm that stranded him and his men for weeks.

HOPE (2006: pop. 6185) This district municipality was named after Fort Hope, a Hudson's Bay Company trading post that was constructed on the site in 1848–49. The fort got its name from the HBC's "hope" to establish a feasible all-British route, one that did not cross into the United States, for their brigades to travel between Fort Kamloops and Fort Langley. (The nearby 49th parallel had recently become the international border.) The townsite, which was laid out around the fort in 1858 at the start of the Fraser River Gold Rush, is located at the junction of the Fraser and Coquihalla rivers, at the mouth of the Fraser Canyon.

HOPE ISLAND Located west of Nigei Island, this island was named by Captain George Richards after Vice Admiral Sir James Hope in about 1864. The admiral had just been appointed commander-in-chief of the Royal Navy's North America and West Indies Station.

HORNBY ISLAND (22.92 km^2) This island was named in about 1850 by Hudson's Bay Company officials in honour of Rear Admiral Phipps Hornby. The admiral was the commander-in-chief of the British Fleet's Pacific Station from 1847 to 1851. The island lies southeast of Courtenay in the Strait of Georgia. The community (2006: pop. 1074) there takes its name from the island.

HORSESHOE BAY The bay and the community (estimated pop. 1000) that shares its name, as well as the residential community of Whytecliff, are located at the northwest end of West Vancouver near the entrance to Howe Sound. The bay was christened Horseshoe Bay because of its shape when a plan to survey the area was filed in 1892.

The southwest tip of the peninsula, located just west of the bay, was known for years as White Cliff Point because of the white cliffs. In 1909, a townsite was surveyed at the location of the present-day community of Horseshoe Bay and was called White Cliff City. That same year, real estate developer Colonel Albert Whyte, who had recently acquired a lot of property around the bay, and Vancouver lawyer Sir Charles Herbert Tupper, a Vancouver lawyer, federal cabinet minister and son of Prime Minister Sir Charles Tupper, opened a summer resort at the bay called WhyteCliff Park Resort. When the Pacific Great Eastern Railway opened a railway station there in 1914, Whyte convinced them to call it Whytecliff. In 1920, White Cliff City was renamed Whytecliff, to reflect the name of the railway station. The village on the bay was rechristened Horseshoe Bay in 1942, to reflect local preference, but the residents on the peninsula have chosen to stick with the name Whytecliff for their seaside community. Coincidentally, Chemainus Bay on Vancouver Island was also called Horseshoe Bay from 1859 to 1895.

HORSEFLY The names of both Horsefly Lake (59 km²) and Horsefly River go back to at least 1871. Each was christened for the pesky insect that appears in droves every summer. The community of Horsefly (2006: pop. 150) was established in 1884 or 1885 and was originally called Harper's Camp, after Thaddeus Harper of the famous Gang Ranch, who owned some mines in the area in the 1880s. Also, from 1895 until 1908, there was another mining town called Horsefly about 10 kilometres north, on the Horsefly River, where the Horsefly Mining Company operated. The issue of the name Harper's Camp came up for public vote in 1920, and all but one person favoured changing it to Horsefly. Horsefly Mountain was officially christened after the lake in 1939. The lake, the river, the community and the mountain (1791 m) are all located 50 kilometres east of Williams Lake.

HOUSTON (2006: pop. 3163) This district municipality was named for John Houston, the first mayor of Nelson and a member of the provincial legislature. He was also, for more than two decades, a famous and colourful muckraking journalist, who ran a number of newspapers across the province. In 1910, the year of Houston's death, the town of Pleasant Valley held a contest to choose a new moniker, and his name won, even though Houston probably never set foot there. The community is about 50 kilometres southeast of Smithers.

HOUSTON STEWART CHANNEL This channel at the south end of Moresby Island has been known by several names, including Ibbertson's Sound, Barrell Sound and Koya's Straits. It received its current name in 1853 from Captain James Charles Prevost, the commanding officer of the HMS *Virago*. The channel was christened after Prevost's predecessor, Captain William Houston Stewart. Almost all the islands in the channel are named after officers of the *Virago* and their friends, and the smaller islets are named after Prevost's children.

HOWE SOUND This body of water north of Burrard Inlet was named in 1792 by Captain George Vancouver for British hero Richard Howe, the 1st Earl Howe. The earl, a retired First Lord of the Admiralty, was called back into duty in 1790 to command the Channel Fleet when the building of a fort by the Spanish at Friendly Cove almost led to war between Britain and Spain. (Vancouver's first assignment off British Columbia's coast in 1792 was to meet with the Spanish at Nootka Sound to implement the treaty that ended the crisis.) Admiral Howe is best known for his victory over the French in 1794 at the naval battle known as the Glorious First of June. When he surveyed Howe Sound in 1859–60, Captain George Richards named all the islands, passages and mountains in and around the sound after various officers and ships that fought in that battle, including Bowen Island, Defence Islands, Gambier Island and the Queen Charlotte Channel.

HOWSER This name refers to two mountains—Howser Peak and Howser Spire—that are only three kilometres from each other, as well as to a creek, a mountain ridge and a community. It all began with Fred Hauser. Fred and his brother, John, were prospectors who lived along Duncan Lake. One summer, Fred found several hundreds of dollars' worth of gold in the waters of what is now Howser Creek, on the north side of the lake. The following summer, Hauser took a partner with him back to the creek, and the two were never heard from again. Exactly when this occurred, or how or why the spelling of the name was changed, is no longer known, but the body of running water was known as Howser Creek by 1887.

H

The nearby lake was called Ecclesion on a map made by Jesuit explorer and missionary Father Pierre-Jean De Smet in 1846, but it was renamed Upper Kootenay Lake 19 years later. The water body was known as Howser Lake by 1892, but it was also often called Duncan Lake after John "Jack" Duncan, a local prospector and politician. Maps from 1896 and 1897 even refer to it as "Duncan or Howser Lake." The lake was officially designated Duncan Lake in 1902, though it was still called Howser Lake by many at least until 1911.

Ironically, the community on the west side of the lake got the name Howser. The settlement was established by 1893 and was originally called Duncan. It became known as Duncan City by 1898. However, postal authorities were constantly confusing the town with Duncan Station on Vancouver Island. Government mining reports were calling the settlement Howser by 1899, so the name of Duncan City was officially changed to Howser in 1900.

Howser Peak (3082 m) and Howser Spire (3412 m), both located in Bugaboo Provincial Park north of the lake, were named in 1911 for the creek. The mountain ridge just west of Duncan Lake officially became Howser Ridge in 1915.

HUDSON'S HOPE (2006: pop. 1012) This district municipality can trace its beginnings back to 1805, when Simon Fraser established a North West Company trading post on this site called Rocky Mountain Portage House. The outpost was closed in 1825 but had been reopened by 1873 by the Hudson's Bay Company as Hudson's Hope or The Hope of Hudson. There are several theories behind the name. One is that it refers to a real or hypothetical prospector and his hope of finding gold. Another is that the moniker was meant as an ironic comment on the prospect of the HBC successfully maintaining a trading post there. Until the late 19th century, place names ending with the word "hope" were common in Scotland and northern England. Finally, it has been said that the old definition of "hope" included "haven," "bay" and "small inlet." Hudson's Hope is on the Peace River, 90 kilometres west of Fort St. John.

HUGH KEENLEYSIDE DAM The construction of this dam, eight kilometres west of Castlegar, was completed by BC Hydro in 1968. It was originally named the Arrow Dam because the water it holds back caused the Upper and Lower Arrow Lakes to merge into one giant body of water. The dam was renamed in 1969 after Hugh Keenleyside, the co-chairman of BC Hydro from 1961 to 1969.

H

I

ICONOCLAST MOUNTAIN (3236 m) Sources differ as to whether it was alpinist Arthur O. Wheeler in 1902 or surveyor Percy Carson in 1907 who named this mountain. All agree that the moniker refers to its steep, black face. The word "iconoclast" is a combination of two Greek words, *eikōn*, which means "image," and *klastēs*, which means "breaker."

INDIAN ARM / INDIAN RIVER This 17-kilometre-long fjord northeast of Vancouver, which runs north from Burrard Inlet to Indian River, was officially called North Arm (because it is the inlet's northern arm) until 1921. At that time, the Vancouver Harbour Commission decided the body of water needed a more distinctive name. Because the name of the Meslilloet River was about to be changed to Indian River to reflect local usage, the Commission suggested Indian Arm and the Geographic Board of Canada agreed.

INVERMERE (2006: pop. 3002) This district municipality on the north side of Windermere Lake was first called Copper City and then Canterbury before it was given its current name in 1924 by Robert Randolph Bruce, a famous mining engineer who was also the president of the Columbia Valley Irrigated Fruit Lands Company. Bruce, who later became lieutenant-governor of British Columbia, owned a major estate in Invermere, and the company owned the townsite where Invermere is located. The name is an amalgamation of two Anglo-Saxon or Middle English words, *inver* for mouth and *mere* for lake, that together mean "at the mouth of the lake."

IOCO For most of the 20th century, this Imperial Oil Company distribution terminal was also the site of a small community built for Imperial Oil's employees. The name is a collection of the Imperial Oil Company's initials (I-O-Co) and dates from at least 1916. Ioco is on the north side of Burrard Inlet, northwest of Port Moody.

J

JAFFRAY (2006: pop. 453) This community was settled shortly after the Canadian Pacific Railway laid its tracks there in 1898. Originally called Cranston, it was renamed in 1901 after Toronto financier and industrialist Robert Jaffray, the president of several companies doing business in the Cariboo and around Cranbrook and Fernie. Jaffray was a powerful and influential member of the federal Liberal Party, and some believe that the CPR christened this town after him to win favour with the Liberals, who were then in power. Others say that Jaffray was honoured because he was the first to invest in the coal mines surrounding the community. Jaffray is 35 kilometres southeast of Cranbrook.

JAMES BAY Located at the eastern end of Victoria Harbour, this bay was named in 1846 in honour of Hudson's Bay Company chief factor James Douglas, who, four years earlier, had chosen the spot overlooking the bay for the site of Fort Victoria. The name was later applied to the peninsula south of downtown Victoria, which overlooks the Juan de Fuca Strait and the entrance to Victoria Harbour.

JANE ISLAND *See* Sarah Island.

JEDEDIAH ISLAND Captain George Richards named this island in 1860 for Jedediah Stephens Tucker. Tucker's father, Benjamin Tucker, was a British naval officer who served for many years as the secretary to Admiral Earl St. Vincent (a.k.a. Sir John Jervis, of Jervis Inlet fame), and young Jedediah used his father's notes and papers to write a biography of the admiral that was published in 1844. The island is located between Lasqueti and

Texada islands, in the Sabine Channel of Georgia Strait. Tucker Bay on Lasqueti Island was also named by Captain Richards, this time, in honour of Jedediah's father, Benjamin.

JEMMY JONES ISLAND Located at the mouth of Cadboro Bay east of Victoria, this island was named in 1870 by Staff Commander Daniel Pender of the Royal Navy for one of British Columbia's most colourful characters, Captain James "Jemmy" Jones. Jones was a coastal mariner who traded between Puget Sound and Vancouver Island from 1854 to 1882. One of his first ships, the schooner *Caroline*, ran aground on this island. In his most famous exploit, in 1865, he was imprisoned for debt in Victoria. His ship, the *Jenny Jones*, had been seized in Washington State. Jones escaped from jail wearing a woman's dress and bonnet, crossed the Juan de Fuca Strait alone in a canoe and managed to retake his ship when the U.S. marshal guarding it went ashore for the night.

JERICHO BEACH This beach on the south shore of Burrard Inlet is part of Vancouver's Point Grey neighbourhood. It was once called Jerry's Cove after pioneer logger Jeremiah "Jerry" Rogers. Over time, the name was shortened to Jericho.

JERVIS INLET Located on the north end of the Sechelt Peninsula, east of Malaspina Strait, this inlet was named by Captain George Vancouver in 1792 for Rear Admiral Sir John Jervis. On the north side of the inlet is St. Vincent Bay, which was also named in honour of the admiral. Jervis became a hero and was made the 1st Earl of St. Vincent after he defeated a Spanish fleet off Cape St. Vincent, Portugal, in 1797. Captain George Richards christened the bay in about 1860.

JOHNSTONE STRAIT Captain George Vancouver named this strait in 1792 for James Johnstone, the master of the armed tender HMS *Chatham* and the first non-Aboriginal to explore this channel earlier the same year. The sea corridor extends 110 kilometres along the northeast side of Vancouver Island, from Alert Bay to Rock Bay.

JORDAN RIVER / RIVER JORDAN The Jordan River was named for Alejandro (or Alexandro) Jordan, a Franciscan priest who accompanied Spanish naval officer Francisco de Eliza y Reventa to Nootka in 1790 and stayed there for a few years. Spanish Navy Sub-Lieutenant Manuel Quimper, the commander of the *Princesa Real* (the captured British merchant sloop *Princess Royal*), named the river Rio Hermoso in 1790 while exploring the southern coast of Vancouver Island from Nootka to the Juan de Fuca Strait. However, the name was changed to Rio Jordan by Quimper's first mate, Gonzalez Lopez de Haro, when Haro drew the maps of the voyage later that same year. The river is on the west coast of Vancouver Island, about 60 kilometres from Victoria. At its mouth is the community of River Jordan. This has been the logging town's official name since its founding in 1919, even though the British Admiralty had previously changed the river's name to Jordan River. Virtually everybody calls the logging town Jordan River.

JUAN DE FUCA STRAIT A book published in 1625 titled *Purchas, his Pilgrimes* includes an account of an Englishman, Michael Lok, who visited Venice in 1596. Lok supposedly met an old Greek mariner whose real name was Apostolos Valerianos but who was commonly called Juan de Fuca. According to Lok, this "ancient Pilot of Shippes" claimed that, four years earlier, the Spanish viceroy of Mexico sent him north up the Pacific Coast to find the Northwest Passage. Juan de Fuca did not find the elusive passage, but he did come across the entrance of a strait. The story was largely ignored for nearly 200 years, until 1787, when Captain Charles Barkley of the *Imperial Eagle* rediscovered the strait exactly where Juan de Fuca said it was and named it after him. The strait separates southern Vancouver Island from Washington State and is part of the Canada-U.S. border. The official American name is the Strait of Juan de Fuca. That was also the Canadian name until colonial governor Frederick Seymour had the moniker changed to Juan de Fuca Strait to distinguish British Columbia from the United States to the south.

JUMBO MOUNTAIN (3437 m) This mountain was originally called Jumbo Peak in 1892 by alpinist Edward Warren Harnden after the Jumbo Mining Claim on the nearby present-day Jumbo Creek. The mine, in turn, was named for the famous elephant, Jumbo, that appeared in the Barnum & Bailey Circus shows in the early 1880s. The peak was renamed Jumbo Mountain in 1917 and is 36 kilometres northeast of Argenta.

K

KAIEN ISLAND Christened when Tuck Inlet was surveyed in 1892, this island is home to the city of Prince Rupert. The moniker was taken from the Tsimshian First Nation word *kai-en,* which means "foam." The name refers to the large quantities of foam that occur on the sea south of the island, sometimes extending for two kilometres or more, which are caused by a combination of rapid tides and heavy rain.

KALAMALKA LAKE For several decades, this extraordinarily deep lake south of Vernon was officially called Long Lake, but the name was changed in 1951 to conform to long-time public usage. The current name dates from at least 1910. Some believe that it is a word brought over by the Hawaiians who were employed in the Pacific Northwest by the Hudson's Bay Company. It is also said that the name is an amalgamation of two First Nations words—one Secwepemc, the other Okanagan—that mean "water" and "soothing" or "healing." An old First Nations chief called Tanamalka lived at the head of the lake in the 1880s. Furthermore, there is a colourful story about a locally well-known chief, Kalamalka, who once lived at the head of the lake. (The two may have been the same person.) In his advanced years, Kalamalka wanted to become a Christian, but he was continually denied baptism because he had four wives. Finally, his spouses decided that a young wife could take over a lot of the household work and allow them to retire, so they had their husband find a young maiden whom he presented to the priest as his only spouse. Kalamalka was baptized and had the one "wife" but continued to support all five women. In any case, it is known that the large Kalamalka Hotel already existed in Vernon in 1891, that the Kalamalka Lake Country Club had been built on the lake's shores by 1910 and that some of Vernon's city fathers started a campaign to replace the name Long Lake with the more distinctive Kalamalka Lake in the 1920s to promote business and tourism.

KALEDEN (2006: pop. 1289) This community's townsite was laid out in 1909 by James Ritchie, who offered a prize of one town lot for whoever came up with the best name for the new settlement. The lot was given to the Reverend Walter Russell, a Baptist evangelist from the Okanagan, who combined the Greek word *kalos*, meaning "beautiful," and the name of the Biblical garden of Eden. Kaleden is 13 kilometres south of Penticton.

KAMLOOPS / KAMLOOPS LAKE The city of Kamloops (2006: pop. 80,376) is located at the junction of the North and South Thompson rivers. North West Company fur trader Alexander Ross established a trading post there in 1812, "at a place called by the Indians Cumcloups." Years later, John Tod of the Hudson's Bay Company wrote in his memoirs that the "Indians called the place Kahm-o-loops, meaning 'the meeting of the waters.'" Ross and Tod almost had it right. The Secwepemc (Shuswap) First Nation name for this location is Tk'emlups, which means "a meeting place." Over the years, there have been some wild interpretations of the name, including "field of wolves." It has also been said that the name comes from the French phrase *champ de loups*, which was supposedly used by the voyageurs. Until 1870, there were so many trading posts by different names in the area that the names Fort Kamloops, Fort Thompson and Thompson River Post became interchangeable. It was not until the first post office was established in 1870 that the city fathers finally settled on the name Kamloops. Ten kilometres west of the city is Kamloops Lake (59 km²), the name of which dates at least from 1877, if not earlier.

KASLO / KASLO RIVER The village of Kaslo (2006: pop. 1072) lies on the west side of Kootenay Lake, about 71 kilometres northeast of Nelson. It was originally named Kane's Landing after two brothers who settled there in 1889, but the following year, the pair renamed the community after the river that flows into Kootenay Lake. One of the brothers, David Kane, wrote in 1905 that he was not sure about the name's origin but that he had heard stories about a French trapper and prospector called John Kaslo (or Kasleau or Casleau), who came to the area decades before with a Hudson's Bay Company expedition and named the river after himself. Another early settler claimed that a Ktunaxa (Kootenay) First Nation woman had told him that Kaslo comes from the First Nations name Ah-Kas-loe, meaning "the place where blackberries grow," but Kane said the story was hogwash. Other theories are that the name is a derivation of *cassoloe*, a Ktunaxa word for "blackberry," or *kala*, the Ktunaxa word for "black hawthorn."

K

KEEFERS This small, unincorporated community was named after George Keefer, a railway construction engineer, who lived there with his family in the 1880s and was in charge of building the Canadian Pacific Railway line between North Bend (about 12 kilometres south of Keefers) and Lytton (about 30 kilometres north). Although the town's official name is Keefers, some refer to it as Keefer's.

KEENLEYSIDE DAM *See* Hugh Keenleyside Dam.

KELOWNA (2006: pop. 106,707) This city, located on the east side of Okanagan Lake, was named after the appearance of a giant, hairy, early settler called August (or Augustus) Gillard. Gillard was a Frenchman who arrived in 1862, after spending some time in the California Gold Rush. A blacksmith, he lived in a partly underground hut. One day, some passing First Nations people saw him crawl out of his abode like a bear from a den and laughingly cried out "*Kimach touche*" to each other. The word has been variously translated as "brown bear," "bear face" and "black bear's face." In any case, the phrase became the local nickname for Gillard and his home. Thirty years later, John Coryell was laying out the townsite, and when the question of the new settlement's name came up, someone suggested Kimach Touche; others thought the moniker too awkward and uncouth, so Kelowna was chosen instead. Kelowna is the Okanagan First Nation word for "female grizzly bear."

Just south of Kelowna is Gillard Creek, which is also named after August Gillard. In 2007, the District Municipality of West Kelowna was established on the west side of Okanagan Lake.

K

KENNEDY An island, a lake and a river are all named for Arthur Edward Kennedy, the last colonial governor of Vancouver Island (1864–66) before it merged with the mainland colony of British Columbia. Kennedy Island is located at the mouth of the Skeena River and was named by Captain Daniel Pender in about 1866. Kennedy Lake (61 km^2) was originally called Lake Kennedy and was christened in 1865 by John Buttle, the leader of that year's Vancouver Island Exploring Expedition. The lake lies 12 kilometres north of Ucluelet. Kennedy River flows through the lake and was probably named by Buttle as well.

KENNEY DAM This dam on the Nechako River, 95 kilometres southwest of Vanderhoof, was built in 1951–54. At that time, it was the largest rockfill, clay-cored dam in the world. Behind the dam is the Nechako Reservoir, the largest lake in British Columbia until the construction of the W.A.C. Bennet Dam in 1968 created the Williston Reservoir. The dam was named for Edward Kenney, the provincial Minister of Lands, and later the Minister of Lands and Forests, from 1944 to 1952.

KENT (2006: pop. 5208) This district municipality was named for the English county of Kent when the community was incorporated in 1895. It was chosen because growing hops is a major local industry in Kent, and Kent, England, was well known for its hops.

KEREMEOS (2006: pop. 1289) The name of this village was adopted by the Hudson's Bay Company when a trading post was established there in 1860. The moniker is a derivation of the Okanagan First Nation word *keremeyeus*, which has been interpreted in many ways, including "wind channel in the mountains," "beautiful stream crossing the flats," "land cut across the middle," "a flat cut through by water" and "where the valleys meet." The community is on the Similkameen River, 42 kilometres southwest of Penticton.

K

KERRISDALE This Vancouver neighbourhood was named in 1905 by one of its original settlers, Helen MacKinnon, who had arrived two years earlier from Scotland with her husband, William. The BC Electric Railway had just built a tram stop in the area, and the company's general manager, Rochfort Henry "Tim" Sperling, initially planned to name it in honour of the MacKinnons. Helen objected and suggested that it be named Kerry's Dale instead, after her family's ancestral home, Kerrydale (Gaelic for "little seat of the fairies") in Gairloch, Scotland. Sperling agreed, but the spelling was quickly changed.

KICKING HORSE PASS / KICKING HORSE RIVER James Hector, a natural scientist with the Palliser Expedition, which was exploring western Canada, was supposedly kicked in the chest by his horse along the banks of the river, about 10 kilometres west of Lake Louise on August 29, 1858. The men accompanying Hector immediately called it the Kicking Horse River. Nearby Kicking Horse Pass (1622 m), on the Alberta border, was officially named after the river in 1924.

KIMBERLEY (2006: pop. 6139) This city was named in 1896 or 1897 by Colonel William Ridpath, a wealthy Spokane, Washington, attorney who invested in several Kootenay mines. It is believed that the moniker reflected Ridpath's hopes that his mine would be as profitable as the diamond mine in Kimberley, South Africa. That South African community, in turn, was named after John Wodehouse, the 1st Earl of Kimberley and the British Secretary of State for the Colonies when diamonds were discovered there.

KINBASKET LAKE / KINBASKET MOUNTAIN The reservoir (529 km^2), located between Golden and Valemount, was created in 1973 with the construction of the Mica Dam on the Columbia River. The body of water completely engulfed a much smaller lake that was also called Kinbasket Lake. The first lake was christened in 1866 by surveyor Walter Moberly after the Secwepemc (Shuswap) First Nations chief, Paul Ignatius Kinbaskit (also known simply as Kenpesq't), whom Moberly hired for the price of two canoes to take him down the Columbia. The name Kenpesq't means "touch the sky." The spelling had changed to Kinbasket by 1884. The reservoir was originally called McNaughton Lake, in honour of General A.G.L. McNaughton, the commander of the Canadian forces in Britain from 1939 to 1943 during World War II. The name Kinbasket was restored in 1980 because of local pressure.

Kinbasket Mountain (2545 m) is on the east side of the north end of the lake. It was officially named after the original lake in 1939.

KINCOLITH *See* Gingolx.

KING ISLAND (814 km^2) This island between Burke and Dean channels was named in 1793 by Captain George Vancouver for the family of Captain James King. King, along with Vancouver, sailed with Captain James Cook on

Cook's third and last voyage of 1776–79. Vancouver originally called it King's Island, but the British Admiralty had shortened the name by 1868. Nearby Dean Channel was named by Vancouver for King's father. There was once another King Island in British Columbia. Located in Barkley Sound, it was named in 1861 by Captain George Richards for Captain Edward Hammond King of Her Majesty's 59th Regiment. The army captain accidentally shot himself on the island earlier that year, while taking his hunting rifle out of his canoe during a deer-hunting expedition, and he died three days later. That island is now called Edward King Island.

KINGCOME Kingcome Inlet and the Kingcome Mountains were both named in 1865 by Captain Daniel Pender for Vice Admiral John Kingcome. The admiral was stationed off the British Columbia coast while he was the commander-in-chief of the British Fleet's Pacific Station from 1863 to 1864. The inlet is east of Gilford Island and the Queen Charlotte Strait, and the mountains are three kilometres east of the inlet. At the head of the inlet is the community of Kingcome Inlet and also the mouth of the Kingcome River, both of which are named after the inlet. Kingcome Point, on Princess Royal Island, was named by Captain Pender in 1867 for the admiral's nephew, Hudson's Bay Company mercantile mariner Captain William Kingcome.

KINNAIRD Until 1974, this neighbourhood in Castlegar was a separate village. When the Canadian Pacific Railway built a station there in about 1904, they named it after Arthur Fitzgerald Kinnaird, the 11th Lord Kinnaird, a Scottish nobleman and CPR stockholder. The community that evolved around the station took its name.

KITAMAAT / KITIMAT Kitamaat Village (2006: pop. 514) and the district municipality of Kitimat (2006: pop. 8987) are across from one another at the head of the Kitimat

Arm of the Douglas Channel. Kitamaat Village, on the east side of the Arm and a few kilometres south of the mouth of the Kitimat River, is on the site of a former Haisla First Nation fishing village. The Tsimshian First Nation name for both the village and its residents was Kitamaat (or Gitamaat), which means "people of the falling snow." (The Tsimshian used to participate in winter ceremonies hosted by the Haisla and often arrived there when it was snowing. The Haisla name for the village was Dsemosa, which means "place of logs" because of the logs that wash up on the beach.) A Roman Catholic mission began on the site of the village in the 1890s. It was originally called Kitamaat, then Kitamaat Mission and, finally, in 1908, Kitimat Mission. That last name, however, had fallen into disuse by the end of the 1930s, and local residents called the community by its current name. The government, however, did not recognize the change until 1976.

Kitimat lies 11 kilometres northwest of Kitamaat Village and just west of the mouth of the Kitimat River. It dates from the early 1950s, when the Aluminum Company of Canada (known as Alcan) built a smelter there. The district municipality took its name from Kitimat Arm, which was so christened in about 1837 by officers of the Hudson's Bay Company.

KITCHENER (2006: pop. 241) The Canadian Pacific Railway established this community in 1899 and named it for Horatio Herbert Kitchener, then Baron Kitchener (and later the 1st Earl Kitchener). Kitchener had won international fame the year before by leading a successful military campaign to reconquer Sudan. Kitchener is 13 kilometres east of Creston. *See also* Sirdar.

KITLOPE The Kitlope Valley is located at the head of the Gardner Canal, 100 kilometres southeast of Kitimat. Kitlope Lake and the Kitlope River are both found within the valley. Kitlope (or Gitlope) was the Tsimshian First Nation name for the people of the Henaaksiala First Nation, who lived in the area until the 1930s.

KITSAULT RIVER This river flows south into Alice Arm. Kitsault is a derivation of the Nisga'a First Nation name for Alice Arm, Gitsoohl, which means "at the back" (as in "at the back" of a strip of land that separates Alice Arm from the Nass River). The current spelling dates from at least 1917 and was officially adopted five years later, but earlier spellings include Chigitsoult, Gitzault, Kitsaulte, Kitzault and Kitzaulte.

KITSILANO (2006: pop. 40,595) This Vancouver neighbourhood was named after S̲k̲wx̲wú7mesh(Squamish) First Nation Chief Khahtsahlanogh. (His name has also been spelled Haatsalano, Kates-ee-lan-ogh, Khahtsahlano and Khahtsalano.) In the late 19th century, the chief resided at a Squamish village called Snauq (or Sun'ahk), which was located on Kitsilano Point, near modern-day Vanier Park, where the south end of the Burrard Street Bridge and Molson's Brewery are found today. The village became the Khahtsalano (or Kitsilano) Indian Reserve No. 6 when British Columbia joined Confederation. (The reserve was closed and its residents forced to move to North Vancouver in 1913.) The Canadian Pacific Railway opened up some land west of the reserve in 1905 to create a new housing division and needed a name for it. The chief's name was suggested, but the spelling was changed so that it would rhyme with Capilano, which is across Burrard Inlet.

KLEECOOT *See* Sproat.

KLEENA KLEENE / KLINAKLINI The names of both the community of Kleena Kleene and of the Klinaklini River (as well as of the canyon, glacier and lake near the river) are derived from a word in the Kwak'wala language of the

Kwakwaka'waka First Nation. The word *t'lina* is pronounced *GLEET-na* and means "eulachon (or oolichan) grease (or oil)." The grease was considered a delicacy by First Nations peoples throughout British Columbia. It was extracted from the small, oil-rich eulachon fish by the First Nations bands on the Pacific Coast and shipped along the famous "grease trails" to be traded in the Interior. Kleena Kleene is 180 kilometres due west of Williams Lake. Its first non-Aboriginal residents arrived in the early 1900s. The Klinaklini River flows southwest from Kleena Kleene to Knight Inlet.

KLOIYA BAY / KLOIYA RIVER Both the bay and the river that flows into it are located just southeast of Prince Rupert. The current spelling of the name dates from 1930. Before that, the bay was known as Cloyah Bay and the river as the Coloyah River. *Kloiya* is a Tsimshian First Nation word meaning "a place to hide valuables." The moniker refers to the fact that, because it was out of the way of their usual path to their fishing grounds on the Skeena River, the bay was an excellent place for the Tsimshians to stash their treasured possessions while they were away.

KNIGHT INLET This 113-kilometre-long fjord was named in 1792 by Lieutenant Commander William Robert Broughton for his old comrade, Captain John Knight. In 1776, during the American Revolution, Broughton and Knight were captured and briefly held as prisoners of war together by the Americans. The mouth of the inlet is just north of Cracroft Island.

KOOTENAY This name is applied to the southeast corner of British Columbia, from the Okanagan Valley to the Alberta border. It is also the name of the large lake (422 km²), the river and the national park located within this region. The current spelling dates from the late 1860s,

K

when colonial governor Frederick Seymour changed the names of the Kootenai and other rivers to distinguish British Columbia's waterways from those in the United States. The name refers to the people of the Ktunaxa First Nation, whose members live in the area; the Ktunaxa (pronounced *tuh-nah-ha-gh*) are also known as the Kootenay (variously spelled Coutonai, Kootanae, Kootenai and Kutenai). Several meanings for Kootenay have been suggested, including "water people" and "deer robes." It could be a derivation of the Kootenays' traditional name for themselves, Ktunaxa, which some believe might come from the name of the Tunaxa people of the Great Plains, to whom the Kootenay might be related. The name might also have come from the Blackfoot, traditional enemies of the Kootenays, who referred to them as the Kutunáiua or "slim people."

K

KOTCHO LAKE / KOTCHO RIVER No one is certain when this lake and river in the far corner of northeast British Columbia received their current names. Kotcho is probably a derivation of the traditional Slavey First Nation name for Kotcho Lake, which is Gōh-chō-deh, "the elders' place." The name refers to the fact that it was the meeting place of all the Slavey people in the area and that, while the younger folk went out hunting, they left their elders there. Another possibility is that Kotcho comes from the Slavey word *k'a cho*—*k'a* means "willow" and *cho* means "big," referring to the diamond willows that are prevalent in the area. Kotcho may also be a combination of *ko*, the Slavey word for "fire" with *cho*, which has led at least one non-Aboriginal source to conclude that Kotcho means "big fire." Finally, Kotcho could come from the Slavey place name Eh kow tu cho, which means "water or lake in that area."

KULLEET BAY This bay north of Ladysmith was officially named by the British Hydrographic Office in 1895.

The bay had earlier been christened Chemainus Bay by Captain George Richards while he was making a survey of the area in 1859, but it was renamed to avoid confusion with the natural harbour on which the settlement of Chemainus is located. One source indicates that the bay was named after the band of the Chemainus First Nation that lived there, but another points out that Kulleet is a derivation of K'elits, the Hul'qumi'num First Nation name for the bay. The word *k'elits* means "sheltered area" or "protected bay."

KUNGHIT ISLAND (212 km²) Kunghit is a derivation of the traditional Haida First Nation name for this island, Gaang.xid Gwaayaay. The name Gaang.xid means "to the south," and Gwaayaay means "island." Kunghit Island is the southernmost island of Haida Gwaii (Queen Charlotte Islands). The isle was renamed Prevost Island in 1853 by British Admiralty surveyors, presumably after Commander James C. Prevost, the commanding officer of the HMS *Virago*, which was sailing around Haida Gwaii that year. However, the Geographic Board of Canada reversed that decision 51 years later, to prevent confusion with the other Prevost Island located near Saltspring Island.

K

KUPER Cape Kuper and nearby Kuper Inlet (originally called Port Kuper), both on the southwest side of Hibben Island, were named in 1852 by Captain George Richards in honour of Captain Augustus Leopold Kuper, the commanding officer of the HMS *Thetis*, while that ship sailed in British Columbia waters from 1851 to 1853. Hibben Island was also christened Kuper Island in 1852 by Richards in Kuper's honour, but it was renamed in 1905 to avoid confusion with another island that Richards named in 1859 after his fellow captain—Kuper Island (8.66 km²), located northwest of Saltspring Island.

KYUQUOT A community, a bay, a sea channel and a sound share this name. They are all located within five kilometres of each other on the northwest coast of Vancouver Island, south of Checleset Bay. Kyuquot refers to the Ka:'yu:'k't'h people who are part of the Ka:'yu:'k't'h'-Che:k:tles7et'h' First Nation (the two groups joined in the 1960s). Kyuquot is the anglicized spelling of Ka:'yu:'k't'h, which has been used for more than 100 years. The name was also variously spelled as Caiyuquat, Cayuquet and Ky-u-kew by 19th-century missionaries and traders. The Ka:'yu:'k't'h are part of the Nuu-chah-nulth (Nootka) First Nation. Ka:'yu:'k't'h means "people of Ka:'yu:k," but some Nuu-chah-nulth elders have also translated it as "different people" or "foreign people."

K

L

LAC LA HACHE A community and a lake share this name. Sometime before 1862, a packhorse or mule that was part of a Hudson's Bay Company brigade of voyageurs was carrying a large load of axes, when the animal fell into the lake. The lake, 25 kilometres north of 100 Mile House, was immediately called Lac la Hache, which is French for "Lake of the Axe." The community (2006: pop. 245) that stretches along the lake's 19-kilometre shoreline was settled in the 1860s and is called the "longest town in the Cariboo."

LAC LE JEUNE This name applies to a lake, a community and a provincial park that are all 35 kilometres south of Kamloops. The lake and community were both known as Fish Lake when, in 1928, the lake was renamed after Jean-Marie Le Jeune, a 78-year-old Oblate missionary in Kamloops. Le Jeune was a Frenchman who came to British Columbia in 1879 and served at missions in the East Kootenay and Williams Lake before he was transferred to Kamloops in 1882. In the 1880s, he created a written alphabet for Chinook Jargon, a language then commonly used from Alaska to California between various First Nations and between First Nations and non-Aboriginals who otherwise would not be able to understand each other. Le Jeune also published a newspaper in Chinook Jargon called the *Kamloops Wawa*, as well as a number of books for First Nations peoples. Lac Le Jeune Provincial Park was established along the lake in 1956. One year later, the name of the community, which was still officially called Fish Lake, was changed to Lac Le Jeune.

LADNER (2006: pop. 21,112) This neighbourhood in Delta was named sometime before 1875 for (depending upon what source you read) one or both of the Ladner brothers, William and Thomas, who were the first pioneers to settle there in 1868. They arrived in British Columbia in 1858 from England via the California gold fields to prospect in the Cariboo. They later became storekeepers and mule packers before moving to Delta to farm. In the 1860s, William was also the first constable on the BC mainland. William later went into politics, and Thomas became rich in the salmon-canning business. Their descendants are still prominent in Lower Mainland business, legal and political circles. The locale was officially known as Ladner's Landing until 1895.

LADY DOUGLAS ISLAND *See* Dowager Island.

LADY PEAK (2178 m) In about 1917, A.S. Williamson, the superintendent of the nearby Lucky Four Mine, named this mountain for alpinist Phyllis Munday and "her mountaineering experience." The peak is located just southeast of Cheam Peak.

LADYSMITH (2006: pop. 7538) This town is named for Ladysmith, South Africa. The community was established in 1899 by industrialist James Dunsmuir for employees of his coal mine, which was located 11 kilometres to the north at Extension. Dunsmuir originally called it Oyster Harbour for the rich oyster beds nearby, but he changed the name in March 1900, immediately upon hearing about the relief of Ladysmith in South Africa. The Boers had been besieging the town for four months, and news of the relief was cause for great celebration throughout the British Empire. South Africa's Ladysmith was founded in 1851 and named after Lady Juana Smith, the wife of Major General Sir Harry Smith. General Smith was a British war hero of the First Anglo-Sikh War and, in 1851, became governor of the Cape Colony in South Africa. Canada's Ladysmith is on the east coast of Vancouver Island, between Duncan and Nanaimo.

LAIDLAW (2006: pop. 163) This community, just west of Hope, is named after early resident, farmer, storekeeper and hotel owner Walter Forbes Laidlaw. It was originally called St. Elmo after both the 1866 bestselling novel by Augusta Evans and the St. Elmo Hotel owned by Laidlaw, which might have been named after the novel. However, when the Canadian Northern Railway wanted to lay its tracks across Laidlaw's farm, he insisted that the CNR name the railway station (and, hence, the town) after him. His neighbours were incensed, but he got his wish.

LAKE COUNTRY (2006: pop. 9606) This district municipality was incorporated in 1995 and is located on the east side of Okanagan Lake, between Kelowna and Vernon. Nearby are Duck Lake, Kalamalka Lake and Wood Lake. The name is clearly descriptive of the community's local geography.

LAKE COWICHAN *See* Cowichan.

LAKE KOOCANUSA This reservoir was created when the construction of the Libby Dam in Montana was completed in 1968. A few names were suggested, and finally a contest was held. The winner was Alice Beers of Rexford, Montana, who recommended a combination of the names Kootenay, Canada and USA. The lake is an expansion of the Kootenay River as it flows south into the United States and lies 70 kilometres west of Cranbrook.

LANGARA / LANGARA ISLAND Both the residential community of Langara in Vancouver and Langara Island in Haida Gwaii (Queen Charlotte Islands) were named directly or indirectly for the 18th-century Spanish naval hero Juan Francisco de Lángara y Huarte. The neighbourhood took its moniker from Punta de Lángara, the name given in 1791 to the southern entrance of Burrard Inlet (now known as Point Grey) by either Spanish explorer Dionisio Alcalá-Galiano or by Spanish Navy Lieutenant Francisco de Eliza y Reventa. The island was christened

Isla de Lángara by Spanish Navy Lieutenant Jacinto Caamaño Moraleja after Lángara in 1792. However, British fur trader George Dixon had earlier named it North Island in 1787 to honour Frederick North (more commonly known as Lord North), Britain's prime minister from 1770 to 1782, and the name remained in common usage. When Commander James Prevost of the HMS *Virago* surveyed Haida Gwaii in 1853, he changed the island's name from Isla de Lángara back to North Island. The moniker was changed, yet again, to Langara Island when Captain Frederick Learmonth of the HMS *Egeria* resurveyed the area in 1907. Langara Island is still frequently referred to as North Island.

LANGDALE There was once a small community with this moniker on the west side of Howe Sound. It was named after its first settler, Robinson Henry Langdale, who arrived from Yorkshire, England, in 1892 or 1893. The site is now a busy BC Ferries terminal.

LANGFORD / LANGFORD LAKE The city of Langford (2006: pop. 22,459) is located just west of Victoria. Langford Lake, in the centre of the community, was named by 1855 for Captain Edward Edwards Langford, a former landowner from Sussex, England, and a veteran of the 73rd Foot Regiment, who arrived in Victoria in 1851 to manage the 600-acre (243-hectare) Colwood Farm, which had been established by the Puget Sound Agricultural Company (a subsidiary of the Hudson's Bay Company). The farm spread from the lake to Esquimalt Harbour and encompassed much of present-day Colwood and Langford. The area surrounding the lake became known as Langford Plains. Various tenants lived on the farm after Langford returned to England in 1861, and the west end of the present-day city was a popular recreational site by the late 1880s. It wasn't until the early 20th century that permanent settlers arrived. When a post office was opened there in 1911, it (and, hence, the local community) was named after the lake. Northeast of Langford Lake is Florence Lake, which was named in 1855 for the captain's fifth and youngest daughter, Florence Isabella. *See* Colwood.

LANGFORD (NUCHATLITZ INLET) Captain Edward Edwards Langford had five daughters. His third, Emma, married John Augustus Bull, master of the HMS *Plumper* and the ship's senior assistant surveyor under Captain George Richards. As a result, a number of spots at Nuchatlitz Inlet were named by Richards for Langford and Emma's four sisters while the *Plumper* was surveying Nootka Island in 1859. These include a harbour called Port Langford. Colwood Inlet was also christened in the captain's honour. (Colwood was the name of Langford's farm in England and of his farmhouse near Victoria.) Other geographical features named for members of Langford's family include Louie Creek, after the eldest sister, Louisa Ellen; Mary Basin, after the second sister, Mary; Sophia Range, after the third sister, Sophia Elizabeth; and Florence Point, after the youngest sister, Florence Isabella.

LANGLEY Two neighbouring municipalities, the City of Langley (2006: pop. 23, 831) and the Township of Langley (2006: pop. 93,726), use this name. They trace their beginnings to Fort Langley, which was built in 1827 as a Hudson's Bay Company trading post along the south bank of the Fraser River, about 30 kilometres east of present-day downtown Surrey. The site was abandoned, and a new Fort Langley was built five kilometres upstream in 1839. The fort was named after Thomas Langley, a director of the HBC, and, over time, a village by the same name grew around it. Another settlement called Langley was later established 10 kilometres to the south. In 1873, the entire area, including these two communities, was incorporated as a district municipality called the Township of Langley. A small portion of the western side of the township that was its trade and service centre was split off in 1955 and incorporated as the City of Langley in 1955. The neighbourhood near the old HBC fort is still known as Fort Langley.

LANTZVILLE (2006: pop. 3661) This district municipality dates from 1917, when a coal mine was opened there. The townsite that grew up around the mine was originally called Grant's Mine, but it was renamed shortly after the mine was sold to the Seattle-based Nanoose Collieries Company three years later. The moniker honours Fraser Harry Lantz, an American investor then living in Vancouver, British Columbia, who was the vice-president and later managing director of the Seattle firm. Lantzville is 10 kilometres northwest of Nanaimo.

L

LASQUETI ISLAND (67 km²; 2006: pop. 359) This island was named in 1791 by José María Narváez, the commanding officer of the *Santa Saturnina*, for fellow Spanish sea captain Juan Maria Lasqueti, who explored the coast of Brazil. Lasqueti Island is southwest of Texada Island.

LAX KW'ALAAMS (also known as Port Simpson) (2006: pop. 679) A Hudson's Bay Company trading post called Fort Nass was established at the mouth of the Nass River in 1831. In September of that year, Captain Aemilius Simpson died there. Simpson was a Hudson's Bay Company hydrographer and surveyor, the captain of the HBC ship *Cadboro*, a distant relative of HBC governor George Simpson and a person who had played a key role in the establishment of the post. Needless to say, the fort was promptly renamed after him. The location of Fort Simpson proved unsatisfactory, so it was moved (Simpson's body and all) in 1834. Both the bay where the new fort was located and the settlement that grew around it came to be known as Port Simpson during the 1880s.

Most of the residents are members of the Tsimshian First Nation and, in 1986, the community was renamed Lax Kw'alaams. The new moniker derives from the Tsimshian name Laxłgu'alaams, which means "place of the wild roses" and has long been used by the local First Nations people as the name of the town. It is also the name of the First Nation band (a part of the Tsimshian Nation) that resides there. The community is located just north of Prince Rupert and is still frequently called by its old name.

LAXQALTS'AP (2006: pop. 474) This Nisga'a First Nation village was officially called Greenville from 1950 until 2000. The name honours the Reverend Alfred E. Green, a Methodist missionary who lived there from 1876 to 1889. In 2000, pursuant to the Nisga'a Treaty, the village's previous name, Laxqalts'ap(misspelled Lachkaltsoup before 1950), was restored. Laxqalts'ap is a Nisga'a place name that means "a dwelling place situated upon an ancient dwelling place" and reflects the fact that there once was another village on the site, Gitxat'in, which was destroyed by fire and renamed Laxqalts'ap when it was rebuilt. The village is located on the north side of the Lower Nass River.

LIARD RIVER A little less than one quarter of this 1115-kilometre-long river is in northeast British Columbia; the rest lies in the Northwest Territories and the Yukon. The traditional Kaska First Nation name for the river was Nêt'i Tué, which means "river flowing from mountains where sheep are snared." French Canadian voyageurs who travelled down this river with Hudson's Bay Company explorer John McLeod in 1834 called it Rivière aux Liards. Cottonwood trees are found in abundance along this river's banks, and *liard* is the French name for this species of poplar. HBC fur trader Robert Campbell renamed it the Bell River four years later, after fellow fur trader and HBC chief factor John Bell, but the name never took. The English translation of Rivière aux Liards was officially adopted as the river's name in 1898.

LIBERATED GROUP This group of mountains just west of Chilko Lake was named in 1976 for 11 Canadians who were leaders in the early movement for women's rights. Those honoured include the world's first female war correspondent, Kit Coleman (Mount Coleman); the first woman professor at a Canadian university, McGill's Carrie Derick (Mount Derick); the founder of the National Council of Women, Henrietta Edwards (Mount Edwards); Canada's first female medical doctor, Emily Howard-Stowe (Mount Howard-Stowe); the first two women elected to a Canadian provincial legislature, Alberta's Roberta MacAdams and Louise McKinney (Mount MacAdams and Mount McKinney); the first woman elected to the House of Commons, Agnes Macphail (Mount Macphail); suffragist and social activist Nellie McClung (Mount McClung); the first female judge in the British Commonwealth, Edmonton's Emily Murphy (Mount Murphy); the first woman provincial cabinet member in Alberta, Mary Parlby (Mount Parlby); and Canada's first woman mayor, Ottawa's Charlotte Whitton (Mount Whitton). A 12th mountain in the group is Why Not Mountain, whose name was taken from the "Why Not?" slogan of the pioneers of the Canadian women's equality movement.

LIKELY This small community dates back to the Cariboo Gold Rush and is located where the Quesnel River flows into Quesnel Lake. It was named Quesnel (or Quesnelle) Dam in 1898, when a dam was built to allow mining in the river. Its moniker was changed in 1923 to honour a popular 81-year-old local miner, John A. "Plato" Likely. The fellow loved Plato and Socrates, and he gave lectures about them to other miners underneath the trees along Quesnel Lake. In return, some of Likely's students provided him with tips on where to find gold, which added to his financial prosperity.

LILLOOET This name is applied to a district municipality (2006: pop. 2324), a glacier, a lake and a river. The district municipality of Lillooet is on the Fraser River, 65 kilometres north of Lytton. It dates from the Fraser River Gold Rush and was called Cayoose Flat, but the name was changed in 1859. One story has it that the name was chosen because the spot overlooks the point at which both the Lillooet River and the Douglas Trail (a major trail starting at Lillooet Lake) meet the Fraser River. Another is that colonial governor James Douglas wanted the community to be known by its original First Nations name; he apparently thought the village of Lillooet was there when, in fact, it was located about 60 kilometres away, at the south end of Lillooet Lake. The name comes from the people of the St'át'imc First Nation, who were once known as the Lillooet; a group of them, known as the Lil'wat, live near Lillooet along the Fraser River, as well as around Anderson and Seton lakes. There is a difference of opinion as to the meaning of the name. The most common interpretations are "wild onion" and "place of the wild onion." One linguist, however, argues that Lillooet is the anglicized version of a St'át'imc word whose meaning is no longer known but was used by the Natives to refer to the northeast side of Lillooet Lake.

The Lillooet River, which flows 145 kilometres from Lillooet Glacier to Harrison Lake, was named by fur trader Alexander Anderson in 1849. It is not clear when Lillooet Lake, where the river widens near Pemberton, or Lillooet Glacier, the head of the river, were named, though it was probably at about the same time.

LITTLE SHUSWAP LAKE *See* Shuswap.

LIONS BAY / LIONS' GATE / THE LIONS The Lions are twin peaks (West Lion, 1654 m; East Lion, 1606 m) in the North Shore Mountains above Burrard Inlet and are easily visible from downtown Vancouver. Previously called The Sisters, the current name was suggested in about 1890, when someone noticed their resemblance to a pair of reclining lions, and the name was formally adopted in 1924. It was also suggested at the time that the entrance to Burrard Inlet should be called Lions Gate. Although the name was never formally approved, ever since the bridge over the inlet opened in 1938, it has been called the Lions Gate Bridge.

The name Lions Bay, which is the moniker of both the bay and the village (2006: pop. 1328) that overlooks it, comes from the Pacific Great Eastern Railway stop that opened there in 1954 and was, in turn, named after the mountain peaks. The bay and village are on the east side of Howe Sound, 11 kilometres north of Horseshoe Bay.

LOGAN LAKE A community and a lake share this name. The district municipality (2006: pop. 2162) was established in 1970 by the Lornex Mining Corporation as a residence for employees of the company's Highland Valley Copper Mine. It was Lornex's suggestion that the community be named after the nearby lake. There are two stories regarding the origin of the lake's moniker. One is that it is a misspelling of the name Tslakan, a local Savona First Nation fur trader and horse rancher who lived there during the 1860s. The other is that Tslakan had a daughter whose English name was Anne Logan and that Logan Lake was named after her. The community and the lake are both about 30 kilometres southwest of Kamloops.

LOST LAGOON This 0.17-square-kilometre lake at the entrance to Vancouver's Stanley Park was once a cove of Coal Harbour. The "lagoon" was created in 1916 when the traffic causeway into the park was completed and separated the two bodies of water. The name comes from a poem by Pauline Johnson, "The Lost Lagoon," which was included in her 1911 anthology, *Legends of Vancouver*. Johnson explained that the "lagoon" was one of her favourite places to canoe but was empty of water and "lost" to her at low tide. The name was officially adopted by the Vancouver Parks Board in 1922, nine years after Johnson's death, the same year that a cairn was erected in Stanley Park in Johnson's honour.

LOUGHBOROUGH INLET This inlet was named in 1792 by Captain George Vancouver for Alexander Wedderburn, the 1st Baron Loughborough and the Chief Justice of the Court of Common Pleas. He would be appointed the Lord Chancellor of Great Britain in 1793. The inlet is west of North Thurlow Island.

LOUISE ISLAND (276 km²) This island in Haida Gwaii (Queen Charlotte Islands) was named by George Dawson in 1878 in honour of Princess Louise, the fourth daughter of Queen Victoria and the wife of John Douglas Sutherland Campbell, the Marquis of Lorne, who had just become the Governor General of Canada.

LOWER ARROW LAKE *See* Arrow Lakes.

LOWER MAINLAND This is an unofficial, but popularly used, term that refers to the city of Vancouver and the surrounding area. Depending upon who is using it, it can mean the territory west of Abbotsford and Mission and include the North Shore, or it can include everything west of Chilliwack and south of Whistler.

LOWER NICOLA *See* Nicola.

LULU ISLAND (110 km²) This island at the mouth of the Fraser River, south of Vancouver is now the site of the city of Richmond. The isle was simply called Island No. 1 when it was surveyed in 1859 but was renamed the following year by Colonel Richard Moody of the Royal Engineers. The engineers had built a theatre in New Westminster, and one of their favourite entertainers was 16-year-old actress and singer Lulu Sweet of San Francisco's Potter Theatre Troupe, the first theatrical troupe to ever perform in that city. As recorded by one of Moody's men: "Her conduct, acting and graceful manners gave great satisfaction, and were appreciated to such an extent by her friends and patrons that the island was named after her." It is also said that on January 12, 1860, as Moody was pointing out various landmarks to Ms. Sweet as their steamship was sailing down the Frase River on their way to Victoria, he commented at one point, "We are now approaching the eastern end of a large island that extends all the way to the Gulf." "What's its name?" she naturally asked. "It has no name," he replied, "except its Indian name, whatever that might be. By Jove! I'll name it after you."

L

LUMBY (2006: pop. 1634) The first non-Aboriginal settlers arrived in the area in the 1860s, and a townsite was laid out in 1888. The village was first named White Valley, after the valley in which it is located, but was rechristened in 1894, in honour of Moses Lumby, a farmer who had settled there in 1870 and died in 1893. Lumby was a justice of the peace and the vice-president of the Shuswap & Okanagan Railway. This community is 25 kilometres east of Vernon.

LYELL ISLAND (169 km²) This island in Haida Gwaii (Queen Charlotte Islands) was named in 1878 by George Dawson after the famous British geologist, Sir Charles Lyell.

LYNN The infamously turbulent and dangerous Lynn Creek on the North Shore was named for John "Jock" Linn. Linn was one of the Royal Engineers who arrived in British Columbia in 1859, and he stayed behind after the unit disbanded four years later. In 1869, Linn and his family moved to a cabin just east of the creek, which was then called Fred's Creek, after an earlier settler who had already left the area. Linn's name was attached to the creek as early as 1878, though it has been misspelled almost from the very beginning. Jock died two years earlier, but his family continued living near the creek for several years.

The canyon through which the creek flows and the lake from which it originates, as well as the neighbourhoods of Lynn Valley and Upper Lynn in the district of North Vancouver, were all named after 1878 for Linn or for the creek. Lynnmour, another neighbourhood in the district of North Vancouver, was named after Lynn Creek and nearby Seymour Creek. Between Lynn and Seymour creeks are the Lynn Peaks (1015 m). There are also two local parks, Lynn Canyon Park and Lynn Headwaters Regional Park, that share the name.

LYTTON (2006: pop. 235) This village sits on the site of an old Nlaka'pamux (Thompson) First Nation community called Camchin or Kumsheen. Miners and settlers arrived with the coming of the Fraser Valley Gold Rush, and the infant non-Aboriginal community was named by colonial governor James Douglas in 1858 for Sir Edward Bulwer-Lytton (later the 1st Baron Lytton). Bulwer-Lytton was the new British Secretary of State for the Colonies, and it was he who sent the Royal Engineers to British Columbia to lay out townsites and build roads. Bulwer-Lytton was also a noted novelist, poet and playwright. In the 1830s, he coined the phrases "It was a dark and stormy night…" and "The pen is mightier than the sword." Lytton is located where the Fraser and the Thompson rivers meet.

M

MABEL LAKE A lake and a community share this name. The lake (56 km²) was christened sometime in the 1870s by Canadian Pacific survey engineer Charles Perry for Mabel Hope Charles. Mabel, who was born in 1860, was the eldest child of William Charles, the Hudson's Bay Company manager at Fort Hope, Fort Kamloops and later Victoria. Mabel Lake is 25 kilometres east of Armstrong. The community, located 12 kilometres south of the lake and just north of Shuswap Falls, was settled in about 1904 and was christened after the lake.

MacBETH GROUP In 1959, mountaineer Robert West visited a large snowfield about 10 kilometres east of Duncan Lake and 15 kilometres southwest of Mount Farnham. Perhaps unaware that the lake was christened in 1902 for recently deceased local prospector John "Jack" Duncan, instead of the ill-fated 11th-century Scottish king in Shakespeare's *MacBeth*, West felt inspired to name three of the surrounding peaks after the leading characters in the play: Mount MacBeth (3054 m), Mount Banquo (2994 m) and Mount MacDuff (3009 m). Other surrounding mountains would later be named Mount Lady MacBeth (2891 m) and Mount Fleance (2904 m). Together, these mountains are informally known as the MacBeth Group.

MacKENZIE (2006: pop. 4539) This district municipality is named for fur trader and explorer Alexander Mackenzie. The community, located on the south end of Williston Reservoir, 193 kilometres north of Prince George, was established in 1966 by Alexandra Forest Industries as a residence for employees who worked at the company's new complex along the lake. Mackenzie passed by the lake in 1793, while on his way to the Pacific Ocean. The town fathers quickly picked the moniker when they discovered that no town or city in Canada had yet been named after the first-known non-Aboriginal to cross North America.

MAIDEN CREEK This creek, between Clinton and Cache Creek, derives its name from a First Nations legend that was told to British Columbia colonial governor Sir James Douglas. As Douglas conveyed the story, there was a young First Nations woman in love with a young chief, who was a great hunter and warrior. The couple was to be married in the winter, but the previous autumn, the groom-to-be went off on a long hunting trip. The girl anxiously waited, always keeping a watchful eye for her betrothed near the spot where this creek flows into the Bonaparte River. Winter came and went, but he did not return. The chief finally arrived in the spring, but with a woman he had married while visiting another band. The young woman died of grief and was buried where she had kept her vigil. According to the legend, from her breasts grew the twin knolls that can be seen near the mouth of the creek.

M

MAILLARDVILLE This Francophone neighbourhood in Coquitlam traces its origin to 1909, when 150 individuals arrived from Québec to work for the Fraser River Saw Mills. The Roman Catholic parish of Notre Dame de Lourdes was founded that same year. More millworkers arrived from Québec, and the community of Maillardville grew around it. It is named after Father Edmond Maillard, the first priest at the church.

MALAHAT On the west side of Saanich Inlet are a community, a 25-kilometre stretch of the Trans-Canada Highway (commonly referred to as The Malahat or as Malahat Drive), a mountain ridge, a summit and a rugged region of heavy forest and steep cliffs that share this name. They were all named directly or indirectly for the Malahat First Nation. The Malahat are part of the Salishan First Nation, and they had one of the largest communities on southern

Vancouver Island when the Europeans first arrived. According to the Malahat, the name comes from the Hul'qumi'num First Nation word *ma'le-'h'xe'l,* which means "caterpillars." (Hul'qumi'num is a Coast Salishan language.) Many Malahat became sick and died when the Europeans brought measles and smallpox to the island, and the Natives incorrectly blamed their illness on the tent caterpillars. The caterpillars were abundant at that time—there was possibly even an infestation of them—and they ate all the leaves off the trees in the area.

MALAKWA (2006: pop. 619) This community is 10 kilometres northeast of Sicamous and was established before 1902. Its name is the Chinook Jargon word for "mosquito."

MALASPINA An inlet, a lake, a mountain, a peninsula and a strait are all named for Alexandro Malaspina. Malaspina was an Italian who, as a captain in the Spanish Navy, was in command of a worldwide exploration and scientific expedition from 1789 to 1794 that took him, in 1791, to the coast of British Columbia. The inlet was christened in 1792 by Spanish naval explorers Dionisio Alcalá-Galiano and Cayetano Valdés y Flores and is located at the northeast end of Georgia Strait. The western shore of the inlet is Malaspina Peninsula. Malaspina Strait was named in 1859 by Captain George Richards and is southeast of Powell River, between Texada Island and the BC mainland. Malaspina Lake is on Vancouver Island, east of Tahsis Inlet. Malaspina Peak (1520 m) is just east of the lake. The mountain was previously called Needle Peak but was rechristened in 1935 to avoid confusion with another mountain of the same name.

MALCOLM ISLAND (82 km²) This island was named in 1846 by Commander George Gordon, the commanding officer of the HMS *Cormorant,* when Gordon surveyed the isle. Gordon christened the island in honour of Admiral Sir Pulteney Malcolm. The admiral is best known for having been the commander-in-chief of the British fleet's St. Helena Station from 1816 to 1817, while Napoleon was a prisoner there. In essence, Malcolm was Napoleon's warden. The island lies off the northeast coast of Vancouver Island, near Port McNeill.

MAPLE RIDGE (2006: pop. 68,949) This district municipality was incorporated in 1874 and named for the abundance of maple trees on a local ridge. The community is on the north side of the Fraser River, just east of Pitt Meadows.

MARPOLE This residential neighbourhood in southern Vancouver was originally named Eburne after its first settler, W.H. Eburne, who opened a store there in 1881. It was renamed Marpole in 1916 after Richard Marpole, the superintendent of construction and operation for the Canadian Pacific Railway's Pacific Division from 1897 to 1907. It was Marpole who planned the development of the suburb of Shaughnessy Heights for the CPR, and he built the first home there in 1909.

M

MASSET This is the common name of an inlet, a sound and two communities, Old Massett (with two *t*'s since 1995) and the village of Masset (often called New Masset; 2006: pop. 940), all located on or near Graham Island in Haida Gwaii (Queen Charlotte Islands). Many say that the name Masset is taken from the moniker of Maast Island, which is located in Masset Inlet, and that Maast is a Haida First Nation place name whose meaning is now unknown. However, Haida tradition and historical records tell a different story. The famous American windjammer, the *Columbia Rediviva*, sailed into the inlet in 1791. Its captain intended to name the body of water Hancock River but discovered that the local Haida already called the harbour "Masheet." According to the Haida, an earlier ship had sailed into the inlet and anchored off the location of present-day Masset. (The first known Europeans to visit Haida Gwaii arrived in 1774.) One of that ship's officers, a man named Masseta, died and was buried on the island in the inlet. The Haida named the isle after him but found his name too difficult to pronounce and settled on Mah-sh-t. The British Navy surveyed Masset Inlet in 1853, and the name appears on Admiralty charts from that date. In 1878, noted geologist George Dawson renamed Mah-sh-t Island to Maast Island during his visit to Haida Gwaii, in the apparent belief that this was the origin of the name Masset.

MASTODON MOUNTAIN (2968 m) This mountain was first named Mount Mastodon in 1921 or 1922 by mountaineer Arthur O. Wheeler while he was in charge of the Interprovincial Boundary Survey. Wheeler thought the shape of the mountain resembled a prehistoric elephant. The name was changed to Mastodon Peak in 1924. The current name was first applied by the Alberta government in 1962 and adopted by British Columbia a year later. Mastodon Mountain is on the Alberta border, near the south end of Mount Robson Provincial Park.

MATSQUI This part of Abbotsford was named for the people of the Matsqui First Nation, who live in the area. The colonial government set aside the "Masquee Reserve" for the Matsqui in 1858, and the first non-Aboriginal settler arrived in 1867. The District of Matsqui was incorporated as a municipality in 1892; when or why the spelling was changed is not clear. Matsqui was merged with the District of Abbotsford in 1995 to form the City of Abbotsford. The Matsqui are part of the Stó:lô First Nation, an alliance of various Halq'emeylem communities along the lower Fraser River, and speak Upriver Halq'eméylem. The name is from the Halq'eméylem name for the area. The Matsqui in the mid-19th century pronounced the word *Mats-whey*, and anthropologist Franz Boaz recorded it as Ma'cQui in an 1890 report. Most sources say the word means "easy portage" or "easy travelling" and refers to the ease with which the Matsqui could travel along the creeks from the

Fraser River and drag their canoes over the land to
the now-drained Sumas Lake or to the tributaries of the
Nooksack River in Washington State. One source, however, says the word means "stretch of higher ground" and
refers to the portage between the Fraser River and Sumas
Lake. Nearby Matsqui Island, in the Fraser River, and
Matsqui Prairie, north of Abbotsford, also take their name
from the Matsqui.

MAURELLE ISLAND (54 km²) Located between Quadra
Island and the British Columbia mainland, this island,
along with Quadra and Sonora islands, were originally
thought by early surveyors to be part of one large island,
which was known as Valdes Island. After the mistake was
realized, Maurelle Island became known as Middle Valdes
Island. It finally acquired its current name in 1903, when
the Geographic Board of Canada christened it after
Francisco Antonia Maurelle, a Spanish naval officer who
made two trips to the BC coast in the late 1770s as second-
in-command under Lieutenant Commander Juan
Francisco de la Bodega y Quadra.

MAYNE ISLAND (23 km²; 2006: pop. 1112) This island was
named in about 1860 by Captain George Richards for
Lieutenant Richard Charles Mayne. Mayne served under
Richards, first on the HMS *Plumper* from 1857 to 1860,
and then, in 1861, on the HMS *Hecate*. Mayne Island is
northeast of Saltspring Island. The main community on
the island is called Mayne. Also named between 1858
and 1861 by Richards after Lieutenant Mayne are Mayne
Bay, off Barkley Sound, and Mayne Passage, between East
and West Thurlow islands.

MAYO LAKE *See* Paldi.

McBRIDE (2006: pop. 660) Located 207 kilometres west of
Prince George, this village was established in 1911 by the
Grand Trunk Pacific Railway and was named after Sir

M

Richard McBride, who was premier of British Columbia at the time. McBride Glacier in Garibaldi Provincial Park is also named after him.

McLEESE LAKE Both a community (estimated pop. 300) and a lake share this name. The two are located 10 kilometres north of Soda Creek. The lake was labelled Mud Lake on an 1871 map and Lac La Hache ("lake of the axe") on a 1913 chart. Another body of water, however, already had the latter name, so the lake was rechristened McLeese Lake the following year. The name honours Robert McLeese, a Soda Creek hotelier, store owner, long-time postmaster and member of the provincial legislature, who owned property near the lake. The community dates from at least 1959, when a post office opened there.

McNEILL BAY The name of this bay was officially adopted in 1924, though the moniker had been in use since at least 1865. The bay was named after Captain William Henry McNeill of the Hudson's Bay Company. This American seaman commanded the HBC's famous vessel, the *Beaver*, from 1837 to 1843. McNeill was later in charge of various HBC posts, including Fort Rupert and Fort Simpson, and became a chief factor in 1856. When McNeill retired in 1863, he settled in the home that he built on 81 hectares near this bay. McNeill Bay is on the south side of Oak Bay, near Victoria. *See* Port McNeill.

MEARES ISLAND (82 km²) In 1862, Captain George Richards named this island in honour of Commander John Meares. Meares was a fur trader who established a trading post at Nootka Sound in 1788 and built the sloop *North West America* there. It was the first vessel of European design constructed on the Pacific Northwest Coast. In 1789, he sent trading ships to Nootka Sound from China; the seizure of those ships by the Spanish almost led to war between Britain and Spain. Meares Island is north of Tofino, in Clayoquot Sound.

M

MERRITT (2006: pop. 7170) Established in 1893, this city went through at least three name changes before it was christened in 1906 after mining engineer William Hamilton Merritt III. That year, the Canadian Pacific Railway built a railway from Spences Bridge to the community to exploit the local coal deposits, and Merritt had been promoting the construction of the line since 1891. The community is southwest of Kamloops, at the junction of the Coldwater and Nicola rivers.

MERVILLE (2006: pop. 2012) This community was established in 1919 for soldiers who were returning from World War I. The veterans named the settlement after the town in France near the Belgian border where the Canadian Army had its first field headquarters in the war. Merville is 14 kilometres north of Courtenay.

MESACHIE LAKE Both a lake and a nearby community on the south shore of Cowichan Lake share this name. It is not known when the lake received this moniker, but the name is a Chinook Jargon word that means "bad," "evil" or "ill-tempered." The people of the local Cowichan First Nation once believed that an old man ("the Mesachie Man") lived in the lake and that anyone sailing or swimming in its waters would be drowned. The community was founded and named by the Hillcrest Lumber Company when it established its sawmill and timber operations there in 1943. In 2006, the combined population of Mesachie Lake and nearby Honeymoon Bay was 610.

M

METCHOSIN (2006: pop. 4795) The moniker of this district municipality is a derivation of the Coast Salish First Nation place name Smets-Shosin. The name has been interpreted in various ways, including "smelly fish," "smelling of oil," "place of oil," "place of stinking fish" and "place smelling of fish oil." The name refers to a dead whale that washed up on a nearby beach. Two whale vertebrae, allegedly from the creature, are on display in the Metchosin School Museum. Hudson's Bay Company chief factor James Douglas was the first to use the name Metchosin when he inspected the site in 1842 as a possible location for a trading post at the southern tip of Vancouver Island; he chose present-day Victoria instead. The community's first European settlers arrived in 1854. Metchosin is southwest of Victoria, between Colwood and Sooke.

METLAKATLA This community is an ancient Tsimshian village, and its name is an adaptation of the Tsimshian place name Metlakah-thla. It was listed on British Admiralty charts as Metlah-catlah in the 1860s and '70s, and the current spelling came into use in the 1880s. The word is believed to mean "a passage between (or connecting) two bodies of salt water." The "passage" the name refers to is probably the Venn Passage, which connects Chatham Sound and Tuck Inlet. The community is just west of Prince Rupert.

M

MIDWAY (2006: pop. 621) This village is located just west of Grand Forks. The community's first permanent settler was Louis Eholt, who built a ranch there in the mid-1880s. By 1889, a small settlement called Eholts had been established. In 1892, Eholt sold his property to Captain R.C. Adams of Montréal and his partners, who planned to build a smelter there. A townsite was laid out in 1893 and called Boundary City because it was less than two kilometres from the American border. However, the name was too similar to that of nearby Boundary Falls (now a ghost town), and the postal authorities wouldn't go along with it, so Adams renamed the community in 1894. It is often assumed that the name was chosen because Midway is between two locations that Adams did not mention. For example, Midway is roughly halfway between the Rocky Mountains and the Pacific Ocean. However, the truth is that Adams had attended the 1893 Chicago World's Fair and was so impressed with the

Midway Pleasance, a walkway showcasing various pavilions and amusements, that he named the village after it.

MILBANKE SOUND This body of water was named in 1788 by Captain Charles Duncan for Vice Admiral Mark Milbanke. Duncan was a former naval officer in command of a merchant vessel called the *Princess Royal*. Milbanke had commanded a warship by that same name from 1777 to 1778. It is not known if this is more than a coincidence. Milbanke Sound is between Campbell and Price islands.

MILL BAY A bay on the west side of Saanich Inlet and the community that overlooks it share this name. The bay received its moniker shortly after an American, Henry S. Shepherd, built a sawmill there in 1861. It was, for a time, the only mill between Esquimalt and Nanaimo, and lumber magnet William Sayward purchased it in 1863. The small community of Mill Bay (2006: pop. 1106) quickly developed around the mill.

M

MINSTREL ISLAND This name is shared by a small island at the mouth of Knight Inlet and a community on the island. The island was named in the late 19th century by a survey crew that was working in the area when a "minstrel boat" arrived. The community was established in 1907. Most agree that the "minstrel boat" was the HMS *Amethyst*, which stopped at the island while taking Frederick Hamilton-Temple-Blackwood, the 1st Earl of Dufferin and Governor General of Canada, and his wife, Lady Dufferin, on a cruise to Metlakatla in 1876. Some of the vessel's crew formed an amateur troupe and performed minstrel shows in blackface for their shipmates. It is presumed that the survey crew that named the island were guests at a performance when the *Amethyst* anchored here. On nearby West Cracroft Island are Bones Bay and Sambo Point, both christened after stock characters (Mr. Bones and Sambo) popular in late-19th-century minstrel shows.

MIOCENE / MIOCENE LAKE The community of Miocene dates from the Cariboo Gold Rush. It and nearby Miocene Lake, both located between Horsefly and Williams Lake, were named after the Miocene Mine on the Horsefly River. The mine takes its name from the fourth geological epoch, which occurred 12 to 26 million years ago.

MISSION (2006: pop. 34,505) This district municipality takes its name from St. Mary's Mission, which was established on the site in 1861 by an Oblate missionary, Father Leon Fouquet. Not one, but two communities grew around the site, one called Mission and the other Mission City, but they merged in 1969. Mission is located across the Fraser River from Abbotsford.

MONARCH MOUNTAIN (3555 m) This mountain was christened in the early 1930s by explorer and mountaineer W.A.D. "Don" Munday in honour of King George V. The peak is in the southwest corner of Tweedsmuir South Provincial Park.

MONASHEE MOUNTAIN / MONASHEE MOUNTAINS The Monashee Mountains are one of the four mountain ranges of south-central British Columbia. Located between the Columbia River on one side and Shuswap Lake and the North Thompson and Okanagan rivers on the other, the mountains extend about 440 kilometres from Valemount to the American border. The range includes two peaks with the name Monashee: Mount Monashee (3274 m), located 40 kilometres northeast of Blue River, and Monashee Mountain (1887 m), which is 18 kilometres southeast of Cherryville. The name is a derivation of a Scottish Gaelic phrase. In 1880 or 1881, prospector Donald McIntyre, an immigrant from the Scottish Highlands, was in the area of Monashee Mountain and faced a day of terrible weather consisting of strong winds with a mixture of rain and snow. As evening came, the wind dropped, the clouds disappeared, and there was a beautiful sunset. "*Monadh sith!*" exclaimed McIntyre. In Scottish Gaelic, *monadh* means "mountain" and *sith* (pronounced *shee*) means "peace." Thus, "mountain peace" or "mountain of peace."

MONTROSE (2006: pop. 1012) Most sources agree that this village was named, directly or indirectly, for the popular resort town in Scotland. How and why it acquired the moniker is a little unclear. Montrose was established in 1942 as a residential community by Montrose Homesites, Ltd., a business created by the Columbia Mining & Smelting Company (now Cominco), which owned most of the land, and A.G. Cameron, a lawyer from Trail. Depending on the source, the community was originally called Beaver Falls or Beaver Heights. One source says the village was renamed for a local rural school called Montrose, which opened in 1928, after the government claimed that too many communities with "Beaver" in the name already existed. Others say it was the village residents who initiated the name change, while some suggest that Cameron himself, who was apparently from Montrose, Scotland, gave the community its current name. In any case, the community officially became Montrose in 1953. Montrose sits on the Columbia River, 11 kilometres east of Trail. Coincidentally, Montrose Peak is not far from the village.

MOODYVILLE *See* North Vancouver.

MORESBY Two Moresby Islands in British Columbia are named after Rear Admiral Fairfax Moresby. Moresby was the commander-in-chief of the British Fleet's Pacific Station from 1850 to 1853. The largest of the two islands (2755 km²) is south of Skidegate Channel in Haida Gwaii (Queen Charlotte Islands). It is the third largest island in British Columbia and was named for Moresby in 1853 by his son-in-law, Captain James Charles Prevost. Both

Moresby Lake and Mount Moresby (1164 m) can be found on the island. The much smaller Moresby Island (7 km²) is located in Haro Strait. Both it and nearby Moresby Passage were christened in 1858 by Captain George Richards. Also in Haida Gwaii (Queen Charlotte Islands) are the Moresby Islets, located on the north side of the entrance to Moore Channel. This group of small islands was named for Gunnery Lieutenant John Moresby of the HMS *Thetis* in 1852 by his captain, Augustus Leopold Kuper. The lieutenant was the admiral's son.

MORICE / MORICETOWN Morice Lake (95 km²) and Morice River were both named in 1910 for Oblate missionary Father Adrien-Gabriel Morice, who explored north-central British Columbia and worked among the people of the Dakelh (Carrier) First Nation from 1883 to 1905. Among his accomplishments was the invention of a written alphabet for the Dakelh; he also wrote the first history of the area, *History of the Northern Interior of British Columbia*, published in 1904. Nearby Mount Morice was named for the river in 1951. Moricetown is a Wet'suwet'en First Nation village that dates back at least 4000 years; it was renamed after Father Morice sometime in the early 1900s. The lake, the mountain and the river are all southwest of Houston. Moricetown is about 90 kilometres to the north, on the west side of the Buckley River, 31 kilometres north of Smithers. Mount Morice (1823 m), located on the east side of Morice River, was named after the river in 1956, though local residents frequently call it Morice Mountain.

MOUNT ABBOTT *See* Abbott.

MOUNT AGASSIZ *See* Agassiz.

MOUNT ALBERT EDWARD *See* Mount King Edward.

MOUNT ALBREDA *See* Albreda.

MOUNT ALEXANDRA *See* Mount King Edward.

M

MOUNT ARTHUR (1619 m) This mountain, as well as nearby Mount Wellington (1727), were both named in 1860 by Captain George Richards for British military hero and statesman, Arthur Wellesley, the 1st Duke of Wellington and the general who defeated Napoleon at Waterloo. Both mountains are located west of Jervis Inlet and were christened while Richards was surveying the inlet.

MOUNT ARTHUR MEIGHEN (3205 m) In 1962, this mountain was named for Arthur Meighen, prime minister of Canada from 1920 to 1921 and, briefly, in 1926. Frequently referred to as Mount Meighen, it is 20 kilometres southwest of Tête Jaune Cache in the Premier Range.

MOUNT ASSINIBOINE (3616 m) This mountain sits along the Alberta border on the southeast corner of Mount Assiniboine Provincial Park, 32 kilometres southwest of Canmore. It is the ninth highest peak in British Columbia, and its name dates back to about 1885. It is assumed that the mountain was christened by geologist George Dawson during his 1884 survey of the area. The mountain was named after the people of the Assiniboine First Nation, who once hunted in the Rocky Mountains from the American border to the North Saskatchewan–Athabasca watershed. Centuries ago, the Assiniboine were part of the Sioux First Nation, and their name comes from the Ojibwa First Nation name Asiniibwaan and from the Cree First Nation name Asinipwat, both of which mean "Stone (or Stoney) Sioux." The name refers to the way the Assiniboine cooked their food, by placing very hot stones into clay vessels full of water to boil their meals.

MOUNT BALDY HUGHES *See* Baldy Hughes.

MOUNT BALFOUR *See* Balfour Pass.

MOUNT BARNARD Two mountains in British Columbia bear this name. The first (3340 m), located on the Alberta border, north of Golden, was named in 1917 by the

Interprovincial Boundary Survey in honour of Francis Stillman Barnard, the lieutenant-governor of British Columbia at the time. The other peak (2491 m), on the Alaska border on the southeast side of Tatshenshini-Alsek Provincial Park, was named in 1923 by the American government for Edward Chester Barnard, the chief topographer from 1903 to 1915 of the International Boundary Commission, which surveyed the British Columbia–Alaska border. Edward Barnard died in 1921, and the Canadian government adopted the name in 1924.

MOUNT BEDAUX *See* Bedaux Pass.

MOUNT BEGBIE Three mountains in British Columbia share this name, and at least two of them were christened after Matthew Begbie, the famous judge who played a key role in maintaining law and order throughout British Columbia from 1858 until his death in 1894. The tallest of the three (2733 m) was named in 1890 by geologist George Dawson and is located 12 kilometres south of Revelstoke. The moniker of the second (1276 m), located 20 kilometres south of 100 Mile House, can be found on a 1913 map. The shortest (640 m) is 19 kilometres west of Port Clements; records are unclear for whom this mountain is christened, though its name dates back to at least 1922.

MOUNT BENNETT *See* Mount Richard Bennett.

MOUNT BIDDLE (3320 m) This mountain is 14 kilometres southwest of Lake Louise. It was christened in 1894 by mountaineer Samuel E.S. Allen for his friend, author and publisher Anthony Joseph Drexel Biddle of Philadelphia, Pennsylvania, who was a fellow alpinist and did a lot of climbing in the area.

MOUNT BISHOP There are three mountains in British Columbia with this name. The first (2839 m), located on the Alberta border, north of Elkford, was named in 1918 after Colonel William "Billy" Bishop, the World War I Canadian ace and recipient of the Victoria Cross. The second (1509 m) is 16 kilometres northeast of North Vancouver. It was christened in 1914 in honour of Joseph Bishop, the noted Vancouver mountaineer and photographer, who was killed the year before when he fell into a crevasse on Mount Baker. The third (1721 m) is located northwest of Lillooet. It was named in 1957 after an old settler.

MOUNT BRYCE (3507 m) This mountain was named in 1898 by visiting British mountaineer J. Norman Collie for a fellow alpinist, the British historian and politician James Bryce. Mount Bryce is near the Alberta border, 61 kilometres northwest of Donald.

MOUNT CAIRNES (3081 m) This mountain was named in 1919 by mountaineer Arthur Wheeler for Delorme Donaldson Cairnes, a geologist who worked for 12 years mapping the Yukon for the Geological Survey of Canada. Mount Cairnes is 34 kilometres northeast of Blaeberry. There are two Mount Cairnes in the Yukon, and both are also named for this person.

MOUNT CARL BORDEN (2118 m) This mountain was officially named in 1981, in response to a suggestion made two years earlier by University of British Columbia geography professor Helen Akrigg. The moniker honours UBC German professor Charles "Carl" Borden, who died in 1978. Borden's hobby was archaeology, and he is described as "the father of scientific archaeology in British Columbia."

MOUNT CLEMENCEAU (3664 m) Originally called Pyramid Mountain, this mountain was renamed in 1919 by the surveyors of the Interprovincial Boundary Survey Alberta Border Commission in honour of George Clemenceau, the prime minister of France, who led his country during the last year of World War I. The peak is

M

just this side of the Alberta border, east of Kinbasket Lake. It is the eighth highest mountain in British Columbia.

MOUNT COLUMBIA (3741 m) This mountain was named in 1898 by British mountaineer Norman Collie for the Columbia River, which had been christened by Captain Robert Gray in 1792 after his ship, the *Columbia Rediviva*. Gray's ship, in turn, was named in honour of Christopher Columbus. Located about 35 kilometres northeast of Kinbasket Lake (into which the Columbia River flows), this peak straddles the Alberta border and is both the seventh highest mountain in British Columbia and the highest point in Alberta. *See* Columbia Icefield.

MOUNT CURRIE Both the mountain (2591 m) and the nearby community (estimated pop. 1400) are named after John Currie, a gold-prospector-turned-rancher from Scotland who settled near Pemberton in about 1885 with his Lil'wat First Nation wife. He was one of the first non-Aboriginal residents of the Pemberton Valley. The mountain and the community are both west of the northern end of Lillooet Lake, near Pemberton. The mountain was named after Currie in 1911, one year after his death. The community dates from the 1870s. It was originally known as Chilsampton, a derivation of the Lil'wat word *shasheel-hitchamton*, meaning "putting on the moccasins." This moniker refers to the fact that First Nations people travelling north along the portage between present-day Pemberton and Lillooet walked barefoot to this point but wore moccasins the rest of the way. The community's name was changed to Creekside by 1932, and then again, after the mountain, in 1956. The community is the centre of the Mount Currie Reserve of the Lil'wat First Nation, a group of the Stl'atl'imx Nation.

MOUNT DAER *See* Selkirk Mountains.

MOUNT DAWSON (3377 m) Located at the south end of Glacier National Park, in the Selkirk Mountains, this mountain was named in 1888 by the British alpinist, the Reverend William S. Green. The mountain was christened in honour of noted geologist George Mercer Dawson, who explored and examined the geology of the Selkirks and other parts of British Columbia. At that time, Dawson was the assistant director of the Geological Survey of Canada.

MOUNT DELPHINE (3406 m) This mountain was named in 1911 by alpinist Edward Warren Harnden for the Delphine mine, which operated on the peak's lower slopes. The mine, in turn, was christened in honour of Delphine (née Francour) Starke, the wife of George Starke, who owned the mine. After Starke sold the mine, he opened the Delphine Hotel in Wilmer, which, until recently, was a bed and breakfast known as the Delphine Lodge. Mount Delphine is 29 kilometres west of Wilmer. The original name, Delphine Mountain, was changed to Mount Delphine in 1960 to reflect the fact that the peak was really named after a person. (According to Canadian mountain naming practices, "Mount" should be used before a given name if the peak is named after a specific person; otherwse, the given name is followed by "Mountain" or "Peak.") Near the mountain are both a creek and a glacier, which were named in 1898 after the Delphine mine.

MOUNT DEWDNEY (2244 m) Previously called Hopeless Mountain, this peak was named in 1936 after Edgar Dewdney, engineer, federal politician and the lieutenant-governor of British Columbia from 1892 to 1897. As an engineer, Dewdney built the Dewdney Trail across southern BC, from Hope to Trail, from 1860 to 1865. The mountain is southeast of Hope.

MOUNT FAIRWEATHER *See* Fairweather Mountain.

MOUNT FARNHAM (3493 m) This mountain was named in 1902 after George Paulding Farnham, the famous designer of jewellery and silver for Tiffany and Company. Between 1898 and 1904, Farnham spent (and lost) much of his personal fortune on the nearby Red Line (Ptarmigan) mines. It is said that, rather than go bankrupt and leave behind a bunch of unhappy creditors, he eventually paid back every penny he owed. Farnham's property was at the base of this mountain, which is located 30 kilometres west of Wilmer and 30 kilometres east of Duncan Lake. His wife was noted sculptress Sally James Farnham.

MOUNT FRASER There are three Mount Frasers in British Columbia. The highest (3313 m) is on the Alberta border, 30 kilometres southwest of Jasper. It was christened in 1917 for explorer Simon Fraser. The second Mount Fraser (1649 m) is located 10 kilometres north of Pemberton and was christened in 1983 for early Pemberton residents Maria and Nelson Fraser. It is not known who the third Mount Fraser, located near Barriere, is named after, but the label appears on maps going back to at least 1930.

M

MOUNT FRESHFIELD (3337 m) In 1897, mountaineer Norman Collie named this peak for explorer and fellow British alpinist Douglas William Freshfield. One-time president of the Royal Geographical Society, Freshfield climbed mountains in the Caucasus, the Himalayas, Italy and many other countries and wrote several books about his adventures. Mount Freshfield is on the Alberta border, north of Golden.

MOUNT GARIBALDI (2675 m) Captain George Richards named this mountain in 1860 in honour of Italian soldier and statesman Giuseppe Garibaldi, who earlier that year had begun his military campaign to unify Italy. Garibaldi Provincial Park, which includes the mountain, was created in 1920. The community of Daisy Lake, located near the lake of the same name, was renamed Garibaldi in 1932, after it became the main access point to the park.

MOUNT GEIKIE (3298 m) This mountain was named in 1898 by James McEvoy of the Geological Survey of Canada for his colleague Sir Archibald Geikie, the director-general of the Geological Survey of Great Britain from 1882 to 1901. McEvoy might also have intended to honour Sir Archibald's brother, James, who was himself a noted geologist. This peak is in Mount Robson Provincial Park.

MOUNT GEORGE V (1931 m) In 1935, this mountain was named by surveyor N.C. Stewart, in honour of King George V's Silver Jubilee that year. The Silver Jubilee marked King George's 25th anniversary on the throne. Mount George V is located south of Mount Albert Edward in Strathcona Provincial Park. This is, however, not the only mountain in British Columbia named after this king. See Mount King George.

MOUNT GOODSIR (also known as Mount Goodsir South Tower) (3567 m) This mountain was named by naturalist James Hector while he was travelling through the Rocky Mountains in 1858. He christened the peak for either (or both) his former instructor, Professor of Anatomy John Goodsir of Edinburgh University, or the professor's brother, Henry "Harry" D.S. Goodsir, who was the assistant surgeon with the ill-fated Franklin Expedition of 1845. The mountain is located in Yoho National Park, east of Golden, and it is the 10th highest peak in British Columbia. Two kilometres to the northwest is a second mountain, officially called simply North Tower (3507 m) but also known as Mount Goodsir North Tower and as Mount Henry Goodsir. Some sources list the North Tower and the South Tower as two summits of the same mountain. Perhaps Hector felt the same way and thought it was therefore appropriate to name it after the two brothers.

MOUNT HARRISON (3360 m) Just when everyone thought that all the mountains in British Columbia exceeding 11,000 feet (3350 metres) had long since been found and named, this one was discovered in the early 1960s. It was named in 1964 to honour 27-year-old RCAF Pilot Officer Francis Arthur Harrison from Cranbrook, who was shot down 20 years earlier while his Lancaster bomber (KB780) was attacking Duisburg, Germany. Just 11 days before his death, Harrison was awarded the Distinguished Flying Cross for his courage in another bombing raid. Mount Harrison is 21 kilometres west of Elkford.

MOUNT HUNGABEE (3490 m) This mountain was named in 1894 by mountaineers Samuel Allen and Walter Wilcox while they camped in nearby Paradise Valley. The peak dominates the scenery at the upper end of the valley and is noticeably higher than any neighbouring mountain. Its appearance so impressed Allen and Wilcox that they chose the Assiniboine First Nation word *hungabee*, which means "chieftain," as its name. The mountain is located on the Alberta border, in Yoho National Park.

MOUNT JOFFRE (3433 m) In 1916, this mountain was named by the surveyors of the Interprovincial Boundary Survey Alberta Border Commission in honour of French general Joseph Jacques Césaire Joffre. At the time, Joffre was busy fighting in World War I as the commander-in-chief of the French army. The mountain is on the Alberta border, at the west end of Elk Lakes Provincial Park.

MOUNT JOHN DIEFENBAKER (2637 m) This mountain was named in 2006 for John Diefenbaker, prime minister of Canada from 1957 to 1963. Frequently called Mount Diefenbaker, it is 19 kilometres southwest of Valemount in the Premier Range. It was pointed out after the mountain was christened that, in 1951, while a prominent attorney, Diefenbaker had successfully defended a telegraph dispatcher who was accused of causing a railway accident at the base of the mountain the previous year in which 21 people were killed. It is possible that naming a mountain after Diefenbaker was delayed so long after his death in 1979 because a lake in Saskatchewan had been christened in his honour in 1967.

MOUNT JOHN OLIVER (3123 m) Discovered in 1916 and originally called Mount Aspiration in 1925, this mountain was renamed in 1928 for British Columbia premier John Oliver, who died the previous year. Frequently referred to as Mount Oliver, it is 20 kilometres southwest of Tête Jaune Cache, in the Premier Range.

MOUNT JULIET (1626 m) This mountain, about 70 kilometres northwest of Campbell River, and Mount Romeo (1663 m), three kilometres west, were named in 1934 for Shakespeare's two great lovers. Between lies Montague Creek (Montague was Romeo's family name) and its tributary, Capulet Creek (Juliet's family name).

MOUNT KING EDWARD (3490 m) In 1906, American explorer Mary Schaffer named this mountain for King Edward VII, who reigned from 1901 to 1910. Mount King Edward is on the Alberta border, 71 kilometres northwest of Donald. Also on the Alberta border, 54 kilometres north of Donald, is Mount Alexandra (3401 m), which was christened in 1902 by mountaineer James Outram for the king's wife, Queen Alexandra. And at the other end of the province, just east of Buttle Lake on Vancouver Island, are two mountains that are also named after the royal couple. Mount Albert Edward (2093 m) and Alexandra Peak (1983 m) were named in 1862 for the future king and queen while they were the Prince and Princess of Wales.

M

MOUNT KING GEORGE (3413 m) While demarcating the British Columbia–Alberta border through the Rocky Mountains in 1917, the surveyors of the Interprovincial Boundary Survey came across seven unnamed mountains, all within five kilometres of each other, including a particularly high one that dominates the landscape in all directions. The surveyors decided to name the highest mountain after the reigning monarch, King George V, and the rest for his wife and children. The mountains are Mount King George (3413 m), Mount Queen Mary (3235 m), Mount Prince Albert (3212 m, for King George V's second son, and the father of Queen Elizabeth II, who became King George VI in 1936), Mount Prince Edward (3225 m, for King George V's eldest son, who briefly reigned as Edward VIII in 1936), Mount Prince George (2879 m), Mount Prince Henry (3219 m), Mount Prince John (3226 m) and Mount Princess Mary (3069 m). These mountains are collectively known as the Royal Group and are 45 kilometres east of Invermere.

M

MOUNT LEFROY (3442 m) There is some confusion as to who named this mountain. Some argue that it was naturalist James Hector during his 1858 expedition through the Rocky Mountains; others argue that it was geologist George Dawson during his 1884 visit through the area. All agree that the mountain was named for Sir John Henry Lefroy, a British military officer who travelled more than 8800 kilometres between 1842 and 1844, making magnetic and meteorological surveys across Canada's northwest. He was also in charge of the observatory in Toronto from 1842 to 1853. The mountain is located on the Alberta border in Yoho National Park.

MOUNT LEHMAN This neighbourhood in Abbotsford is located on an area of raised ground in the Fraser Valley. The first settler arrived in 1874, but the community had been named by 1884 after Isaac Lehman, who arrived in the area to farm in 1875. He was later a prospector in the

Cariboo, a blacksmith in New Westminster and an undertaker in Ashcroft.

MOUNT LESTER PEARSON (3086 m) This mountain was named in 1973 for Lester B. Pearson, prime minister of Canada from 1963 to 1968 and Canada's first winner, in 1957, of the Nobel Peace Prize. Frequently called Mount Pearson, it is located 21 kilometres west of Valemount, in the Premier Range.

MOUNT LOUIS ST-LAURENT (3045 m) This mountain was named in 1964 for Louis St-Laurent, prime minister of Canada from 1948 to 1957. Frequently referred to as Mount St-Laurent, it is 34 kilometres southwest of Tête Jaune Cache. Although it is in the Premier Range, St-Laurent was still alive when the peak was named after him, even though the mountains in that range are supposed to be christened after deceased prime ministers.

MOUNT LYELL (3498 m) Naturalist James Hector named this mountain while he was travelling through the Rocky Mountains in 1858. He named it for the famous British geologist, Sir Charles Lyell. Mount Lyell is on the Alberta border, 51 kilometres north of Donald.

MOUNT MACBETH (2639 m) This mountain in Garibaldi Provincial Park was named by mountaineers Neal Carter, Karl Ricker and others in 1964 to commemorate the Bard's 400th birthday. They named other mountains in the park to honour Shakespeare, including, from *Romeo and Juliet*, Mount Benvolio (2613 m), and from *Othello*, Mount Iago (2506 m). There is also a second Mount MacBeth near Duncan Lake. *See* MacBeth Group.

MOUNT MACDONALD (2883 m) This mountain was named in 1887 for Sir John A. Macdonald, Canada's first prime minister, who served from 1867 to 1873 and again from 1878 to 1891. It had been christened Mount Carroll the previous year to honour a member of the

Canadian Pacific Railway survey party that visited the area in 1884–86. The peak was pointed out to Macdonald as his train passed by during his 1887 intercontinental tour, and, through a pair of binoculars, he saw the pole that had been placed on its summit. Mount Macdonald is three kilometres east of Rogers Pass in Glacier National Park.

MOUNT MACKENZIE Three mountains in British Columbia share this name. One (2143 m) is located in Tweedsmuir Park and was named for Alexander Mackenzie, the famous fur trader and explorer, who passed by in 1793 while on his way to the Pacific Ocean. It is unclear when the moniker was adopted, though Mackenzie Pass and the Mackenzie Valley are located nearby. The second peak (2459 m) is eight kilometres southeast of Revelstoke and was named in 1887 for Alexander Mackenzie, Canada's prime minister from 1873 to 1878. The third (816 m) is four kilometres north of Pemberton. It does not yet have an official name, but because it is located near the Mackenzie Basin, it is frequently referred to as both Mount Mackenzie and Mackenzie Peak. (According to Canadian mountain naming practices, "Mount" should be used before a given name only if the peak is named after a specific person; otherwise, the given name comes first, followed by "Mountain" or "Peak.")

MOUNT MACKENZIE KING (3234 m) This mountain was named in 1962 for William Lyon Mackenzie King, who served as prime minister of Canada three times: 1921 to 1926, 1926 to 1930 after a brief hiatus and 1935 to 1948. The peak was previously called Mount Hostility. Frequently referred to as Mount King, this peak is 31 kilometres southwest of Tête Jaune Cache, in the Premier Range.

MOUNT MAXWELL *See* Baynes Peak.

MOUNT McBRIDE There are two mountains by this name in British Columbia. One (2083 m), in Strathcona Provincial Park, was named in 1919 for British Columbia Premier Richard McBride, who died two years earlier. The other (2500 m), located about 50 kilometres west of Nelson, was named in 1962, in honour of 24-year-old Canadian Army Captain Kenneth Gilbert McBride of the Seaforth Highlanders. Captain McBride was from Nelson and was killed in action in Italy in 1944. Another mountain in BC is named after Premier Richard McBride. Mount Sir Richard (2681 m) in Garibaldi Provincial Park was named for the premier in 1930.

MOUNT MERRITT (903 m) This mountain was named in 1944 for World War II hero Charles Cecil Ingersoll Merritt. A Vancouver lawyer, Merritt was a lieutenant colonel in command of the South Saskatchewan Regiment at Dieppe, France, in 1942. During that operation, Merritt successfully led an attack across a bridge, after earlier groups had been mowed down by German machine-gun fire. Later, although twice wounded, he stayed behind to give his men cover as they were evacuated from the beach. Merritt was taken captive and was still a prisoner of war when the mountain was christened in his honour. He was awarded the Victoria Cross—Canada's first in the war—for his leadership and bravery. Merritt served in Parliament after the war and was the great-grandson of Canadian Prime Minister Sir Charles Tupper. Mount Merritt is on Hunter Island, south of Bella Bella.

M

MOUNT MIKE (3313 m) Located 25 kilometres west of Elkford, this peak was christened for Private Sebastian Mike of Cranbrook, who was killed in action during World War II.

MOUNT MUMMERY (3331 m) This mountain is 29 kilometres northeast of Blaeberry. It was named in 1898 by mountaineer J. Norman Collie for the famous British alpinist, Albert Frederick Mummery, who disappeared three years earlier while attempting to climb Nanga Parbat in the Himalayas.

MOUNT MUNDAY (3356 m) Located just southeast of Mount Waddington, this mountain was named in 1928 after W.A.D. (Don) Munday who, with his wife Phyllis, made numerous mountaineering expeditions in this area between 1926 and 1936. Munday also led a climbing party onto Mount Waddington in 1926.

MOUNT MURCHISON / MOUNT RODERICK These two mountains, located west of Squamish, are less than five kilometres from each other and are both named for the famous British geologist, Sir Roderick Impey Murchison. Mount Murchison (1731 m) was named in 1858 by Dr. James Hector; it was Murchison who recommended Hector as geologist for the Palliser Expedition (1857–60), which explored western Canada. Hector had also named Alberta's Mount Murchison after his mentor earlier that same year. Hector probably named Mount Roderick (1478 m) as well; its name appears on British Admiralty charts from 1865 onward.

MOUNT NELSON British Columbia boasts seven Mount Nelsons. The highest (3313 m) is 22 kilometres west of Wilmer and was named in 1807 by explorer David Thompson in honour of Admiral Horatio Nelson. Although Nelson had been killed at the Battle of Trafalgar two years earlier, the news of his death had just reached Thompson. Another Mount Nelson (2187 m), located 35 kilometres north of Cherryville, was christened in the 1890s for Nels Peter Nelson of the British Navy. Nelson jumped ship in Vancouver in 1891 and settled in the Okanagan. While there, he heard that a pot of gold had supposedly been hidden on the mountain by the local First Nations people, and Nelson spent quite a bit of time looking for it.

MOUNT NKWALA (1019 m) This mountain was officially given the highly objectionable name of Niggertoe Mountain in 1955, though it was a well-established local moniker long before then. Fortunately, the mountain was rechristened 11 years later. No one knows for certain how the peak got its original name, but it may date from Christmas 1908, when three black men who worked at a hotel in Summerland got lost at the foot of the mountain in a snowstorm after celebrating Mass in Penticton. Two of the three died. In 1965, the Boy Scouts suggested renaming the peak Jamboree Mountain, in recognition of the Boy Scout gathering to be held in Penticton the following year. In 1966, the Okanagan Historical Society recommended that the peak be called Nkwala Mountain, because Nkwala was the name of several important ancestral Okanagan chiefs as well as the title of an award-winning novel about a Salish boy who lived near Okanagan Lake. The mountain is four kilometres northwest of Penticton. See Nicola.

M

MOUNT PETER (3360 m) This mountain, located 30 kilometres west of Wilmer, was originally named Mount St. Peter in 1915 by alpinist Winthrop Stone. It was rechristened nine years later in honour of another mountaineer, Peter Kerr, who climbed the peaks in the area in 1914 and was killed three years later in France in World War I.

MOUNT PETERS (1966 m) Located 10 kilometres northwest of Nelson, this peak was named in 1946 after the city's favourite son and Victoria Cross recipient, Captain Frederick Thornton Peters. Peters was awarded the VC for ramming his ship through the booms protecting the Oran, Algeria, harbour in 1942, during the Allied invasion of North Africa in World War II.

MOUNT PIERRE ELLIOT TRUDEAU (2650 m) In 2006, this mountain was named for Pierre Elliot Trudeau, prime minister of Canada from 1968 to 1979 and from 1980 to 1984. Frequently referred to as Mount Trudeau, it is located 12 kilometres west of Valemount in the Premier Range. Although the other peaks in the area named for prime ministers are all more than 3000 metres in height, this one is only 2650 metres high. Trudeau was himself a mountaineer, and it was felt that, to honour him, the peak bearing his name should be easily accessible to the public (this one is near the Yellowhead Highway) and offer non-technical climbing and exploring opportunities for all outdoor enthusiasts.

MOUNT PREVOST *See* Prevost.

MOUNT PTOLEMY (2813 m) Mountaineer Arthur O. Wheeler named this mountain in 1914 or 1915. Wheeler thought the mountain looked like the chest and head of a man with folded arms lying prone and gazing at the stars, and it reminded him of the famous second-century Egyptian astronomer and geographer. Mount Ptolemy is 10 kilometres southeast of Crowsnest Pass.

MOUNT QUEEN BESS (3298 m) This mountain was named after Queen Elizabeth I of England. It is fittingly the highest of a number of peaks located to the west and south of Chilko Lake named after Elizabethan people and events. Other peaks include Mount Raleigh (3132 m), named after explorer Sir Walter Raleigh; Mount Sir Francis Drake (2705 m), named after the captain who sailed the first English vessel into the Pacific (and possibly as far north as Vancouver Island); Mount Grenville (3126 m), after Richard Grenville, another Elizabethan sailor and explorer; Pembroke Peak (2779 m) after the ducal name of the Herberts, a politically prominent Elizabethan family; Silver Swan Mountain (2877 m), after "The Silver Swan," a popular Elizabethan song; and Armada Mountain (2735 m), after the Spanish Armada, the great invasion fleet defeated by England in 1588.

Most of these names were officially adopted in 1935, after being suggested in 1928 by Richard P. Bishop while he was conducting surveys in the area.

MOUNT QUINCY ADAMS (4150 m) Named after John Quincy Adams, the sixth president of the United States, this mountain is the second highest peak in British Columbia. It is located in the northwest tip of British Columbia, in the Tatshenshini-Alsek Provincial Wilderness Park, but its eastern and southern flanks are actually in Alaska. The mountain was named in 1923 by the United States to commemorate Adams' successful challenge in 1823, as Secretary of State, to Russia's attempts to extend its territorial claims to most of British Columbia's coastline. The BC government adopted the name in 1966.

MOUNT RICHARD BENNETT (3190 m) This mountain was named in 1962 for Richard Bennett, prime minister of Canada from 1930 to 1935. Frequently referred to as Mount Bennett, the peak is located west of Valemount in the Premier Range.

M

MOUNT RICHARDS (359 m) Located two kilometres west of Crofton, this mountain was christened in 1905 by Captain John F. Parry of the HMS *Egeria* after Admiral Sir George Richards. From 1856 to 1863, as a British Navy captain in command of the HMS *Plumper* and, later, the HMS *Hecate*, Richards conducted extensive surveys of the coasts of Vancouver Island and the British Columbia mainland and named hundreds of harbours, islands and other locations.

MOUNT ROBSON (3958 m) This mountain is the fourth highest peak in British Columbia and the highest in the Canadian Rockies. Its name was officially adopted in 1912 but was in common usage by 1863, and a fur trader referred to it as Mount Robinson in his 1827 diary. There are at least 10 theories as to how the mountain got its name. Among the most probable is that the mountain was named after a Hudson's Bay Company foreman named Robson, who was in charge of the HBC's hunting parties in the area. Another theory is that it was named after Colin Robertson, an HBC official in BC's Peace River region who, in 1820, sent a company of fur traders into the area. Possibly, the name was corrupted over the years from Robertson to Robinson and, finally, to Robson. The mountain is located in Mount Robson Provincial Park, along the Alberta border.

MOUNT RODERICK *See* Mount Murchison.

MOUNT ROGERS (3169 m) This mountain, 29 kilometres southwest of Donald, was christened in 1890 by mountaineer Carl Sulzer in honour of Major Albert B. Rogers, the railway engineer and surveyor who discovered nearby Rogers Pass nine years earlier.

MOUNT ROOT (3928 m) This mountain is nine kilometres south of Fairweather Mountain, and, like Fairweather, part of it is located in Alaska. It is the fifth highest mountain in British Columbia. The United States named this peak in 1908 after Elihu Root, who was then the U.S. Secretary of State. He was also part of the commission that settled the Alaska-BC boundary dispute in 1903. The name was adopted by the Geographic Board of Canada in 1924.

MOUNT SCOTT There are two Mount Scotts in British Columbia. The highest (3296 m) is located on the Alberta border, 48 kilometres south of Jasper. Mountaineers Arnold Mumm and Edward Howard christened the peak in 1913 for Antarctic explorer Robert Scott, who died the year before at the South Pole. The other Mount Scott (2448 m) is west of Fort Nelson. It was named in 1982, in honour of Canadian Army Private William Campbell

Scott of Victoria, who was killed in action in Italy in 1943 during World War II.

MOUNT SEYMOUR Three mountains in British Columbia bear this name. The highest and most famous (1449 m) is located 12 kilometres northeast of North Vancouver. It was once called Third Pump Peak because a mountaineering party exploring the peak in 1908 thought a tree stump near the summit looked like a pump. Exactly when the current moniker came into use is not known. British Admiralty charts from the mid-19th century mark, but do not name, the mountain. The earliest known use of the label on a map is from 1914. The peak was named after Frederick Seymour, the colonial governor of British Columbia from 1864 to 1869.

The second Mount Seymour (620 m) is on Graham Island, about 13 kilometres southwest of the village of Queen Charlotte. This mountain was christened sometime before 1872 (possibly in 1865 by Captain Daniel Pender of the *Beaver*, who named nearby Seymour Inlet that year) and is probably also in honour of Governor Seymour.

The third Mount Seymour (619 m) is on Quadra Island, north of Campbell River. Its name can be found on British Admiralty charts from 1860. The peak was possibly named by Commander George T. Gordon of the HM steam sloop *Cormorant*, in honour of Rear Admiral Sir George Francis Seymour. Gordon had named the nearby Seymour Narrows for the commander of the British Navy's Pacific Station in 1846.

MOUNT SHACKLETON (3327 m) Surveyor and mountaineer Arthur O. Wheeler named this mountain in 1923 for Antarctic explorer Sir Ernest Shackleton, who died the previous year while leading his fourth expedition to the South Pole. The peak is located near the Alberta border, 79 kilometres south of Jasper.

M

MOUNT SHAUGHNESSY (2750 m) This mountain, located 28 kilometres southwest of Donald, was named in 1900 or 1902 (sources differ) after Sir Thomas G. Shaughnessy, the president of the Canadian Pacific Railway.

MOUNT SHORTY STEVENSON (2000 m) Located 14 kilometres north of Stewart, this mountain was originally named Mount Stevenson in 1924 after Hiram "Shorty" Stevenson, an old-time prospector from New Brunswick who made his living as a miner around Stewart and at the now-abandoned mining community of Jedway on Moresby Island. Stevenson was a "giant of a man" and a special uniform had to be ordered from Ottawa to fit him when he enlisted to fight in World War I. He was killed in action in France in 1917. The mountain was given its current name in 1953.

MOUNT SIR ALEXANDER (3275 m) This mountain was christened in 1917 for fur trader and explorer Sir Alexander Mackenzie, but only after it went through a couple of rapid name changes. The peak was first called Mount Kitchi in 1915, reflecting its well-known name among mountaineers. It was renamed Mount Alexander Mackenzie the following year, at the suggestion of Professor S. Prescott Fay of New York's Museum of Natural History, who saw the peak in 1914 but did not climb it. The recommendation was adopted by the Geographic Board of Canada, even though Mackenzie never saw it himself. It is unclear why the moniker was changed again in 1917; perhaps it was to avoid confusion with Mount Mackenzie, which was also named after the hero. Mount Sir Alexander is located at the northern tip of the Candian Rockies.

MOUNT SIR ALLAN MACNAB (2297 m) In 1974, this mountain was named for Sir Allan MacNab, the premier of the colony of Upper Canada (now the province of Ontario) from 1854 to 1856. Frequently called Mount

MacNab, it is located 35 kilometres south of Valemount, in the Premier Range.

MOUNT SIR DONALD (3284 m) This mountain is located 31 kilometres southwest of Donald. The highest mountain in the Sir Donald Range, it was originally named Syndicate Peak by Major Albert B. Rogers in 1881, in honour of the group of financiers who backed the Canadian Pacific Railway. The peak was renamed four years later after Sir Donald Smith (later the 1st Baron Strathcona and Mount Royal), who was the head of that syndicate. The Sir Donald Range, located south and east of Rogers Pass, as well as nearby Sir Donald Glacier, were also christened in 1885 after the banker.

MOUNT SIR DOUGLAS (3411 m) The surveyors of the Interprovincial Boundary Survey named this mountain in 1916, during the middle of World War I, for General Sir Douglas Haig. Haig had been named commander-in-chief of the British forces in France and Belgium the year before. Mount Sir Douglas is in Mount Assiniboine Provincial Park, on the Alberta border.

MOUNT SIR JOHN ABBOTT (3398 m) Formerly known as Mount Kiwa, this mountain was renamed in 1927 for Sir John Joseph Caldwell Abbott, who served as Canada's third prime minister from 1891 to 1892. Frequently referred to as Mount Abbott, it is west of Valemont in the Premier Range.

MOUNT SIR JOHN THOMPSON (3349 m) This mountain was named in 1927 for Sir John Sparrow David Thompson, Canada's prime minister from 1892 to 1894. It was originally christened Mount David Thompson in 1924 by a climbing party that mistakenly thought a nearby pass was the source of the North Thompson River. Frequently called Mount Thompson, the peak is located 32 kilometres southwest of Tête Jaune Cache, in the Premier Range.

MOUNT SIR MACKENZIE BOWELL (3301 m) In 1927, this mountain was named for Sir Mackenzie Bowell, Canada's prime minister from 1894 to 1896. It was originally called Mount Welcome by mountaineer Allen Carpe when he climbed it in 1924. Frequently called Mount Bowell, it is located 26 kilometres southwest of Tête Jaune Cache, in the Premier Range. Two kilometres to the north is an unnamed mountain (2829 m) that is often referred to as Mackenzie Bowell N2.

MOUNT SIR RICHARD *See* Mount McBride.

MOUNT SIR ROBERT (2388 m) Frequently referred to as Mount Borden, this mountain was named in 1917 for Sir Robert Borden, Canada's prime minister from 1911 to 1920. It is located northeast of Terrace. Nearby is Borden Glacier, also named after the prime minister in 1917.

MOUNT SIR SANDFORD (3519 m) Mountaineer Arthur O. Wheeler named this mountain in 1901 for railway engineer Sir Sandford Fleming. In the late 19th century, Fleming played a key role in developing the time zones into which the world is now divided. Mount Sir Sandford, 10 kilometres west of Kinbasket Lake, sits virtually on top of the line demarcating the Pacific from the Mountain Time Zone. Wheeler also named Fleming Peak on Mount Rogers in 1901.

MOUNT SIR WILFRID LAURIER (3516 m) This mountain was named in 1927 for Sir Wilfrid Laurier, prime minister of Canada from 1896 to 1911. Frequently called Mount Laurier, it is 28 kilometres southwest Tête Jaune Cache, in the Premier Range. Hundreds of kilometres away, in Graham-Laurier Provincial Park in northern British Columbia is another mountain named for the prime minister. Mount Laurier (2361 m) was originally christened Laurier Peak in 1928, but the moniker was changed in 1945. Also in the park is Mount Lady Laurier (2369 m), named in 1928 for the prime minister's wife, Lady Zoe Laurier.

MOUNT SPROAT *See* Sproat.

MOUNT STANLEY BALDWIN (3256 m) This mountain was named in 1927 for British Prime Minister Stanley Baldwin. He visited Canada earlier that year and, in doing so, became the first prime minister of Britain to see Canada while in office. Frequently called Mount Baldwin, the peak is 20 kilometres southwest of Tête Jaune Cache, in the Premier Range. Just five kilometres away is another mountain, still unnamed, that is commonly referred to as Stanley Baldwin SW5.

MOUNT TERRY FOX (2643 m) This mountain was named in 1981, one month after the death of 22-year-old Terry Fox, the Port Coquitlam athlete who, after losing his right leg to bone cancer in 1977, decided to run across Canada with an artificial limb to raise money for cancer research. Fox started his "Marathon of Hope" on April 12, 1980, at St. John's, Newfoundland, and ran the length of a full marathon (42 kilometres) almost every day until he was forced to quit at Thunder Bay, Ontario, on September 1, when it was discovered that the cancer had spread to his lungs. Fox ran 5373 kilometres in 143 days and raised millions of dollars; hundreds of millions more have been raised since his death in the annual Terry Fox Run fundraisers held every September around the world. The mountain is 11 kilometres north of Valemount and was chosen to honour Fox because, at the time, it was the highest unnamed peak in British Columbia within sight of a public highway.

MOUNT TIEDEMANN (3838 m) In 1928, this mountain was named for Herman Otto Tiedemann, explorer and British Columbia's first professional architect. Tiedemann designed the province's first legislative buildings—the famous "Birdcages"—and many other prominent Victoria buildings. Tiedemann also nearly drowned while exploring the Homathko River, and in the 1860s, he was involved in Alfred Waddington's unsuccessful construction of a wagon road from Bute Inlet to Fort Alexandria. This mountain is just northeast of Mount Waddington and is the sixth highest peak in BC.

MOUNT TRUTCH (3246 m) This mountain was christened in honour of Joseph Trutch, who was a surveyor, engineer and British Columbia's first lieutenant-governor from 1871 to 1876. The mountain was originally named Trutch Mountain in 1920 and renamed Mount Trutch in 1957. (According to Canadian mountain naming practices, "Mount" is used before a given name if the peak is named after a specific person; otherwise, the given name is followed by "Mountain" or "Peak.") Mount Trutch is on the Alberta border, 31 kilometres northeast of Donald.

MOUNT TUAM (606 m) The name of this mountain on Saltspring Island is an anglicized version of its Cowichan First Nation name Tseween, which means "where the land or mountain comes down to the water." Officially adopted in 1934, the name is found on British Admiralty charts dating from 1861.

MOUNT TUPPER (2816 m) Originally called Mount Hermit, this mountain was renamed in 1887 for Sir Charles Tupper. A Father of Confederation, Tupper was, at the time, a prominent federal politician, cabinet member and Canada's High Commissioner to the United Kingdom. He later served as prime minister for a few weeks in 1896. Mount Tupper is 29 kilometres southwest of Donald. Nearby is a glacier that was also named after the future prime minister.

MOUNT TZOUHALEM *See* Tzouhalem.

MOUNT VAUX (3310 m) The name of this mountain is pronounced *vox* as if it rhymed with "fox." Mount Vaux was christened by British naturalist James Hector as he travelled through British Columbia in 1858. Hector named the peak after his friend, William Vaux, who was the resident antiquarian at the British Museum in London, England. The mountain is east of Golden, in Yoho National Park. Vaux Glacier is about 60 kilometres away, southeast of Glacier National Park. One would initially assume that it too was named for William Vaux, but it was actually christened for his distant relatives, the Vaux family (Mary Vaux and her brothers, George Jr. and William) of Philadelphia, who frequently stayed at Glacier House at nearby Rogers Pass and made a detailed study of the glaciers of British Columbia from the 1890s to the 1910s.

MOUNT VICTORIA Two mountains in British Columbia share this name. The first (3464 m) was christened in 1897 by British mountaineer J. Norman Collie, in honour of Queen Victoria (the year 1897 marked the 60th anniversary of Victoria's accession to the throne). Collie was among the first to climb the mountain, which is located on the Alberta border, in Yoho National Park. The other Mount Victoria (2088 m), located at the north end of Jervis Inlet, was named in 1860 by Captain George Richards while he was surveying the area. Richards chose the moniker to honour Queen Victoria's three-year-old daughter, Her Royal Highness Princess Beatrice Mary Victoria.

MOUNT WADDINGTON (4019 m) This mountain is the third highest peak in British Columbia and the highest entirely within the province. (The first and second highest, Fairweather Mountain and Mount Quincy Adams, both sit on the Alaska border and are partially in the United States.) The mountain is located in the middle of the Coast Mountains, about 55 kilometres north of Bute Inlet. It was unknown to non-Aboriginals until 1922. The names Mount Cradock—after World War I hero Sir

Christopher Cradock—and Mystery Mountain were suggested, but the government named the peak in 1928 after Alfred Waddington. Waddington was a wealthy Victoria businessman who unsuccessfully tried to build a wagon road in the 1860s from the head of Bute Inlet up the Homathko River, through the Coast Mountains and on to Fort Alexandria. In 1858, he wrote the first book (aside from government publications) to be published in British Columbia. There was once another Mount Waddington located in Mount Robson Provincial Park that was named after Alfred Waddington in 1917, but its name was changed to Waddington Peak in 1951 to avoid confusion.

MOUNT WARBURTON PIKE *See* Saturna / Saturna Island.

MOUNT WASHINGTON (1585 m) Despite one local artist's claim in the 1930s that, when viewed from Comox, the mountain resembles George Washington, this peak was not named for America's first president, but for British admiral John Washington. Washington was the Royal Navy's chief hydrographer from 1855 to 1863, and the mountain was named in 1864 by his successor, Captain George Richards, who had just spent several years surveying the lower coast of British Columbia. Mount Washington is in Strathcona Provincial Park.

MOUNT WELLINGTON *See* Mount Arthur.

MOUNT WHEELER There are two mountains by this name in British Columbia. The tallest (3336 m) is located 37 kilometres southwest of Golden, in the Selkirk Mountains. The peak was named in 1904 for surveyor and alpinist Arthur O. Wheeler, who began his high-mountain surveys of the Selkirks in 1901. He later co-founded and became president of the Alpine Club of Canada.

The second Mount Wheeler (1221 m) is 16 kilometres northwest of Kamloops. It was named in 1982 after

John Wheeler, an early settler who arrived in the area in the 1870s.

MOUNT WHITEHORN (3399 m) This mountain was originally christened the White Horn in 1907 or 1908 by geologist, academic and mountaineer Arthur Coleman, during one of his attempts to climb Mount Robson. The current name was officially adopted in 1912. The name is descriptive, but not everyone agrees with the description. Coleman's fellow alpinist Arthur Wheeler wrote: "Mt. Whitehorn is a very striking feature…but it is not very white and does not convey the impression of a horn."

MOUNT WHYMPER There are two mountains by this name in British Columbia. The first (1539 m), located 14 kilometres north of Honeymoon Bay, was named in 1864 by Robert Brown of the Vancouver Island Exploring Expedition for the famous artist Robert Whymper. The 27-year-old Whymper was a member of the expedition party. The other Mount Whymper (2844 m), 23 kilometres south of Lake Louise, was christened in 1901 after Robert's brother, Edward, who became an international celebrity for being the first to climb the Matterhorn in 1865.

MOYIE A community, two lakes, a mountain and a river share this name. All are located in or near the Moyie Valley, approximately 31 kilometres south of Cranbrook. Explorer and fur trader David Thompson named the waterway McDonald's River after his clerk, Finan McDonald, when the pair came to the area in 1808. Hudson's Bay Company governor George Simpson called it Grand Quête River in 1847 in honour of a local First Nations chief, who had a very long pigtail—a *quête*, in French. The explorer Captain John Palliser christened it the Choe-coos River in 1857. However, French Canadian voyageurs have long called it Moyie (originally pronounced *moo-YAY*, but now more commonly *moy-EE*) because of its moist conditions. *Mouillé* is French for "soggy" or "wet," and *mouiller* is French for "to (make) wet." Walter Clutterbuck and James Lees, during their visit to British Columbia in 1887, complained about "this water-logged Mooyie [sic] Valley." The river's name was officially adopted in 1900. The two lakes are separated by a two-kilometre stretch of the Moyie River. They were once collectively called Moyie Lakes and individually known as Lower and Upper Moyie Lake, but in 1915, they were lumped together with the singular name of Moyie Lake, to reflect long-time local usage. The community of Moyie (estimated pop. 450) was established and christened before 1899. Moyie Mountain (2086 m), located 11 kilometres northeast of the community, was so named by 1915.

MS MOUNTAIN This mountain in Strathcona Provincial Park was named in 1975 by the Island Mountain Ramblers Mountaineering Club of Nanaimo for its female members, who participated in the club's first climb of the mountain. A few kilometres away is Rambler Peak, which was also named by the Island Mountain Ramblers.

MURDERER CREEK This creek is named after the notorious American robber, murderer and cannibal Boone Helm, who, in 1862, was suspected of killing two merchants (Harris Lewin and David Sokolowsky) and their packer (Charles Rouchier or Bouchier) and of stealing their $18,000 in gold. It is said that he buried his ill-gotten gains under a cedar tree somewhere along this gulch east of Quesnel Forks and that the gold has never been recovered.

MURTLE LAKE (67 km²) This lake, located on the southeast side of Wells Gray Provincial Park, was named in 1874 by Canadian Pacific Railway surveyor Joseph Hunter after the Scottish town where he was born.

N

NAHMINT A bay, a lake, a river and a mountain on the west side of Alberni Inlet all share this name. The first three were named in 1864 by John Buttle, a member of the Vancouver Island Exploration Expedition. Robert Brown, the leader of the expedition, referred to the bay as Nahumet Bay later that same year. Other early spellings included Nah-mint, Na'mint and Nam'int. The mountain (1564 m) was named by 1938 after the lake and the river. The moniker comes from the name of the Nam'int?ath First Nation, a group of the Nuu-chah-nulth (Nootka) First Nation, whose people once had a large village at the bay, before they were driven away by the Yuu-tluth-aht (Ucluelet) First Nation.

NAKUSP (2006: pop. 1524) This village on the east side of Upper Arrow Lake was settled in 1892. Nakusp is a derivation of the Okanagan First Nation place name Nakipus or Neqo'sp, which has been interpreted to mean "closed in," "come together" or "the bay behind the long point." All the suggested meanings refer to the village's location, which is at the point where the lake closes in or narrows, thus providing canoes safe harbour from wind and storm.

NAMU Evidence indicates that First Nations people have lived in this fishing community for at least 11,000 years, making it the longest continuously occupied place in Canada. The first non-Aboriginal settlers arrived in 1893. *Namu* is a Heiltsuk (Bella Bella) First Nation word that has variously been translated as "place of high winds" and "closely alongside." This town is near the mouth of Burke Channel, southeast of the community of Bella Bella.

NANAIMO (2006: pop. 78,692) The name is a derivation of Snuneymuxw, a Hul'qumi'num (Halkomelem) First Nation name. Today, it refers to the people of the Snuneymuxw First Nation, who are a part of the Hul'qumi'num First Nation linguistic group and still live around the city of Nanaimo. Five different Snuneymuxw villages were located in the general area surrounding Nanaimo Bay, on the east coast of Vancouver Island, 110 kilometres north of Victoria, when the Hudson's Bay Company and the Royal Navy started poking around in the 1840s. When the HBC and the navy arrived, Snuneymuxw was also the Natives' name for this place. Many interpretations of the word touch on the idea of a shared locale, including "the whole," "meeting place" and "gathering place." Other interpretations indicate cooperation or intermingling among the villagers, including "the great people," "big strong tribe," "group of many people" and "people of many names." In 1791, explorer Jose Maria Narvaez called the bay Boca de Winthuysen, in honour of a Spanish rear admiral Francisco Xavier de Winthuysen. However, it was still commonly referred to as "Nanymo bay," after the Hudson's Bay Company built a post there in 1849, and the Spanish name completely disappeared in the 1850s. The current spelling of Nanaimo was first used by colonial governor James Douglas in 1853. The HBC established a settlement in the area called Colvile Town (after the HBC's company governor, Andrew Colvile), but by 1860, even that name was no longer used and everybody referred to the growing city, as well as the neighbouring harbour, lakes and river, by the name Nanaimo.

NANOOSE BAY / NANOOSE HARBOUR Nanoose Harbour is actually the official name of the inlet commonly referred to as Nanoose Bay. In contrast, Nanoose Bay is the official name of the community (2006: pop. 5246) that overlooks the harbour. Both are located 15 kilometres north of Nanaimo. Nanoose is a derivation of the Snaw'naw'as First Nation word *nuas*, which means "to push or work in." When applied to the bay, it means "the bay tending inward." The Snaw'naw'as are part of the Hul'qumi'num (Halkomelem) First Nation linguistic group, and they still live around Nanoose Bay. The name Nanoose Bay, in reference to the harbour, first appeared on a map in 1859, and non-Aboriginal settlement of the area began in the 1880s. The community of Nanoose Bay was originally called Arlington Hotel; the name was changed in 1916.

NARAMATA (2006: pop. 1787) Founded in 1905 by prominent land developer John Moore Robinson, this community was originally called East Summerland. However, the name caused too much confusion with the nearby town of Summerland, which Robinson also established. Robinson then considered the name Brighton Beach, after the resort village in England, but changed his mind when he attended a séance officiated by Mrs. J.M. Gillespie, the wife of the local postmaster. While she was in a trance, the spirit of Sioux chief Big Moose entered Mrs. Gillespie's body and, through Gillespie, spoke tenderly of his wife, Nar-ra-mat-tah. Robinson was so struck by this that he decided to rename the community after Big Moose's loved one. Skeptics have pointed out that Gillespie's husband was from Australia and that Gillespie, consciously or unconsciously, might have been thinking of the Australian Aboriginal word *naramatta*, which means "place of water." Naramata is 16 kilometres north of Penticton.

NASS This name applies to a small community (Nass Camp), a bay, a harbour, a lake and a river. All derive their names from the Tlingit First Nation place name Ewen Nass. When Captain George Vancouver first arrived in the area in 1793, he noted in his journal that this was the name given to the present-day Nass Harbour by the First Nations people he met. (It turned out that he had encountered some visiting Tlingit and not the Nisga'a, who still live there.) Vancouver knew that *ewen* meant "great" or "powerful." However, he did not know that Nass was the Tlingit name for the river that flows into the bay and that it means "the stomach," "food basket," "food depot" and "satisfier of the belly." The name refers to the enormous eulachon and salmon runs that occur there. The bay, the harbour and the river are all about 75 kilometres north of Prince Rupert. Nass Camp, which was settled in the 1970s, is near the Nass River, 90 kilometres north of Terrace. About 90 kilometres away from the mouth of the Nass River is Nass Lake; the lake is the headwater of the river, and the adoption of its name in 1987 reflected long-time local usage.

NAUTLEY RIVER Nautley is a derivation of the Dakelh (Carrier) First Nation name for the river, Nadleh K'oh, which means "where the salmon return." It is not known when the name was first used or by whom. The river drains Fraser Lake into the Nechako River.

NECHAKO Nechako is a derivation of the Dakelh (Carrier) First Nation name for the Nechako River, Ncha K'oh, which means "big river." The river flows east into the Fraser River at Prince George. At the head of the river is the Nechako Reservoir (847 km²), located 130 kilometres west of Prince George behind the Kenney Dam. The reservoir was to be called the Alcan Reservoir, because it was created in the early 1950s to supply water to an Aluminum Company of Canada (Alcan) hydro-power project, but the name was changed before the Kenney Dam was completed.

The Nechako urban residential neighbourhood in Kitimat, as well as the ghost town of Nechacco, the Nechako Canyon and the Nechako Range were all named after either the reservoir or the river.

NELSON (2006: pop. 9258) The city fathers who established this community in 1887 had trouble deciding which politician to impress. First, they called their town Salisbury, after Robert Cecil, the 3rd Marquess of Salisbury, who was then the British prime minister. Next they named it Stanley, after Frederick Stanley, the 16th Earl of Derby, who was the Governor General of Canada. However, that name was soon rejected by the postal authorities because another community with the same name (now a ghost town), nine kilometres east of Quesnel, already existed. Finally, in 1888, they settled on Nelson, in honour of Hugh Nelson, the new lieutenant-governor of British Columbia.

NELSON ISLAND (100 km²) This island was named in about 1860 by Captain George Richards, in honour of Vice Admiral Horatio Nelson, the 1st Viscount Nelson and the British naval hero killed at the Battle of Trafalgar in 1805. Nelson Island lies at the mouth of Jervis Inlet.

NEPEAN SOUND This body of water was named in 1788 by Captain Charles Duncan for Evan Nepean. Duncan had been in the British Navy before he joined the King George's Sound Company in 1785. Nepean was also in the navy from 1773 to 1782, but whether the two men ever served together is unknown. In 1788, Nepean was Under-Secretary of State (the second in command, or what is commonly called the deputy minister) at the British Home Office. The Home Office was then responsible for Britain's wars and colonies, and Nepean was in charge of managing its many varied tasks. Nepean Sound is between Banks, Campania and Pitt islands.

N

NEROUTSOS INLET This inlet, located east of Quatsino Sound, was named in 1927 at the suggestion of the Hydrographic Service's H.D. Parizeau, in honour of Captain Cyril Demetrius Neroutsos (nicknamed "the Skipper"), who was the assistant manager of the Canadian Pacific Railway's Coastal Service.

NEW AIYANSH (2006: pop. 806) This Nisga'a First Nation community is on the west side of the Nass River, about 75 kilometres from the river's mouth. Upstream a short distance was a large Nisga'a village called Gitlakdamiks. That ancient community's name meant "people of the ponds." In 1883, Anglican missionary James McCullagh established a mission six kilometres downriver from Gitlakdamiks and named it Aiyansh, which means "place of the first leaves," "early leaves," "leafing early" or "place of early blooming" in Nisga'a. But after a series of floods, another settlement was established in 1961 about five kilometres southwest across the river and on higher ground. That new community was called New Aiyansh. After a fire in the early 1980s, what was left of the homes and businesses at Aiyansh moved to New Aiyansh.

NEW BRIGHTON *See* Gambier Island.

NEW DENVER (2006: pop. 512) When it was established in 1891, this village was named El Dorado, after the mythical city of gold. It did not take long, however, for the community to realize that its wealth lay in lead and silver, rather than in the yellow metal. According to one story, a town meeting was called in 1892 to determine a new town name. Thomas Latheen, from Denver, Colorado, said that the community could one day be even greater than his old hometown and convinced the residents to christen the place New Denver. Another tale has it that the village was renamed for the American city in 1892 by the local gold commissioner, Captain Napoleon Fitzstubbs, in the hope that the new name would bring better luck to the local miners. New Denver is on the east side of Slocan Lake.

NEW HAZELTON *See* Hazelton.

NEW WESTMINSTER (2006: pop. 58,549) This city was first called Queenborough in 1858 by Colonel Richard

Moody of the Royal Engineers, when he selected the site to be the future capital of the new mainland colony of British Columbia. Objections were immediately made by the residents of Victoria, who felt that the name too closely resembled their community's nickname, Queen City. An *s* was added to make it Queensborough, but that did not end the dispute. Colonial governor James Douglas finally laid the whole matter in the lap of the British government, with the comment that "it will be received and esteemed as an especial mark of royal favour" were the new community to be named after Queen Victoria or some member of the royal family. The Queen herself named the city after her residence, Westminster Palace. New Westminster is on the north shore of the Fraser River, 20 kilometres east of Vancouver. The once-rejected name, Queensborough, later became the moniker of a neighbourhood in New Westminster.

NEWCASTLE ISLAND This island on the north side of Nanaimo Harbour was named in 1853 by officers of the Hudson's Bay Company and possibly by Joseph Pemberton himself (see Pemberton), who was, at the time, surveying the Nanaimo area for the HBC. Coal was discovered on the island, so it was named after the English community of Newcastle-upon-Tyne in Northumberland, England, which has been famous for centuries for its coal industry. By coincidence, Newcastle Island is in the Northumberland Channel.

NICOLA Two communities, Lower Nicola (2006: pop. 1047) and Nicola, as well as a lake and a river share this name. The lake and the river were both named after Chief Hwistesmetxö'qen (also spelled Hwistesmetx'quen, Hwistesmethpegan, Hwistesmelxquen and Nwistesmeekin), the famous early 19th-century leader of the local Spaxomin First Nation. The Spaxomin, also known as the Upper Nicola, are a branch of the Okanagan First Nation. (One source says the chief was not of the Spaxomin but of the neighbouring Nlaka'pamux, formerly the Thompson, First Nation.) The chief's name translates as "walking grizzly bear." He was also called Shiwelean. The fur traders at Fort Kamloops could not pronounce Hwistesmetxö'qen, so they called him "Nicholas" (and various spellings thereof, such as Neckilus) because it sounded vaguely similar to the chief's Spaxomin name. An 1849 map labels the lake and the river as Lac de Nicholas and Nicholas River. Ironically, the First Nations people had trouble pronouncing Nicholas, so the nickname eventually became N'kuala (or Nkwala) and then Nicola. The monument at the chief's gravesite bears the name Inkula. The current spelling, Nicola, was officially adopted by the Geographic Board of Canada for the lake and the river in 1913 but had been in use long before then. The once-thriving community of Nicola, on the south end of Nicola Lake, was founded in 1871 and named after the nearby lake and river. It is now the site of the famous Nicola Ranch. Lower Nicola is an old Sce'exmx First Nation village, just northwest of Merritt. The Sce'exmx (a branch of the Nlaka'pamux) originally called it Shulus. *See* Mount Nkwala.

NIGEI ISLAND (61 km²) Located just west of Port Hardy, this island was originally christened Galiano Island in 1792 by Spanish explorers Dionisio Alcala Galiano and Cayetano Valdés y Flores. The moniker was changed in 1900 by the Geographic Board of Canada because there was another Galiano Island in the Straight of Georgia. Nigei is the hereditary name of the principal chief of the Nahwitti First Nation, a branch of the Kwakwaka'wakw people of northern Vancouver Island. According to one source, the Geographic Board was thinking of one particular chief who was known for gathering food on the island.

NIMPKISH A lake, a river and two small communities (Nimpkish and Nimpkish Heights) share this name. Nimpkish Lake (36.5 km²) is on Vancouver Island, just south of Port McNeill. The Nimpkish River flows north from Vernon Lake into Nimpkish Lake and from there into Broughton Strait. The river was named by Captain George Richards in 1860; the christening of the lake and the communities came later. Nimpkish is a derivation of the name of the people of the 'Namgis First Nation, one of the many Kwakwaka'wakw First Nations of northern Vancouver Island. 'Namgis means "halibut at the bottom" and is derived from two Kwak'wala words. 'Nam is from 'namxiyalegiyu, which means "something terrible" and was the name of a huge, mythical, halibut-like sea monster that allegedly causes the powerful riptide at the mouth of the Nimpkish River. The suffix *gis* suggests that the creature lives at the bottom of the ocean. Put together, the two mean "halibut at the bottom." (It should be noted that an alternate translation, "those who are one when they come together," has also been suggested.) The lake and river lie within the traditional territory of the 'Namgis, though most of them now live in and around Alert Bay on Cormorant Island.

NITINAT The name of a lake and two rivers (Nitinat and Little Nitinat) in southwestern Vancouver Island, Nitinat is a derivation of the name of the diitiid7aa7tx (or di:ti:dʔa:ʔt$_x$) people of the Ditidaht First Nation. The da7uu7aa7tx were the original First Nations people who lived around Nitinat Lake. They were later joined by the diitiid7aa7tx, who came across the Strait of Juan de Fuca from Tatoosh Island, off Cape Flattery in Washington State, and settled at present-day Jordan River before heading to Nitinat Lake. The name diitiid7aa7tx means "people of diitiida," and diitiida is the Ditidaht name for the Jordan River. The meaning of diitiida is apparently no longer known. (It should be noted that, according to some

Nuu-chah-nalth elders, Ditidaht translates into "people from a place in the forest." The Ditidaht are not a Nuu-chah-nalth First Nation, but they do have cultural links to them and speak a similar language.) Ditidaht, which is pronounced *dee-tee-daht*, is the anglicized version of diitiid7aa7tx̱ and is often pronounced *nitinaht* because, in the Westcoast (Nootka) First Nation language, the letter *d* is pronounced as an *n*.

The names of Nitinat Lake and the Nitinat River were officially adopted in 1934 and 1947, respectively, to reflect long-time local usage, but the name of the lake dates back to about 1864.

NOOTKA This name is shared by a bay, an island, a small community and two short mountains on the west coast of Vancouver Island. It was said that Spanish explorer Juan Perez first stopped at Nootka Sound in 1774 and named it Boca San Lorenzo, but it is now believed that Perez was referring to another harbour about 15 kilometres to the southwest, near Estevan Point. Captain James Cook christened the bay King George's Sound after George III when Cook visited the area in 1778. Cook quickly renamed it Nootka Sound, after what he incorrectly thought was the local First Nation people's name for the sound. *Nootk sitl* is a verb in the language of the Nuu-chah-nulth (Nootka) First Nation that means "to go around" or "to make a circuit." *Nootka-a, noot-ka-eh* or *nuutxaa* (different sources use different spellings) is the verb's imperative, which means "Go around!" and *nu-tka-pičim* means "go around the harbour." It has been suggested that Cook heard some version of *nootk sitl* when he asked the Nuu-chah-nulth what they called the sound.

One version of the story is that the Natives that Cook spoke with were either dancing or running in a circle on the beach when he made his inquiry, and they thought he was asking what they were doing. The other version is that the Natives misinterpreted the sweeping motions that Cook made with his arms when he was asking his questions and thought that he was referring to his trip around the bay.

Nootka Island (520 km²), just north of the bay, was originally called Isla de Mazarredo in 1791 by Francisco de Eliza y Reventa, for Spanish naval officer Josef de Mazarredo, but the name had been changed to Isla de Nutka by 1795, to reflect Cook's name for the sound. Nootka Island is the largest island off the west coast of Vancouver Island. The small village of Nootka is on the south tip of the isle. Also on the island are two mountains, Nootka Cone (493 m), named by the British Admiralty in 1862, and Santa Cruz de Nuca Mountain (915 m). The latter was either named by H.D. Parizeau of the Hydrographic Service in the early 1930s, to recall the Spanish presence at Nootka Sound, or by the Spanish, who built a fort at the harbour in 1791. The name Santa Cruz de Nuca means "Holy Cross of Nootka," and it was at that mountain where the Spanish claimed British Columbia for their king.

NORTH COWICHAN *See* Cowichan.

NORTH ISLAND *See* Langara Island.

NORTH PENDER ISLAND *See* Pender Islands.

NORTH SAANICH *See* Saanich.

NORTH TOWER *See* Mount Goodsir.

NORTH VANCOUVER A city (2006: pop. 45,165) and the district municipality (2006: pop. 82,562) that surrounds it share this name. Both are located on the north shore of Burrard Inlet and were christened after Captain George Vancouver, who explored the inlet in 1792. The District of North Vancouver was incorporated in 1891 and encompassed everything along the north shore from Deep Cove to Horseshoe Bay, except for the community of Moodyville. West Vancouver seceded from the district in 1912. Moodyville was named after Sewell Prescott Moody, a lumberman who built the first large sawmill there in the early 1860s. Moodyville changed its name to North Vancouver City in 1902 and was incorporated as the City of North Vancouver five years later.

NORTHUMBERLAND CHANNEL This sea passage east of Nanaimo was named in 1852 by officers of the Hudson's Bay Company for Algernon Percy, the 4th Duke of Northumberland. The duke was an admiral and, for most of 1852, the First Lord of the Admiralty.

NUCHATLITZ INLET This inlet on the west side of Nootka Island was named Ensenada de Ferrer (which means "Ferrer's Inlet") by Spanish explorer Dionisio Alcalá-Galiano and Cayetano Valdés y Flores in 1792. The moniker possibly refers to either Lorenzo Ferrer Maldonado, a seaman who claimed in 1588 to have found the Northwest Passage, or St. Vincent Ferrer, a 14th-century Dominican missionary. One historian suggested that Ensenada de Ferrer was actually christened by Spanish explorers José Espinos and Ciriaco Cevallos in 1791, in honour of Spanish naval officer Vincente Ferrer. In any case, the inlet was renamed (and the name misspelled) in 1860 after either the Nuchatlaht people, a branch of the Nuu-chah-nulth (Nootka) First Nation who once lived on Nootka Island, or after the village of the same name on the northwest side of the island. The name Nuchatlaht has been translated by Nuu-chah-nulth elders as "people of a sheltered bay," but others have also suggested "people from a place with a mountain behind the village."

N

OAK BAY (2006: pop. 17,908) Although this district municipality was incorporated in 1906, the moniker was used to describe the area as far back as 1847. The name comes from the large number of oak trees in the area. The community is immediately east of Victoria, and a natural harbour, also called Oak Bay, lies just east of that.

OBSERVATORY INLET This long, northern arm of Portland Inlet begins at the mouth of the Nass River and was named by Captain George Vancouver in 1793, when he explored the inlet. He also stopped at a cove there to reprovision his ship and to set up an observatory to correct his fixing of latitude and longitude and check his ship's chronometers. In addition, Vancouver christened three tracts of land that extend into the inlet after three astronomers and mathematicians: Wales Point, after William Wales, an astronomer and mathematics instructor, who taught the sciences of navigation and nautical astronomy to Vancouver during Captain James Cook's second voyage (1772–75); Maskelyne Point, after Edmund Maskelyne, the royal astronomer; and Ramsden Point, after Jesse Ramsden, a famous maker of sextants and other mathematical instruments used in navigation and astronomy.

OCEAN FALLS (estimated pop. 40) Located at the head of Cousins Inlet, about 30 kilometres northeast of Bella Bella, this community was established in 1906. The name is a translation of the Heiltsuk (Bella Bella) First Nation word *tuxvnaq*, which means "big sea, out in the ocean." The word was the Heiltsuk name for the head of Cousins Inlet and refers to a spectacular wave that once broke over a big rock in the middle of the waterfalls, where Link Lake empties into the inlet. An 18-metre-long hydro dam now sits where the falls were. Ocean Falls receives an average of almost 4400 millimetres of rain every year and is the rainiest inhabited location in Canada.

OKANAGAN The Okanagan, also known as Okanagan Country and the Okanagan Valley, is a region in south-central British Columbia between Vernon and the American border, with the Monashee Mountains on the east and the Thompson-Okanagan Plateau on the west. The valley, as well as the Okanagan River that flows through it, extend into the United States southward to where the river flows into the Columbia River. A large lake (348 km^2), a mountain (12 kilometres southeast of Peachland; 1576 m), a mountain range and four communities (Okanagan Centre, Okanagan Falls, Okanagan Landing and Okanagan Mission) also share the name. All of these locations were named directly or indirectly for the people of the Okanagan (Syilx) First Nation. The Okanagan still live in the valley and speak the Syilx'tsn language.

There are many theories as to the origin of the name. Some argue that the moniker is a derivation of the Syilx'tsn word *s-ookanhkchinx*, which means "transport toward the head or top end" and refers to the use of Okanagan Lake and the Okanagan River as a traditional transportation route. Others believe the name is an anglicization of the Syilx'tsn word *uk^{w}naqínx*, the Okanagan name for the people living in the Okanagan River basin. Another explanation is that the name is an amalgamation of the Syilx'tsn words *kana*, which means "the place of," and *gan*, which translates into "water" or "lake." A fourth possibility is that the name is a derivation of the Syilx'tsn word *au-wuk-ane*, which means "men with short hair."

Explorers Lewis and Clark were the first non-Aboriginals to see the river and referred to it as the Otchenaukane when they passed it while travelling west on the Columbia in 1805. Fur trader David Thompson came across the lake in 1811 but could not make up his mind and spelled the name four different ways (Oachenawawgan, Ookanawgan, Ookenawkane and Teekanoggin). After that, more than 40 other known spellings were used by explorers and fur traders for the lake, the river and the valley, including Okawaujou, O'Kina hain, Okunaakan, Oo-ka-na-kane and Otchenaukane. Okanagan Lake was identified as Big Okanakan Lake on an 1827 chart and as Great Okinagan Lake on an 1867 map. The first known use of the current spelling, Okanagan, was in 1840, but the name Okanogan was more commonly used, at least to refer to the river, until the late 1860s, when colonial governor Frederick Seymour changed the names of the river and other waterways that crossed into the United States to distinguish British Columbia's jurisdiction from that of the Americans.

The first settlers arrived at Okanagan Centre in the early 1900s and, by 1908, a post office had been opened and a townsite laid out. The community is now part of the district municipality of Lake Country. Okanagan Falls, on the shores of Skaha Lake, 20 kilometres south of Penticton, was known as Dogtown until 1899. The community takes its current name from the twin falls that once existed nearby, before a modern flood-control system was built that destroyed them. Okanagan Landing, 12 kilometres southwest of Vernon, began as the southern terminus of the Shuswap and Okanagan Railway line from Sicamous, which was completed in 1892. A settlement was established there by 1898 and merged with Vernon in 1993. Okanagan Mission, just south of Kelowna, was settled by 1872 and takes its name from a nearby mission founded by Fathers Charles Pandosy and Pierre Richard in 1859 or 1860.

OLALLA (2006: pop. 393) This community was settled in the 1890s and is located six kilometres north of Keremeos. The name comes from the Chinook Jargon or Salishan First Nation word *olallie*, which means "berries" and refers to the plentiful Saskatoon berries in the area.

OLD HAZELTON *See* Hazelton.

OLIVER (2006: pop. 4370) This community was established in 1921 after the South Okanagan region was irrigated by the provincial government to provide farmland to soldiers returning from World War I. The town was named after John Oliver, who was then premier of British Columbia. Oliver is located 40 kilometres south of Penticton.

OLIVER'S LANDING This name was submitted to the British Columbia Geographical Names Office in 1999 for the waterfront community that was subsequently built south of Britannia Beach. The site is located at the mouth of Furry Creek, where it flows into Howe Sound. Both the town and the creek are named for trapper Oliver Furry, who discovered copper nearby in 1898, which led to the development of an extensive copper mine at Britannia Beach. The creek had been christened after Furry by 1901.

O

OOTISCHENIA (2006: pop. 856) In 1908, a group of Doukhobors from Saskatchewan settled at an abandoned mining camp just southeast of present-day Castlegar airport. They gave the place a Russian name, Dolina Uteshenaya, which means "valley of consolation." Over the years, Dolina was dropped, and the remainder of the name was respelled Ootischenia. This was the first and, for a while, the largest Doukhobor community in the province.

OPPY MOUNTAIN (3311 m) This mountain was named in 1918 after a village located 10 kilometres southeast of Lens, France, where many Canadians had been killed the year before in World War I. Oppy Mountain is on the Alberta border, 53 kilometres north of Donald.

OSOYOOS / OSOYOOS LAKE The name of the town (2006: pop. 4752) and lake is pronounced *soo yoos*. It is a derivation of Suius, the Syilx'tsn (Okanagan) First Nation place name for the area, which has been variously translated to mean "where the lake narrows," "where two lakes come together," "a shallow crossing," "sand bar across" and "a sheet of water divided in two by a narrow extension of land from opposite sides," all of which refer to the long strip of land that virtually cuts the lake in two. Some suggest that the *o* was added by Peter O'Reilly, the High Sheriff of the mainland colony of British Columbia, who thought the name would be more dignified with the extra letter. Others say that local cattle rancher and judge John C. Haynes added the *o*. The people of the Okanagan First Nation say the letter was added before the area's first non-Aboriginal settlers arrived. In any case, although more than a dozen spellings were in use over the years (Soyoos was popular for a long while), one 1859 map does refer to the lake by its current spelling, which was formally adopted in 1924. The community was first settled by non-Aboriginals in 1861, and its name has always been spelled Osoyoos.

OWINKENO LAKE (102 km²) This lake is about 120 kilometres northeast of Port Hardy. It was labelled as Owekano Lake on an 1895 map and was known as Oweekayno Lake for decades before that. The current spelling came into use in 1912. The moniker is a derivation of the name of the Oweekeno (now called the Wuikinuxv) First Nation, whose people live in the area. Several translations of the name have been suggested, including "portage makers" and "those who carry on the back," both of which refer to the Oweekeno travelling across the portage between the lake and nearby Rivers Inlet. Other translations are "right-minded people" and "people talking right."

OYAMA The first settler arrived in Oyama in 1870, but this Lake Country neighbourhood did not receive its current name until 1906. A local post office was established that year in the home of Dr. W.H. Irvine, the community's acting postmaster, and his mother suggested that the post office be named after Iwao Oyama, the Japanese field marshal who defeated the Russians in Manchuria in 1905, during the Russo-Japanese War. Oyama's name was prominent in the newspapers during that short conflict. Furthermore, Britain and Japan had recently become allies, and in early 1906, Oyama and two other Japanese war heroes were awarded the Order of Merit by King Edward VII. The name Oyama was quickly applied to the entire neighbourhood.

O

P

PALDI Located 10 kilometres west of Duncan, this small community is named after the village of Paldi in Punjab, India. It was originally called Mayo or Mayo Siding after Mayo Singh, who established a sawmill there in 1917. However, postal authorities frequently confused Mayo with another town with the same name in the Yukon, so it was renamed Paldi, after Singh's hometown, in 1936. Nearby Mayo Lake was named after Mayo Singh in 1962.

PANTHEON RANGE This mountain range north of Mount Waddington, as well as a number of peaks within it, were named by mountaineer Dick Culbert and other climbers who explored this region in 1964. Among the peaks they christened after various ancient gods are Mount Astarte, Hermes Peak, Mount Juno, Manitou Peak, Osiris Peak and Mount Vishnu.

PANTHER LAKE This lake near Mount Washington on Vancouver Island was named by John Brown, who prospected in the area in the 1920s. Brown said a family of cougars had chased him up a tree there.

PARKSVILLE (2006: pop. 10,993) Located on the east coast of Vancouver Island, this city was first settled in 1883 and was initially called Englishman's River, after the nearby river. The community was renamed in 1887 after its first postmaster, Nelson Parks, when its post office opened.

PATRICIA BAY / PAT BAY HIGHWAY Patricia Bay is located on the east side of Saanich Inlet. It was named in 1912 after the beautiful 26-year-old Princess Patricia of Connaught, the daughter of Canada's new Governor General, Prince Arthur, the 1st Duke of Connaught and

Strathearn, and the granddaughter of Queen Victoria. The duke and his youngest child visited Vancouver Island in 1912, and the girl was a hit with the local residents. Years later, when Highway 17, which connects Victoria to the north end of the Saanich Peninsula was completed, it became known as the Pat Bay (short for Patricia Bay) Highway.

PEACE RIVER This river flows 1923 kilometres from Williston Reservoir to the Slave River in Alberta. It is the only river that runs through the entire Rocky Mountain range. The people of the Sekani First Nation called it Thû-tcî-Kah (or Isetaieka or Tse-tai-e-ka), which has been translated as "the river that runs by the rocks," referring to the canyon that the river flows through as it transits the Rockies. The name might also mean "great water" and "important river."

The Dene-thah (Slavey) First Nation knew the Peace River as the Chin-ch-ago, which means "beautiful river." The Cree called it the A-mis-kwe-i-moo-si-pi, which means "the Beaver (Dunne-za) River." The people of the Dunne-za (Beaver) First Nation knew it as the Unchagah (also spelled Unchaga, Unjaja and Unjigah), which is their word for "peace." Both Alexander Mackenzie in 1793 and George Dawson almost 90 years later referred to it as the "Unjigah or Peace River." The current moniker was officially adopted in 1912, but maps from as far back as 1785 identify the river as the Peace River. The name is taken from a point (i.e., Peace Point) near Lake Athabasca in Alberta where, in the 1710s, the Cree and the Dunne-za agreed to end their wars and use the Peace River as a boundary between their territories. An 1822 journal entry from the Hudson's Bay Company's Fort Chipewyan called it Rivière de Brochet, but that name did not stick. *Brochet* is the French name for the freshwater northern pike fish that were once found in the river.

PEACHLAND (2006: pop. 4883) A mining camp known as Camp Hewitt, after local prospector and logger Augustus ("Gus") Hewitt, once existed on this site in the early 1890s. A few years later, in 1897, John Moore Robinson was looking for gold in the area when he tasted a peach from a nearby farm. He instantly realized the full potential for horticulture in this former ranchland and laid out a townsite that he called Peachland. This district municipality is on the west side of Okanagan Lake, between Kelowna and Penticton.

PEARSE ISLAND (218 km²) In 1868, Captain George Pender named this island on the west side of Portland Inlet for Captain Charles H. Peirce of the 2nd United States Artillery. Peirce was in command of Fort Tongass on Tongass Island in the Alaska Panhandle near the Canada-U.S. border from 1868 to 1870. The fort was the first American military outpost established in Alaska after the United States purchased that territory from Russia in 1867. Pearse Island was claimed by the Americans until the location of the border was finally settled in 1903. Either Pender or the mapmakers at the British Admiralty made a spelling error (Pearse for Peirce), and the mistake has never been corrected.

PEARSE ISLANDS This group of islands in Broughton Strait was named in about 1860 by Captain George Richards in honour of Commander William Alfred Rumbulow Pearse. Pearse was the commander of the HMS *Alert* while it was stationed in British Columbia waters from 1858 to 1861.

PEMBERTON (2006: pop. 2192) This village, located 160 kilometres north of Vancouver, was named after Joseph Despard Pemberton, a Hudson's Bay Company surveyor who made some of the first surveys in the Pemberton area. He was also active along the lower Fraser River and on southern Vancouver Island, where he was surveyor general from 1859 to 1864. A community called

Port Pemberton was established in 1858 about 12 kilometres east on the north end of Lillooet Lake. The word "Port" had been dropped from the moniker by 1862. As the Fraser River Gold Rush died down in the early 1860s, people left and resettled around the site of present-day Pemberton. The new locale was first called Pemberton Meadows (now the name of a small community northwest of Pemberton), then, in 1912, it was called Agerton before finally being renamed Pemberton in February 1931.

PENDER Until 1903, what are now North and South Pender islands (2006: pop. 1996 and 236, respectively) in Haro Strait were a single isle called Pender Island. Captain George Richards named the island in 1859 to honour his second master on the HMS *Plumper*, Lieutenant Daniel Pender. Pender would later play a major role in the surveying and naming of hundreds of locations along British Columbia's coast. The island had previously been christened Isla de Zayas (or Sayas) in 1791 by Juan Pantoja y Arriaga, a Spanish naval officer on the *San Carlos*. It is believed that he did so in honour of fellow naval officer Juan Martinez y Zayas. Spanish Navy Lieutenant Francisco de Eliza y Reventa, who commanded the *San Carlos*, later rechristened the place Isla San Eusebio. Between 1903 and 1911, the Pender Canal was constructed through the island's narrow isthmus ("the Portage"), creating the two separate islands.

Pender Harbour (2006: pop. 1225) is actually a collection of bays, islands and lagoons between Powell River and Sechelt on the Sunshine Coast; it was also named by Captain Richards for his second master in 1860.

PENNY MOUNTAIN This mountain was named in 1949 by mountaineer Arnold Wexler when he found a sardine can with a penny inside on the peak. The can and the penny were left behind in 1916 by alpinists Andrew Gilmour and

Professor Edward Holway. The mountain lies near Valemount, north of the head of the Canoe River.

PENTICTON (2006: pop. 31,909) The first non-Aboriginal settler in this area was Thomas Ellis, who arrived in 1865. He began a cattle ranch, which he called the Penticton Ranch, that eventually encompassed an astounding 120 square kilometres (more than 30,000 acres), from Okanagan Lake to Osoyoos Lake, with 20,000 head of cattle. A small nearby community on the south end of Okanagan Lake calling itself Penticton existed as early as 1889, with Ellis as its first postmaster. All agree that the name is a derivation of a First Nations word, but there are many ideas as to what that word was and what it meant. One source said in 1918 that the original word (apparently without indicating what the word was) translated into "place where water passes beyond." Some point to the Okanagan word *pen-tak-tin*, which means "a place to stay forever" or "a place of permanent abode where waters pass by." Others suggest that it is from the Okanagan place name Pente-hik-ton, which means "ever" or "forever" and was applied to the spot where Okanagan Lake flows year round into the Okanagan River (in contrast to other nearby streams and creeks that dry up during the summer). The name could also come from the Okanagan word *sin-peen-tick-tin*, which loosely translates into "permanent place." Yet another possibility is the Interior Salish word *snpintktn*, which translates as "a place to stay forever" or as "a place where people live year-round." Finally, it has also been said that Penticton comes from *snpniniyatn*, a word from the extinct Nicola-Similkameen language that means "place where deer net was used."

PINCHI Two unincorporated communities—the old Dakelh village of Pinchi and the much newer Pinchi Lake—share this name with a lake (56 km²), a mountain (1267 m) and a bay on Stuart Lake. The first time the term is known to have been used by a non-Aboriginal was in 1811, when

North West Company fur trader Daniel Harmon, while stationed at nearby Fort St. James, noted the existence of "Pinchy Lake." The name has also been spelled as Binche, Pinche and Pinchie. It is believed that the first non-Aboriginal visitors to the area applied the moniker of the existing Dakelh village to the lake. Sources differ as to the origin of the name. Some say that *pinchi* is a Dakelh (Carrier) First Nation word meaning "lake outlet." Others believe it is a derivation of a Dakelh place name, either Tesgha or Tesghabun. The prefix *tes* refers to the bottom or bed of a lake, while *gha* translates into "furry," "hairy" or "mossy," and *bun* means "lake." Hence, the name refers to the condition of the lakebed. Another interpretation, however, is that *tes* means "bed" or "bedding" and that Tesgha means "resting place for waterfowl."

PITT An archipelago, an island and a mountain were named after William Pitt. Best known as Pitt the Younger, in 1783, at the age of 24, the statesman became the youngest prime minister in British history. He held the post until 1801 and again from 1804 until his death in 1806. Captain George Vancouver named the 160-kilometre-long archipelago between Chatham and Nepean sounds in honour of the prime minister in 1792. (The moniker, Pitt's Archipelago, is not used much anymore, and when it is, it is frequently given as Pitt Archipelago.) Vancouver named Pitt Island (1357 km²), which lies between Banks Island and Grenville Channel, after the archipelago in 1793. It is the fifth largest island in British Columbia. Mount Pitt (665 m), on the BC mainland near the south end of Pitt Island, was christened in 1946. Chatham Sound was named after Pitt's older brother, John Pitt, the 2nd Earl of Chatham.

The archipelago and island off British Columbia might not be the only geographical sites named after William Pitt. The Pitt River in the Lower Mainland flows into the Fraser River near Port Coquitlam. The earliest known reference to the river is in an 1827 journal entry by James McMillan, the founder of Fort Langley. He called it "Pitt's River," and although McMillan did not specify who Pitt was, most assume that he was probably referring to the late prime minister. The river had been renamed Pitt River by 1858. Pitt Lake (54 km²) is where the river widens just before it drains into the Fraser. South of Pitt Lake are two locales called Pitt Meadows. One, a city (2006: pop. 15,623) located on the northeast side of the junction of the Fraser and Pitt rivers, was part of Maple Ridge before it became a separate municipality in 1914. The other is an unincorporated community two kilometres north of the first, on the east side of the Pitt River. Both communities take their name from the river. Mount Pitt (2487 m) in Garibaldi Provincial Park was also named after the river.

PLUMPER PASS *See* Active Pass.

POINT ATKINSON The northern entrance to Burrard Inlet on the west end of West Vancouver was originally named Atkinson Point by Captain George Vancouver, either in 1792, when he was exploring the waters off present-day Vancouver, or three years later, when he returned home to England. The name was officially changed in 1958 to reflect local usage. It is not clear who Atkinson was—Vancouver merely recorded that he was a "particular friend." Vancouver received his lieutenant's commission in 1779, and three Atkinsons were commissioned as lieutenants in the Royal Navy in 1778 or 1779: George Augustus Atkinson (d. 1782), John Anson Atkinson (d. 1791) and Jonathan Atkinson (d. 1782). There was also a young master's mate named Edmund Atkinson onboard the HMS *Chatham*, the vessel that accompanied Vancouver's HMS *Discovery* on its exploration of the Pacific Coast. However, most historians believe that Vancouver was referring to Thomas Atkinson, a British naval officer 10 years Vancouver's junior, who was the master of Lord

P

Horatio Nelson's flagship, the HMS *Victory*, during the Battle of Trafalgar in 1805.

POINT ELLICE This point in Victoria Harbour was named in 1846 by Hudson's Bay Company officers in honour of Edward Ellice. Ellice was a prominent British politician and London banker and merchant. He joined the North West Company in 1805 and, as its major partner, played a key role in the NWC's merger with the HBC in 1821.

POINT GREY The southern entrance to Burrard Inlet on the west end of Vancouver and the residential community adjacent to it share this name. The entrance was originally named Grey Point by Captain George Vancouver in 1792 after his friend, George Grey, the post captain of the HMS *Boyne*. Grey was 10 years younger than Vancouver and, like Vancouver, had joined the Royal Navy at the age of 14. The name was later changed to reflect local usage. The site had previously been christened Punta de Lángara in 1791, by either Spanish explorer Dionisio Alcalá-Galiano or by Spanish Navy Lieutenant Francisco de Eliza y Reventa, in honour of the 18th-century Spanish naval hero Juan Francisco de Lángara y Huarte. The community was established in 1892 and was an independent municipality from 1908 to 1929, before becoming part of the city of Vancouver.

POOLEY ISLAND (161 km^2) It is not clear when this island, located between Finlayson and Mathieson channels north of Bella Bella, received its name, though the moniker was officially adopted in 1946. It is certain that the island was christened after Charles Edward Pooley (1845–1912), a prominent British Columbia attorney who became wealthy working for the Dunsmuirs (Vancouver Island industrialist Robert and his son, James). Pooley also served in the provincial legislature for 22 years.

PORCHER ISLAND (525 km²) This island in Chatham Sound, south of Prince Rupert, was named in about 1867 by Captain Daniel Pender for Commander Edwin Augustus Porcher, the commander of the HMS *Sparrowhawk*, which sailed off British Columbia's coastline from 1865 to 1868. A small community there takes its name from the island.

PORT ALBERNI (2006: pop. 17,548) This city is at the head of, and is named after, Alberni Inlet on Vancouver Island. In fact, until 1967, two communities on the fjord shared similar names. A sawmill was established at the end of the inlet in 1860, and, the next year, Captain George Richards and the officers of the visiting HMS *Hecate* named the small community surrounding it Alberni Settlement. The name was later shortened to Alberni. The community was called Sayward-Alberni (probably after William Sayward, the pre-eminent lumber dealer on Vancouver Island at the time) from 1886 to 1891. Another city emerged in about 1900 a little to the south on the east side of the inlet. This upstart was first called New Alberni and then, beginning in 1910, Port Alberni. The two communities merged in 1967.

PORT ALICE (2006: pop. 821) This village is located on the east shore of Neroutsos Inlet, near Quatsino Sound. It was originally established four kilometres from its current location in 1917 by the Whalen Pulp and Paper Company, which built a pulp mill there, but the entire community was moved to its present location in 1965. Everyone agrees that the village was named for Alice Whalen, but sources disagree as to whether she was the mother of the brothers that ran the company or one of their wives or daughters.

PORT CLEMENTS (2006: pop. 440) Settled in 1907 by Eli Tingley, this village was originally called Queenstown, but the postal authorities rejected that moniker because another town in Ontario already had a similar name.

P

So, in 1914, Tingley renamed the community after Herbert Sylvester Clements, who was, at the time, the local member of Parliament. (It's said that, in appreciation, Clements got the federal government to build a wharf there.) Port Clements is between Masset and Skidegate on Graham Island.

PORT COQUITLAM *See* Coquitlam.

PORT EDWARD (2006: pop. 577) The townsite of this district municipality was laid out in 1908 and named after the reigning British monarch, King Edward VII, by speculators who hoped that the Grand Trunk Pacific Railway would choose it for its Pacific Coast terminus. Prince Rupert was chosen instead, but Port Edward survived and grew nevertheless. The community lies just south of Prince Rupert.

PORT HARDY (2006: pop. 3822) This district municipality was founded in 1904 and named after nearby Hardy Bay, which, in turn, was named by Captain George Richards of the Royal Navy for Vice Admiral Sir Thomas Masterman Hardy, while Richards was surveying the area in 1860. Admiral Hardy is perhaps best known for holding the dying Lord Horatio Nelson in his arms after Nelson was shot at the Battle of Trafalgar in 1805. Port Hardy is at the north end of Vancouver Island.

PORT McNEILL A bay and a community share this name. When the town (2006: pop. 2623) was established as a logging community in 1937, it was placed at the entrance of a bay that had already been called Port McNeill for 100 years. In 1837, officers of the Hudson's Bay Company named the bay for William Henry McNeill. The same year the bay was christened in his honour, this American sea captain took command of the famous HBC vessel, the *Beaver*. It was also the same year that McNeill reported to HBC governor George Simpson that Camosun (now

P

present-day Victoria) was a suitable place for a settlement or trading post. Port McNeill is on the northeast side of Vancouver Island. *See* McNeill Bay.

PORT MOODY Both a bay on the southeast side of Burrard Inlet and the city (2006: pop. 27,512) located there share this name. Captain George Richards named the bay in 1860, in honour of Lieutenant Colonel Richard Moody of the Royal Engineers. Moody was the colonial commissioner of lands and works, and he built roads and surveyed townsites all across British Columbia. The year before, one such road was cut through the forests between New Westminster and this bay. The community was established in 1879.

PORT NEVILLE This is the name of both an inlet and of a small community at its mouth. The inlet was christened by Captain George Vancouver in 1792. The captain did not indicate who he was thinking about when he chose the name, but most seem to think that it was Lieutenant John Neville of the Queen's Regiment of the Royal Marines. The lieutenant was killed two years later onboard Admiral Lord Howe's flagship, the HMS *Queen Charlotte*, at the naval battle known as the Glorious First of June. The community that takes its name from the inlet was established in 1891.

PORT RENFREW This small community (estimated pop. 190) is located on the south side of the inlet known as Port San Juan. For years, settlers along the inlet frequently found their mail misdirected to the San Juan Islands in the United States, so when they applied to the federal government for a regular post office in 1895, they asked that it (and, hence, their community) be called Port Renfrew. The name was an obvious choice. The first settler arrived in the area in 1889, and the townsite was laid out three years later. The first survey of the region was made in 1885 and, by then, the area was already known as

Renfrew. The moniker is probably in honour of Prince Albert Edward, the Prince of Wales and later King Edward VII. The Baron of Renfrew is one of the many titles the prince held, and when he travelled across the United States in 1860, he would often go incognito as Baron or Lord Renfrew.

PORT SAN JUAN / SAN JUAN RIVER The inlet of Port San Juan, located on the west side of Vancouver Island, was originally named Puerto de San Juan o de Narváez ("the Port of St. John or of Narváez") in 1790 by Spanish Navy Sub-Lieutenant Manuel Quimper, when he commanded the *Princesa Real* (the captured British merchant sloop *Princess Royal*). The nearby San Juan River takes its name from the inlet. It is believed that the inlet's original name came from the fact that Spanish explorer José María Narváez arrived there on St. John the Baptist's Day (June 24) the year before. The moniker was probably shortened and partially anglicized by the British Admiralty after the Royal Navy surveyed the area in 1847. The English fur trader John Meares had named the inlet Port Hawkesbury in 1788 after Charles Jenkinson, the 1st Baron Hawkesbury and the president of the Board of Trade, but even though Meares was the first to "discover" the site, the name did not stick.

PORT SIMPSON *See* Lax Kw'alaams.

PORTLAND CANAL / PORTLAND INLET Portland Canal is a 145-kilometre-long channel that extends northward from Wales Island to the community of Stewart. Now part of the border between British Columbia and Alaska, it was named in 1793 by Captain George Vancouver for William Henry Cavendish-Bentinck, the 3rd Duke of Portland, a prominent British politician who briefly served as prime minister in 1783 and became Home Secretary in 1794. Portland Inlet, which extends south from Wales Island to the mouth of the Nass River, was originally named Brown Inlet by Vancouver (possibly for Captain William Brown of the *Butterworth*), but the inlet was renamed in 1924 to reflect common public usage. *See* Bentinck.

PORTLAND ISLAND Located southeast of Saltspring Island, this island was named in 1858 by Captain George Richards for the HMS *Portland*. The vessel was the flagship of Rear Admiral Fairfax Moresby when he commanded the British Fleet's Pacific Station from 1850 to 1853.

POUCE COUPE / POUCE COUPÉ RIVER The village of Pouce Coupe (2006: pop. 739), located 10 kilometres southeast of Dawson Creek, was settled in 1898 and named for the nearby river. The earliest known use of the river's name is found in an 1806 entry in Simon Fraser's journal. Only the river's name has an accent; it disappeared from the community's moniker when the village was incorporated in 1932. Most residents pronounce the name *poos COOPee*, but *poos COOP* and *poos coo-PAY* are also heard. There are two theories behind the name. One is that the river was named after a member of the Dunne-za (Beaver) First Nation called Pooscapee, who trapped along the waterway in about 1800. His name supposedly meant "place where the beavers had a dam and went away and left it" or "(one who) lives near an abandoned beaver lodge." The other is that the river was named after a Sekani First Nation chief or trapper who was nicknamed Pouce Coupé (French for "cut thumb" or "thumb cut off") by both the French Canadian voyageurs and the local First Nations people. He had a hunting cabin along Cut Thumb Creek, north of Mackenzie, and he also hunted in what is now called Pouce Coupé Prairie, between Dawson Creek and the Pouce Coupé River. Depending on which version of the tale you hear, Pouce Coupé either cut off or severely cut his thumb while butchering a moose at Cut Thumb Creek or shot it off by accident, possibly while cleaning his gun.

P

POWELL LAKE / POWELL RIVER Both the lake and the river were named in 1880 by Lieutenant Commander Vere Bernard Orlebar of the HMS *Rocket* for Dr. Israel Wood Powell. At the time, the *Rocket* was taking Powell, who was then British Columbia's Superintendent of Indian Affairs, on a tour of the BC coast. The lake (123 km^2) is on the BC mainland, about 130 kilometres northwest of Vancouver, between Jervis and Toba inlets. It drains into the river that flows into the west end of Malaspina Strait. Logging camps were established near the mouth of the river in the early 1880s, followed by a townsite in 1910 (now a city; 2006: pop. 12,957), which adopted the river's name as its own. It has been said that the First Nation name for the river was Tees Quot (meaning "big river") and that there was a Native village at the river's mouth called Teshquoit, but it has also been suggested that this is local folklore without any basis in fact.

PREMIER RANGE This mountain range (called the Premier Group until 1962) is 10 to 50 kilometres to the west and south of Valemount. In 1927, to mark Canada's 60th birthday, the British Columbia government and the Geographic Board of Canada set aside all the unnamed peaks in this area that exceed 10,000 feet (3048 m) so they could be named as time went on to honour the country's former prime ministers. Four mountains were christened that year, after Sir John Abbott, Sir John Thompson, Sir Mackenzie Bowell and Sir Wilfrid Laurier. A fifth peak was also named for Stanley Baldwin, who, in 1927, became the first British prime minister to visit Canada while in office. Because there were already mountains in BC named for Sir John A. Macdonald, Alexander Mackenzie, Sir Charles Tupper and Sir Robert Borden, it was decided not to christen any more after them. A mountain was named in 1929 for BC Premier John Oliver, who died a year earlier. No further mountains were christened until 1962. Peaks have since been named for Arthur Meighen, Richard Bennett,

Mackenzie King, Louis St-Laurent, John Diefenbaker, Lester Pearson and Pierre Trudeau, as well as for 19th-century Ontario politician Sir Allan MacNab. There are still seven unnamed peaks in the Premier Range that exceed 10,000 feet.

THE PRESIDENT / THE VICE PRESIDENT The President (3123 m) is a mountain located at the north end of Yoho National Park. It was originally named Mount Shaughnessy, after Sir Thomas G. Shaughnessy, the president of the Canadian Pacific Railway, but it was quickly discovered that another mountain in the Selkirks already had that name. At the suggestion of Edward Whymper, the climber of the Matterhorn, the peak was rechristened in 1904 with Shaughnessy's job title. Within five kilometres is another mountain, The Vice President (3077 m), which was also christened that same year after CPR vice-president David McNicoll.

PREVOST Prevost Hill (70 m), seven kilometres northeast of Victoria, was named in 1858 by Captain George Richards in honour of Captain James Charles Prevost. There is also a Prevost Island, east of Saltspring Island, a Prevost Passage, south of Moresby Island in Haro Strait, a Prevost Point on the east side of Kunghit Island and a Mount Prevost (788 m), just northwest of Duncan. All were also christened by Richards in honour of his fellow captain. Prevost commanded the HMS *Virago* in 1853 and the HMS *Satellite* from 1857 to 1860, while those ships were stationed off the British Columbia coast.

PRICE ISLAND Two islands once shared this name; one still has it. Price Island (172 km²), between Laredo and Milbanke sounds, was named by Captain Daniel Pender in 1866 for Captain John Adolphus Pope Price, who commanded the HMS *Scout* while that ship was stationed off the British Columbia coast from 1865 to 1868. The origin

P

of the name of the other Price Island, located off Barkley Sound, is unknown, though one source suggests that it, too, might have been named after Captain Price. The second island was known by that name as far back as 1865. It was renamed Chalk Island in 1945, after William Max Chalk, a native of New Westminster who was a clerk and stenographer with the Pacific Coast Hydrographic Service.

PRINCE GEORGE (2006: pop. 71,030) Simon Fraser established a North West Company trading post on this site in 1807 and called it Fort George, after the reigning British monarch, King George III. Over the following century, not one, but four towns were established in the area: Fort George, Central Fort George, South Fort George and Prince George. The Grand Trunk Pacific Railway (GTP) founded the community of Prince George in 1913. Three explanations have been offered as to the origin of the name. First, GTP vice-president Morley Donaldson said in 1914 that the town was named after the reigning monarch, King George V. However, GTP documents from 1911 indicate that the company picked the name merely to distinguish Prince George from the other three communities (which were not GTP company towns) and that it had no particular "George" in mind. A much more recent theory is that the community was named after 11-year-old Prince George, the youngest son of King George V. In any case, when Central Fort George, South Fort George and Prince George merged in 1915, a vote was taken to decide on the name of the new community. The name Prince George won over Fort George by a vote of 153 to 13. The town of Fort George had disappeared by 1945. Prince George is located 780 kilometres north of Vancouver, near the geographical centre of British Columbia.

PRINCE OF WALES REACH *See* Princess Royal Reach.

PRINCE RUPERT (2006: pop. 12,815) This city on Kaien Island, near the mouth of the Skeena River, was named for

Prince Rupert, the Count Palatine of the Rhine and Duke of Bavaria, who was also a cousin of King Charles II. The king made Rupert the first governor of the Hudson's Bay Company in 1670. The city was established in 1906 by the Grand Trunk Pacific Railway, which determined that it was to be the western terminus of its transcontinental line. To pick a name for the new metropolis, the GTP held a nationwide contest for which more than 12,000 entries were submitted. The winner of the $250 prize (a lot of money back then) was Miss Eleanor Macdonald of Winnipeg, who was the only one to suggest Prince Rupert. However, she also broke the rules and someone made a stink about it. You see, the submitted names were to have no more than three syllables or 10 letters, and Prince Rupert has 12 letters! In the end, the GTP also awarded $250 prizes to the two people who suggested the name Port Rupert.

PRINCESS LOUISA INLET *See* Princess Royal Reach.

PRINCESS ROYAL ISLAND (2248 km²) In 1778, Captain Charles Duncan of the King George's Sound Company (a fur-trading company) named this island for his sloop, the *Princess Royal*. The island lies north of Bella Bella. Princess Royal Island is the fourth largest island in British Columbia. Princess Royal Channel, which separates the island from the BC mainland, was named for the island in 1926.

P

PRINCESS ROYAL REACH This branch of Jervis Inlet, located between Queens Reach and Prince of Wales Reach, was named in honour of Princess Victoria, the Princess Royal and eldest daughter of Queen Victoria, who had recently married Prince Friedrich (Frederick) of Prussia. The prince would later become the Emperor of Germany. Prince of Wales Reach was christened after Princess Victoria's brother, Prince Edward, the Prince of Wales, who would later become King Edward VII. Queens

Reach was named, of course, after Queen Victoria. On the east side of Queens Reach is Princess Louisa Inlet, which was named in honour of Queen Victoria's mother. Less than five kilometres away is Mount Victoria (2088 m), which was christened after Queen Victoria's three-year-old daughter, Her Royal Highness Princess Beatrice Mary Victoria. All these places were named by Captain George Richards in 1860 while he was surveying Jervis Inlet.

PRINCETON (2006: pop. 2677) Located at the junction of the Similkameen and Tulameen rivers between Hope and Penticton, this town was established in 1859 and went through many name changes in its first year. Among the monikers were Red Earth Forks and Vermilion Forks, because of the red ochre found along the banks of the Tulameen River. The ochre was used as face paint by the local First Nations people. (Vermilion is a brilliant red or orange-red coloured pigment.) The community was also known as Allison's after John Fall Allison, the town founder, and as Similkameen after the nearby river. In 1860, colonial governor James Douglas settled the matter by renaming the place Princeton in honour of Prince Albert Edward, the Prince of Wales, who had visited eastern Canada earlier in the year.

P

PROCTER This small resort community near Nelson was founded by real estate speculator Thomas Gregg Procter. He laid out a townsite in 1897 and christened it Kootenay City, but within three years it had been named after him. Maps and Canadian Pacific Railway timetables frequently misspelled the name as Proctor for several decades, perhaps because there was once a local rancher by that name. There was also a Canadian Pacific Railway construction engineer named Proctor who worked the line that went through this town.

PROGRESS This small community, 33 kilometres west of Dawson Creek, was settled in 1916. At a meeting to choose a name for their village, the secretary of the local school board noticed a watermark that read "progress" on his notepaper, and everyone thought it was a perfect moniker for their town.

PROPHET RIVER This river flows just south of Fort Nelson and was called Prophet's River in a 1912 report, before the current moniker was adopted three years later. The name is a translation of its Sekani First Nation name, Na-tint-te. The Sekani prophet that the name refers to might have been Zacharie Dakodoa, who encouraged resistance to local non-Aboriginal settlement, or to one of two other Sekani prophets, Decutla and Notseta.

PURCELL MOUNTAINS This mountain range extends from the Montana border to the south end of Kinbasket Lake and stretches as far west as Kootenay Lake. It was christened in 1859 by Dr. James Hector, one of the chief explorers of the Palliser expedition, in honour of Dr. Goodwin Purcell. Hector took Purcell's classes in therapeutics and medical jurisprudence while attending medical school in Edinburgh. In addition, Purcell and Hector were on the committee that selected the Palliser Expedition's personnel.

P

Q

QUADRA ISLAND (271 km²) Located at the north end of Georgia Strait near Campbell River, this island, along with Maurelle and Sonora islands, was originally thought by early surveyors to be part of one large isle known as Valdes Island. Quadra Island acquired its current name in 1903, when the Geographic Board of Canada christened it after Spanish naval explorer Lieutenant Commander Juan Francisco de la Bodega y Quadra. Quadra visited the British Columbia coast in the late 1770s and again in the early 1790s.

QUADRA MOUNTAIN (3174 m) The Geographic Board of Canada officially adopted this mountain's name in 1924 on the recommendation of mountaineer and surveyor Arthur O. Wheeler. The name refers to the fact that the mountain has four peaks. The moniker was changed to Mount Quadra in 1952 because somebody got the mistaken impression that the mountain was named after Spanish explorer Juan Francisco de la Bodega y Quadra. (According to Canadian mountain naming practices, "Mount" should be used before a given name if the peak is named after a specific person; in all other cases, the given name is followed by "Mountain" or "Peak.") The name was changed back in 1983. Quadra Mountain is on the Alberta border, in Kootenay National Park.

QUALICUM Settlers first arrived at the mouth of the Little Qualicum River in 1878. The river is on the east coast of Vancouver Island approximately halfway between Comox and Nanaimo. A townsite was laid out and christened Qualicum Beach (2006: pop. 8502) in 1910.

Just a few kilometres to the northwest are the larger Qualicum River, as well as a harbour and a small community (2006: pop. 397), both called Qualicum Bay after the rivers. In 1864, explorer Robert Brown called the waterway the "Quall-e-hum River," and the name might be even older, because Adam Grant Horne opened a trail between Qualicum River and the Alberni Inlet in 1856. The name of the rivers was also spelled Quallchum during the 19th century. Qualicum is a derivation of the Pentlatch First Nation word *sqal-li* or *sqaul-li*, which means "where the dog salmon run."

QUATHIASKI COVE Both the cove and the community (2006: pop. 382) named after it are located on the southwest side of Quadra Island. No one knows who chose the name or when it was first applied to the cove, but the moniker is found on British Admiralty charts from 1862. The community was established sometime during the late 19th century, and a post office opened there in 1899. Quathiaski is a derivation of the Comox First Nation word *qafsásken*, which has been variously translated as "island in the mouth" and "small item in large mouth," both of which refer to the small islet, Grouse Island, at the cove's entrance.

Q

QUATSINO / QUATSINO SOUND Quatsino Sound is a fjord on the northwest coast of Vancouver Island that goes east about 18 kilometres from the Pacific before it branches off into Holberg, Neroutsos and Rupert inlets. The community of Quatsino (2006: pop. 234) is located on the north shore of Quatsino Sound. The sound was labelled Quatsinough Harbour on 1849 British Admiralty maps. History does not record who first applied the name to the sound; it is shown, but not labelled, in Commander Dionisio Alcala Galiano's charts of the area from 1792 and on Captain George Vancouver's maps from 1792 to 1794. The community was established in 1894–95 as a colony for Norwegian immigrants from North

Dakota and was called Scandia (as in Scandinavia) until it was renamed Quatsino in 1896. Some sources incorrectly say that Quatsino is a derivation of the name of the Koskimo (or Koskimox, now spelled G_u sgimukw) tribe of the Quatsino First Nation. However, in the 19th century, the G_u sgimukw resided in the inner waters of Quatsino Sound. Instead, the name comes from the Quatsino, or Quatsinox, now spelled Gwat {sinux_w, of the Quatsino First Nation, who lived along the shore of northwest Vancouver Island. The Quatsino First Nation is one of the Kwakwaka'wakw (Kwakiutl) First Nations whose members speak the Kwakw'ala language. *Gwat {sinux_w* is a Kwak'wala word that has been variously translated to mean "people of the north country," "the downstream people" and "people who live on the other side" (i.e., the other side of Vancouver Island).

QUEEN CHARLOTTE This is the name of a sound, a strait, a village, and a mountain range. It was also once the name of a large group of islands located across Hecate Strait from Prince Rupert.

Queen Charlotte Sound extends 175 kilometres from the south tip of Kunghit Island to the north end of Vancouver Island. Most authorities say it was named in 1786 by Mr. S. Wedgborough of the trading vessel *Experiment* in honour of King George III's wife, Queen Charlotte. Although Captain George Vancouver wrote in his journal that Wedgborough was the commander of the *Experiment*, it has been suggested that Wedgborough was either only in temporary command or merely an officer on the ship. Also, one historian says it wasn't Wedgborough, but English fur trader James Strange who named the sound in 1786 during a boat excursion up the Goletas Channel. If true, then what Strange christened as "Queen Charlotte Sound" was actually Queen Charlotte Strait. The strait, located between the north end of Vancouver Island and the British Columbia mainland, was not named until 1920. Until that time, maps just labelled it as part of Queen Charlotte Sound, but after some discussion between the British Admiralty's Hydrographic Service and British Columbia's chief geographer about the difference between a "strait" and a "sound," it was decided to call this body of water a "strait."

North of Queen Charlotte Sound and about 130 kilometres west of Prince Rupert across Hecate Strait is an archipelago that was known until recently as the Queen Charlotte Islands. They were given that name in 1787 by Captain George Dixon of the King George's Sound Company for his ship, the *Queen Charlotte*, which in turn was named for the king's bride. An agreement was reached in 2009 between the Haida First Nation, who reside on the islands, and the British Columbia government to officially rename the Queen Charlotte Islands as Haida Gwaii, which means, in the Haida language, "Islands of the People."

The community of Queen Charlotte (2006: pop. 948), on the southeast side of Graham Island (the largest island in Haida Gwaii), grew around a sawmill that opened in 1908. Once simply called The Townsite, it was quickly renamed Queen Charlotte. Its moniker was later changed to Queen Charlotte City in 1980 and to the Village of Queen Charlotte in 2005. The Queen Charlotte Mountains extend from the north end of Graham Island to the south end of Moresby Island.

QUEEN CHARLOTTE CHANNEL This channel on the south end of Howe Sound and east of Bowen Island was named by Captain George Richards in about 1860 for the HMS *Queen Charlotte*. The 110-gun vessel was the flagship of Admiral Richard Howe, the 1st Earl Howe, at the 1794 naval battle known as the Glorious First of June.

QUEENSBOROUGH *See* New Westminster.

QUEENS REACH *See* Princess Royal Reach.

QUESNEL A lake, a river, two communities and a famous ghost town share this name. North West Company explorer and fur trader Simon Fraser named the Quesnel River in 1808 for Jules Maurice Quesnel, a NWC clerk who accompanied him when he explored the river. The waterway flows northwest and meets the Fraser River 117 kilometres south of Prince George. Quesnel Lake (256 km²) is 75 kilometres southeast of the city of Quesnel and drains into the Quesnel River. It is the deepest lake in British Columbia and the deepest fjord-lake in the world. The lake was named after the river; it is labelled Quesnel Lake on 1871 maps, but the name might be older, because gold mining began along the lake in 1859.

The city of Quesnel (2006: pop. 9326) sits at the point where the Fraser and Quesnel rivers meet. The community was established in the early 1860s during the Cariboo Gold Rush and was initially called Quesnelle Mouth because it is located at the mouth of the Quesnel River. The smaller community of Quesnel View lies just south of the city. The ghost town of Quesnel Forks (originally spelled Quesnelle Forks) was located near the west end of Quesnel Lake. Settled in 1860, for a brief time during the gold rush, it was the largest community on the British Columbia mainland.

Q

R

RADIUM HOT SPRINGS This name is shared by a hot springs and the village (2066: pop. 735) that surrounds it. Local First Nations people had used the springs for centuries before Hudson's Bay Company governor George Simpson visited the area in 1841. The first non-Aboriginal name for the springs was Sinclair Hot Springs. James Sinclair was hired by the HBC in 1841 to bring settlers from the Red River community in present-day Manitoba to Oregon, and he did so by way of the Sinclair Canyon, which is near the springs. Sources differ as to whether the springs were named after the canyon or after Sinclair himself. The settlement that grew around the springs was first called Sinclair, but both the springs and the community were renamed in 1915. The moniker comes from the high radium content (and, hence, a high level of radioactivity) in the hot springs' water.

RAMBLER PEAK *See* Ms. Mountain.

READ ISLAND (56 km²; 2006: pop. 62) One of the Discovery Islands at the north end of Georgia Strait, this island was named by Captain Daniel Pender in about 1864 for Captain William Viner Read, who was, at the time, the naval assistant to the British Admiralty's Hydrographic Office in London, England.

REDONDA ISLANDS This pair of islands is located at the mouth of Toba Inlet. Spanish explorers Juan Francisco de la Bodega y Quadra and Cayetano Valdés y Flores spotted them in 1792, thought they were a single island and christened them Isla Redonda. In fact, East and West Redonda islands (100 km² and 172 km², respectively) are separated by Waddington Channel. The individual names for the two islands were not officially conferred until 1952. *Redonda* is the Spanish word for "round" and is presumably associated with the shape of Isla Redonda on Quadra's and Valdés' 1795 charts.

REID ISLAND (0.91 km²) This island, located between Galiano and Thetis islands, was named by Captain George Richards in 1859 in honour of James Murray Reid, a seaman whose 28-year career with the Hudson's Bay Company culminated in his being, from 1852 to 1854, the captain of the HBC's brigantine *Vancouver,* which sailed off British Columbia's coast. The *Vancouver* ran aground in a storm and was burned to prevent its cargo of rum from falling into the hands of the Haida First Nation, thus ending Reid's association with the HBC. Reid was a successful merchant in Victoria when Richards christened the island after him.

RESPLENDENT MOUNTAIN (3408 m) This mountain was named in 1908 by geologist and academic Arthur P. Coleman when he explored the area. According to the dictionary, an item is resplendent when it is vividly bright or shines with a brilliant lustre and that was the word that came to Coleman's mind when he saw the light glimmering off the snow on this mountain. Resplendent Mountain is at the north end of Mount Robson Provincial Park.

REVELSTOKE (2006: pop. 7230) This city is on the Columbia River between Golden and Vernon. Its general location was originally called The Eddy, after a large circling current of water in the Columbia that had eroded the river's west bank. It was renamed Second Crossing in the 1870s when the Canadian Pacific Railway surveyed the area; the railway's proposed line would first cross the Columbia River near Donald, and then a second time at Revelstoke. A government surveyor, Arthur Farwell, laid out a townsite on the east bank of the river in 1880 and named it after himself. A small community was quickly established, but when the CPR finally arrived in 1885, it refused to pay Farwell's high price for a right-of-way on his land. In retaliation, the company laid out its own townsite just to the east, built a railway station there and called it Revelstoke. As a result, the city had two distinct business districts well into the 20th century. The Farwell post office, which had been open for only four months at this time, was renamed Revelstoke in June 1886.

The name Revelstoke honours Edward Charles Baring, the 1st Baron Revelstoke, who was the head of the Baring Brothers banking house in London, England. During the last days of the building of the transcontinental railway line, Baring Brothers purchased $15 million of CPR stock, thus averting a financial crisis. Eight kilometres away is Mount Revelstoke (1959 m), which was named after the community in 1910. Also nearby is the Revelstoke Dam, which was built in the 1970s, and the reservoir created by the dam, Lake Revelstoke, which was named in 1985.

RICHMOND (2006: pop. 174,461) This city is located south of Vancouver on Lulu and Sea islands at the mouth of the Fraser River. It began with Hugh McRoberts, who came to British Columbia in 1858 for the Cariboo Gold Rush. McRoberts was the first settler on Sea Island in 1861 and acquired 630 hectares in 1862 for farming. According to one source, it eventually became the largest farm in the British Empire. McRoberts called his place Richmond or Richmond View, and, in 1862, the *British Columbian* newspaper printed a story called "A Visit to Richmond." Most sources say the name was chosen by McRobert's daughter to commemorate one of her favourite places in Australia, possibly the town of Richmond near Sydney. (McRoberts was Irish but lived in Australia before coming to BC.) However, it has been pointed out that McRobert's wife was a native of Richmond in Yorkshire, England. Also, Mary Boyd, who did not arrive in Richmond until 1863

R

but was the wife of Hugh Boyd, the first "warden" (i.e., reeve or mayor) of the city, claimed that the community was christened after her hometown, which, coincidentally, was also Richmond in Yorkshire, England. Finally, it has also been suggested by some that the city was named after Richmond in Surrey, England.

RIONDEL (2006: pop. 291) This retirement community on the northeast side of Kootenay Lake was originally a mining town and the site of the famous Bluebell Mine. It was originally called Hendryx, after the Hendryx brothers, Andrew and Wilbur, who formed a syndicate that mined and processed the galena deposits found in the area from 1885 to 1896. The village was rechristened in 1907 after Count Edouard Riondel, the president of the French-owned Canadian Metal Company, which had acquired the Bluebell mine two years earlier. Company executive S.S. Fowler chose the name when he applied to the government for a post office.

RISKE CREEK The first settler of this small community, 47 kilometres southwest of Williams Lake, was a Polish immigrant named L.W. Riskie, who arrived there in 1868. (Notice the misspelling in the village's name.) When the post office opened in 1886 with Riskie as the first postmaster, it (and, hence, the town) was called Chilcoten. The spelling of that moniker was changed to Chilcotin in 1911, and the current name was adopted the year after that.

RIVER JORDAN *See* Jordan River.

RIVERS INLET This 48-kilometre-long fjord is located west of where Fitz Hugh and Smith sounds meet. The inlet was named Rivers Channel by Captain George Vancouver in 1792 after British politician and writer George Pitt, the 1st Baron Rivers. Thomas Pitt, a midshipman on Vancouver's vessel, the HMS *Discovery*, was a relative of the baron. From the 1880s to the 1950s, a number of

R

canneries, along with logging and trapping, supported a once-thriving community, also called Rivers Inlet, on the inlet's shores.

ROBERTS CREEK (2006: pop. 1966) This community on the Sunshine Coast between Gibsons and Sechelt and the creek that runs through it were both named for its earliest settlers, Thomas William "Will" Roberts and his family, who arrived in 1889.

ROBSON (2006: pop. 464) Founded in 1891, this community was originally named Sproats Landing after the local gold commissioner, Gilbert Sproat. It was rechristened in 1892 after John Robson, the recently deceased premier of British Columbia. Robson is four kilometres northwest of Castlegar.

ROCKY MOUNTAINS The largest mountain range in North America extends 4800 kilometres from northern Mexico, through the western United States, British Columbia and Alberta, to Alaska and the Yukon. Various First Nations peoples have known about and crossed the mountains over the centuries, and each has their own name for the range. The first non-Aboriginal reference to the mountains is found in a 1716 entry in the diary of John Knight, the governor of York Factory, in which he wrote that some "Mountain Indians" told him that they came from a place that was "very mountainous and of a prodigious height." The earliest known reference to the mountains by their current name was by French Canadian soldier Jacques Legardeur de St-Pierre, who called them "Montagnes de Roche" in his journal in 1752.

RODERICK ISLAND (238 km²) Located on the east side of Finlayson Channel, this island was named in about 1866 by Captain Daniel Pender for Roderick Finlayson. A Hudson's Bay Company official, Finlayson was made second-in-command at the HBC post at Fort Victoria in 1843 and was in charge there from 1844 to 1849. He is regarded by many as the founder of Victoria. Finlayson Channel, as well as other islands in the channel, are also named after Finlayson and members of his family. *See* Finlayson Channel.

ROGERS PASS This famous passage through the Selkirk Mountains was discovered by American engineer and surveyor Albert Bowman Rogers on his 52nd birthday, May 28, 1881. At the time, Rogers was in charge of the Mountain Division of the Canadian Pacific Railway and was responsible for finding a route through the Rocky and Selkirk mountains for the CPR's transcontinental line. The pass was named for Rogers by railway builder and CPR director James J. Hill, who promised that if Rogers found a useful pass, he would christen it after him. Rogers Pass is in Glacier National Park.

ROLLA (2006: pop. 119) This community is about 12 kilometres northeast of Dawson Creek. Its first settler and postmaster was L.H. Miller, who arrived in 1912 and named the community after his hometown of Rolla, Missouri.

ROOSVILLE Located on the east side of Lake Koocanusa on the American border, this small community dates back to at least the late 1890s. It was once called Phillips, possibly after nearby Phillipps Creek or after Michael (or Michel) Phillipps, a long-time Elko resident, Hudson's Bay Company employee and Indian Agent for the government, for whom the creek was named. (The creek's moniker was frequently misspelled as Phillips on old maps and documents.) The settlement was rechristened in 1908 when Fred Roo, who arrived there in 1899 and built a store and hotel, became the first postmaster and named the post office (and, hence, the town) after himself. Just across the border is Roosville, Montana.

R

ROSSLAND (2006: pop. 3278) There are two stories about how this city acquired its name, and both involve local miner Ross Thompson. In one, Thompson acquired 65 hectares in the area in 1890 or 1893, laid out a townsite and started to build. He named the place Thompson after himself, but the postal authorities thought the name might cause some confusion because there was already another settlement called Thompson Landing (now a ghost town) on the shores of the Arrow Lakes. As a result, Thompson rechristened the townsite Rossland in 1894. The other story is that Thompson had staked four mining claims in the area in 1889–90. He also lived and hunted in the area, and his neighbours jokingly referred to his cabin and the surrounding territory as Ross' Land. Supposedly, when the townsite was established, the name stuck. Rossland is 10 kilometres west of Trail. Rossland Pass and the Rossland Range are nearby.

ROY This ghost town is located on the southeast side of Loughborough Inlet. It began as a mining settlement in the 1890s, and logging and a salmon cannery later became major employers. There are two versions of how Roy acquired its name. One is that it was simply named after a "Mr. Roy," who was an early settler. Another is that the first postmaster, D. McGregor, named the post office (and, hence, the town) in 1896 after the famous Scotsman Rob Roy because Roy's real surname was MacGregor.

ROYAL GROUP *See* Mount King George.

ROYAL ROADS In 1846, Captain Henry Kellet, the commanding officer of the HMS *Herald*, christened this body of water Royal Bay. Royal Bay and Royal Roads were both given on navigational charts, but the latter became more and more generally used, until the Geographic Board of Canada made it the official name in 1910. The name refers to the fact that the city named after Queen Victoria is on one side of the bay, and on the

R

other side is Albert Head, which was named after her consort, Prince Albert.

ROYSTON (2006: pop. 1718) This community's first settlers, William Roy and his family, arrived in 1890. Twenty years later, Roy and real estate promoter Frederick Warren laid out a townsite that they called Royston. The moniker is a tip of the hat to both Roy and to the fact that Warren came from Royston in Cambridgeshire, England. Royston is five kilometres south of Courtenay.

RYKERTS This small community lies on the American border south of Creston. It dates back to 1883, when former North West Mounted policeman John Charles Rykert was sent there to build a customs office. The Bedlington and Nelson Railway built a station at the site in 1898, and the village that grew around it was called Bedlington. The current moniker was adopted in 1948.

R

S

SAANICH This name is shared by a peninsula, an inlet, a bay (Saanichton Bay), three incorporated municipalities (Saanich, 2006: pop. 108,265; Central Saanich, 2006: pop. 15,745; and North Saanich, 2006: pop. 10,823) and three unincorporated communities (East Saanich, South Saanich and Saanichton), all of them just north of Victoria. The moniker dates back to the 1860s, when the first non-Aboriginal settlers arrived on the peninsula. Saanich is a derivation of the name of the Wsanec (Saanich) First Nation, who live on the peninsula. Wsanec means "raised up" and, when applied to the land, refers to the fact that the area appears higher than the surrounding territory when viewed from a distance. When referring to the people of the Wsanec First Nation, the name takes on a similar meaning—"emerging people."

SALMO / SALMO RIVER The river was originally christened Salmon River in 1859 for the fish that were abundant in its waters before a local dam destroyed the runs. The village (2006: pop. 1007) that sits on its banks was originally established as Salmon Siding in 1893. The community, and probably the river as well, was renamed Salmo four years later. *Salmo* is Latin for salmon.

SALMON ARM (2006: pop. 16,012) Located at the southwest end of Shuswap Lake, there once were two communities, an incorporated district municipality and a village, that shared this name. The two merged in 1970. The name dates back to the mid-1880s, when the creeks and rivers flowing into the southwest arm—the Salmon Arm—of the lake were so full of salmon that early settlers used

S

pitchforks to pluck them out of the water for use as fertilizer on their farms.

SALMON RIVER Seven rivers in British Columbia share this name, but by far the longest stretches 74 kilometres, from the mountains of Strathcona Provincial Park on Vancouver Island to the Johnstone Strait. It is not clear when the name was attached to this river, but it was certainly during the 19th century. The moniker derives from the fact that the river is reputed to contain the largest steelhead salmon on Vancouver Island.

SALTAIR (2006: pop. 538) This small community is located just southeast of Ladysmith. The entire area as far as Chemainus was originally known as the "Oyster District in the Chemainus Country" or, more simply, as Oyster, because of the rich oyster beds. When Ladysmith, which is located in the middle of the old "Oyster District," was established and took its name in 1900, the remaining pieces of the district were called North and South Oyster, but that led to a lot of confusion. Finally, in 1910 (or 1912, depending on the source), a new railway station was built in South Oyster, and a number of submissions were made as to what it should be called. The one picked by the Esquimalt and Nanaimo Railway was Mrs. W.W. Southin's suggestion, Saltair, which is descriptive of the air along the nearby Strait of Georgia. Like many other communities, the new name of the railway station also became the name of the town.

SALTSPRING ISLAND (**informally called Salt Spring Island**) (179 km²; 2006: pop. 9780) The largest island in the Strait of Georgia has gone through several names. It was called Chuan Island in an 1854 report from Vancouver Island's colonial governor, James Douglas. The name was also spelled Chouan elsewhere. Douglas got the moniker from the Cowichan First Nation name for Mount Tuam, which is located on the south end of the island.

S

The Cowichan called the peak Tsuween, which means either "facing the sea" or "where the land or mountain comes down to the water" and the island Klaathem, which translates as "salt." The Saanich First Nation referred to the island as Cuan, which means "each end," in reference to the small mountains at either end of the island.

In 1856, the isle was christened Salt Spring Island by Hudson's Bay Company officers because of the large number of springs containing briny or salty water, which the company hoped to exploit. Captain George Richards then renamed the place Admiral Island in 1859 after Rear Admiral Robert Baynes, the commander-in-chief of the British Pacific Station. Baynes had arrived in British Columbia with the HMS *Ganges* the year before. That remained the island's official name for several decades, but the local residents simply ignored it and continued to call the place Salt Spring Island. The Geographic Board of Canada succumbed to local usage and changed the name in 1910, but only after putting the words "salt" and "spring" together into "saltspring," as the Board often does when it comes to multiple-word names. Most locals, however, still call their home Salt Spring Island. Several places on the island retain the names that Richards gave them in 1859, such as Baynes Peak (formerly Mount Baynes) and Ganges Harbour.

SANDON This famous ghost town was named after John Sandon, the man who discovered silver in the area in 1891. Other settlers and miners quickly started to arrive and, when a post office was opened there four years later, both it and the community were christened after Sandon. The settlement was incorporated as a city in 1898 and once had a population of 4000, but it has been virtually abandoned since 1941. Sandon is located 10 kilometres east of New Denver.

SAN JUAN RIVER *See* Port San Juan.

SANDSPIT (2006: pop. 387) This community on the north-east tip of Moresby Island was preceded by at least one ancient Haida First Nation village, which was called Kil. Sandspit is located on one of the only two natural spits (points of flat, low land that extend from a shore into a body of water) in Haida Gwaii (Queen Charlotte Islands). The first permanent non-Aboriginal settlers arrived in about 1900 to establish a cattle ranch on the spit. It is not clear when the name was first used, but it was officially adopted in 1946.

SARAH ISLAND (92 km²) This island in Finlayson Channel was named after Sarah Finlayson, the wife of Hudson's Bay Company official Roderick Finlayson, for whom the channel was christened. Sarah Finlayson said in her later years that the island was given its moniker by Captain Charles Dodd of the HBC steamer *Beaver* in about 1845. Other sources say, however, that it was Captain Daniel Pender who, as a later commander of the *Beaver*, gave the island its name in 1866 or 1867. The latter is more likely, because Sarah did not marry Finlayson until 1849. Directly across Sarah Passage, which is also named for Sarah Finlayson, is Jane Island. There is no doubt that Captain Pender named this smaller island for Sarah Finlayson's sister (and Dr. William Tolmie's wife), Jane Tolmie. Dr. Tolmie is the namesake of nearby Tolmie Channel.

S

SARATOGA BEACH (2006: pop. 1587) This community, south of the city of Campbell River, was named after a nearby resort and trailer park. The resort was christened in the 1930s, though sources differ as to whether it was named for Saratoga, California, or after the popular tourist destination of Saratoga Springs, New York.

SARDIS Settlers began to arrive at this present-day Chilliwack neighbourhood in 1866. One of them, Adam Swart Vedder, came four years later. When his wife was asked to name the community, she opened her Bible at random and placed her finger on a page from the Book of Revelation. It landed on Revelations 3:4, on the name Sardis. Sardis was one of the "seven churches of Asia" and now sits in ruins in western Turkey.

SATURNA / SATURNA ISLAND (31 km²) Saturna Island was named in 1791 by Spanish naval officer and explorer José María Narváez for his ship, the *Santa Saturnina*. Spanish charts as far back as 1795 mislabelled the place as Isla de Saturna because of a map engraver's error, and the mistake was never corrected. Settlers began to arrive in the 1870s. The community of Saturna (2006: pop. 359) was originally called Pikes Landing after wealthy English big-game hunter Warburton Pike, who moved to the island and established a sheep ranch in 1886. The land that Pike owned on the island included what is now called Mount Warburton Pike (401 m). Saturna Island is southeast of Saltspring Island.

SAVONA (estimated pop. 650) This community is located on the southwest side of Kamloops Lake, where the Thompson River flows out of the lake. It was named for François Saveneux, a stockman from Corsica, who arrived in BC in 1858. His surname was so difficult to pronounce that he became known by the name of his native city, Savona. Saveneux established a ferry that crossed between the north and south sides of Kamloops Lake for the miners who had arrived to participate in the Cariboo Gold Rush. On the north side, where the ferry picked up and dropped off passengers, was a Hudson's Bay Company post, and the settlement that grew around the post was called Savona's Ferry. In the early 1880s, the Canadian Pacific Railway was laying tracks on the south side of the lake, and another town, called Port Van Horne (after CPR general manager William Cornelius Van Horne), was established directly opposite Savona's Ferry. The residents of Savona's Ferry all moved to Port Van Horne but applied their old town's name to their new residence. Perhaps this

S

was because Van Horne himself once visited Port Van Horne and apparently felt that it was beneath him. The name Port Van Horne quickly disappeared, and the town on the south side of the lake became the new Savona's Ferry. The moniker was shortened to Savona around 1910. Visitors should note that he community's name is pronounced *SAV-an-aw* not *sa-VONE-ah* like the town in Italy.

SAYWARD (2006: pop. 341) This village is located southwest of the mouth of the Salmon River on Vancouver Island. Originally called Salmon Arm when the first settlers arrived in the 1890s, it became known as Port Kusam when a post office opened there in 1899 and was rechristened Sayward 12 years later. This logging community took its current moniker from the surrounding Sayward Land District, which, in turn, was named after William Parsons Sayward, the largest lumber merchant on the island in the late 19th century.

SEA ISLAND This island is south of Vancouver at the mouth of the Fraser River. It is one of the two islands on which the city of Richmond is located. It is also the home of the Vancouver International Airport. It was initially called McRoberts' Island after Hugh McRoberts, the first settler, who arrived on the island in 1861 and established a farm that he called Richmond or Richmond View. It eventually became the largest farm in the British Empire. It is not clear when the island's name was changed, but it is believed to have been done by Colonel Richard Moody of the Royal Engineers in 1862 or 1863 when his men surveyed the Lower Mainland.

SEAFORTH CHANNEL This sea passage, east of Milbanke Sound, was named after British politician and general Francis Humberston Mackenzie, who was ennobled the Lord Seaforth, Baron Mackenzie of Kintail. His most famous act was to raise a regiment that later became part of the famous Seaforth Highlanders, from which Canada's Seaforth Highlanders take their name. The exact details are no longer known, but the channel was apparently christened by officers of the Hudson's Bay Company sometime in the mid-19th century. The name is found on British Admiralty charts as far back as 1872.

SECHELT A peninsula, an inlet, a lake, a district municipality and an Indian Government District on the Sunshine Coast, all about 50 kilometres northwest of Vancouver, share this name. It is not clear when the name was first used by non-Aboriginals, but a Roman Catholic Oblate mission was established at the site of the present-day community (2006: pop. 8454) in 1868. The first settlers arrived in 1893, and a post office called Sechelt opened in 1896. Other spellings recorded through the years include Seashelth, Seshal and Sicatl. Most sources say that Sechelt is a derivation of the name of the Shíshálh (Sechelt) First Nation, who live in the area. A Northern Coast Salish people, the Shíshálh speak the Sháshíshálem (or Salishan) language, and the word *shíshálh* means "land between two waters." This refers to the fact that a little strip of land no more than one kilometre wide (where the present-day community of Sechelt sits) separates Sechelt Inlet from the Strait of Georgia and connects the Sechelt Peninsula with the British Columbia mainland. It has also been suggested that Sechelt is an anglicization of ʃíʃáł, which is a Comox First Nation place name for the Sechelt Peninsula.

S

SELKIRK MOUNTAINS Explorer David Thompson named this mountain range Nelson's Mountains in 1807, in honour of British naval hero Lord Horatio Nelson, who was killed two years earlier at the Battle of Trafalgar. However, when the Hudson's Bay Company and the North West Company merged in 1821, the mountains were rechristened after Thomas Douglas, the 5th Earl of Selkirk, who died the year before. Selkirk was a part owner of the

HBC, with a large enough share that he practically controlled its board of directors. He is also well known for bringing Scottish colonists to Canada. The mountain range extends 350 kilometres from the junction of Kinbasket Lake and Lake Revelstoke south to the American border, between Kootenay Lake and the Arrow Lakes. It is one of the four mountain ranges in south-central British Columbia that make up the Columbia Mountains system.

Northeast of Invermere, in Kootenay National Park, are two mountains also named after the earl, Mount Selkirk (2930 m), christened in 1886 by geologist George Dawson during his travels, and Mount Daer (2950 m). It is not clear when Mount Daer first got its name, but it may have been from Dawson as well. Lord Daer was the title of the heirs of the Earldom of Selkirk, and Thomas Douglas held the title before he became the 5th Earl in 1799. There is a third mountain that bears Selkirk's name—Selkirk Peak (2324 m), which lies four kilometres southwest of Sandon, in the Selkirk Mountains.

SETON A lake, a river, a community and a ghost town share this name. Seton Lake, located west of Lillooet on the west side of Fraser River, was named in 1858 by fur trader Alexander Caulfield Anderson, who came across it while searching for a passable route between Harrison Lake and Lillooet. The lake was named for Anderson's relative, Lieutenant Colonel Alexander Seton, who commanded the soldiers on the HMS *Birkenhead*, a British troopship that sank near the Cape of Good Hope in 1852. While allowing their wives and families to take the few lifeboats on the ship, Seton and 453 of his men famously lined up at attention and met their fate. Just west of the lake is the community of Seton Portage (estimated pop. 250). Originally called Seton Lake, it was established soon after the Fraser River Gold Rush began in 1858, and, in 1861, it became the site of the first railway in British Columbia.

Its name was changed to Seton Portage in 1952. Locals pronounce it the English way, *POR-tij*, and not the French way, *port-AWZH*. Just north of the town is Seton River. Named Birkenhead Strait by Anderson in 1858, it connects Anderson and Seton lakes. Its name was changed to Seton Creek in 1917 and to Seton River in 1951. On the east end of Seton Lake was once the village of Seton (also sometimes called Seton Foot), which is now a ghost town. *See* Anderson Lake and Birken/Birkenhead.

SEYMOUR INLET / BELIZE INLET Seymour Inlet, a long fjord on the coast of the British Columbia mainland at the north end of Queen Charlotte Strait, and the even longer Belize Inlet to its immediate south, were both discovered and named in 1865 by Captain Daniel Pender of the *Beaver*. The inlets were named in honour of Frederick Seymour, who was then the colonial governor of British Columbia. Belize was the name of the capital of British Honduras (now the country of Belize), where Seymour had been the colonial governor before he came to British Columbia in 1864.

SEYMOUR NARROWS This sea passage northwest of Campbell River was named in 1846 by Commander George T. Gordon of the HM steam sloop *Cormorant*, in honour of Rear Admiral Sir George Francis Seymour. The admiral was then in command of the British fleet's Pacific Station.

S

SHALALTH / SOUTH SHALALTH The small community of Shalalth (estimated pop. 400) is on the northwest shore of Seton Lake, and the community of South Shalalth is at the west tip of the lake. Shalalth is an old St'át'imc (Lillooet) First Nation village. From 1927 to 1937, it was called Bridge River, after the nearby river that flows from Seton Lake into the Fraser River, just north of Lillooet. South Shalalth was built in the 1920s as a company town during the Bridge River hydroelectric power project.

It was initially christened Bridge River but was often simply called "camp" by its residents. The current name was taken from the Pacific Great Eastern Railway station that was built here. Shalalth is a derivation of the St'át'imc place name for Seton Lake, Tsal'álh, which means "the lake." Tsal'álh was also the St'át'imc name for the village that is now known as Shalalth.

SHAUGHNESSY The large block of land that comprises this Vancouver neighbourhood was once owned by the Canadian Pacific Railway. In the years just before the beginning of World War I in 1914, the CPR turned this area into an exclusive residential community for Vancouver's elite. It was named Shaughnessy Heights, after CPR president Sir Thomas G. Shaughnessy. *See also* Marpole.

SHAWNIGAN LAKE A lake (5.4 km²) between Duncan and Victoria and the community (2006: pop. 1262) on its northeast corner share this name. The first time the moniker is known to have been applied to the lake is on an 1859 map. The community's first permanent residents arrived in 1886, and the name was quickly applied to the settlement as well. There are several theories as to the moniker's origin. Many are secondhand stories suggesting that Shawnigan comes from some First Nation word (which never seems to be identified), and a large number of interpretations have been suggested, including "lake of many shadows," "the place where Indians went to hunt and camp," "something is happening that I don't understand" and "shady gulch." One story has it that the local First Nations people called the lake Sha-ni-gan, meaning "abode of evil spirits," because they angered their gods when they fought a senseless battle on the lake. Because the bloody fight was the result of greed and injustice, the gods in their wrath vowed to kill any First Nation person who afterwards tried to cross the lake. No linguist, however, has been able to connect Shawnigan

S

with any known First Nation word from British Columbia. It has been suggested that the moniker is a combination of the names of two early settlers, Shaw and Finnegan, but there is no record of anybody with either name living in the area when the name was first applied to the lake. Some think the lake was christened by a colourful local mid-19th-century First Nation guide, Tomo Antoine, who apparently knew many languages and possibly took the moniker from one of them. Finally, a recent history of the local Cowichan First Nation suggests that the name may come from the Cowichan place name for the lake, Sha'weluqun.

SHUSWAP Two lakes, a river and two communities share this name. The large, H-shaped Shuswap Lake (315 km^2) is 75 kilometres northeast of Kamloops. Little Shuswap Lake is just west of it, near Chase. The river is directly south of Shuswap Lake, and the community of Shuswap (2006: pop. 169) lies southwest of Little Shuswap Lake. About 30 kilometres east of Vernon is Shuswap Falls (2006: pop. 145). All are named after the people of the Secwepemc First Nation—Shuswap is an anglicization of the name Secwepemc. Evidence indicates that the Secwepemc have lived around Shuswap Lake for more than 9000 years, and there were a number of Secwepemc villages around the lake in the mid-19th century. Today, the Secwepemc mostly live near the west end of the lake. Non-Aboriginal settlement of the area began in the 1880s, with the arrival of the Canadian Pacific Railway.

S

Explorer David Thompson named the river the Sheewap River on his 1813 map, and a chart from 1832 labels Shuswap Lake as Schewhap Lake. An 1837 map refers to both Shoushwap Lake and the Shoushwap River. Fur traders also spelled the name She Whaps and Shoo-Schawps. The current spelling of Shuswap was in common usage by 1871. The river was also called the Spallymsheen, the

Spellmacheen and the Spillemeechene in the 1860s and '70s. *See* Spallumcheen.

SICAMOUS / SICAMOUS NARROWS The first settlers arrived in Sicamous (2006: pop. 2676) in 1885. The district municipality on the southeast end of Shuswap Lake was named for the nearby Sicamous Narrows, which separate Mara Lake from Shuswap Lake. The narrows were labelled as Schikmouse Narrows on an 1866 map and as Schickmous Narrows on an 1871 map. George Dawson called them the Shick-a-mows Narrows in an 1877 report. The narrows, in turn, were named after a branch of the Secwepemc (Shuswap) First Nation that called them the Scheckmoos or Schickamoos. The name has been interpreted to mean "narrow," "in the middle" or "place cut through" and is believed to refer to the narrows' location between Mara and Shuswap lakes.

SIDNEY / SIDNEY ISLAND The town of Sidney (2006: pop. 11,315), located near the tip of the Saanich Peninsula, was settled in the 1880s and named after Sidney Island (8.9 km²), which lies five kilometres offshore. The island, in turn, was originally called Sallas Island, though sources conflict as to whether that was the name given to it by officers of the Hudson's Bay Company in about 1850 or by the local Coast Salish First Nation people. Captain George Richards gave the isle its current name in 1859. It is presumed that he did so in honour of Lieutenant Frederick W. Sidney, a hydrographer in the British Admiralty who entered the service only a few months after Richards and who, like Richards, joined the surveying branch of the navy.

SILVERTON (2006: pop. 185) There is some uncertainty about the origin of this village's name. It was originally called Four-Mile City when it was established in 1892; some sources say the moniker came from Four-Mile Creek (now Silverton Creek), which flows through the community, while others suggest that it came from the fact that the village was four miles south of New Denver. The name was changed to Silverton in 1894. The source of that moniker is also disputed. Some indicate that it refers to the many silver mines in the area; others say the community was christened either after the famous Silverton Mine or after Silverton, Colorado, where that mine was located. One thing is for certain—with its small population, Silverton is British Columbia's smallest incorporated municipality.

SIMILKAMEEN RIVER This river begins in the Cascade Mountains and flows north and east before turning south into the United States. Fur trader Alexander Ross travelled down the waterway in 1812. He called it the Samilkameigh River and listed the Samilkameigh people as one of the 12 tribes that comprise the Okanagan First Nation. Early records also spell the name as Samilkumeigh and Similkameugh. The ending was changed at some point by non-Aboriginals so it would rhyme with Tulameen, which is the moniker of the Similkameen River's tributary. Similkameen is a derivation of Smelqmix, the Syilx'tsn name for the people of the Okanagan (Syilx) First Nation, who live in the Similkameen Valley.

SIR DONALD RANGE *See* Mount Sir Donald.

SIRDAR This small community, 18 miles north of Creston, was founded in 1900, when the Canadian Pacific Railway constructed a depot and a maintenance facility on the site. The neighbouring townsite was owned by Fred Little, Creston's founder, and he named it Sirdar after Horatio Herbert Kitchener. The famous military man had won international fame two years earlier by leading a successful military campaign to reconquer Sudan. In addition to being the Baron Kitchener, one of the other titles the British field marshal held was that of "sirdar," or

S

commander-in-chief, of the Egyptian Army, an honour that he acquired in 1892. *See* Kitchener.

SKAGIT RIVER Located southwest of Princeton, this river flows south across the American border into Washington State. It was christened after the people of the Skagit First Nation, a Coast Salish Nation, who live along its shores. The moniker dates back to an 1871 map, and though the spelling has remained the same in British Columbia, other locations named after the Skagit in Washington have been spelled Scaadget, Scaget, Skait and Scatchet. The meaning of the word is unknown, but "hide or conceal" has been suggested.

SKAHA LAKE This lake (20 km²), just south of Okanagan Lake, was labelled "Du Chien L." and "L. du Chien" (French for "Dog Lake") on maps in the 1860s and '70s. Charts from 1915 and 1930 call it Dog Lake. The lake was given its current name in 1930 to agree with local usage. The name Skaha is a derivation of the Secwepemc (Shuswap) First Nation word *sqéx̌e*, which means "dog." The identical word in the Syilx'tsn language of the Okanagan (Syilx) First Nation means "horse."

SKEENA RIVER This 621-kilometre-long river flows south and west from the Gunanoot Mountains to the Pacific Ocean near Prince Rupert. It was already called Ayton's River by fur traders when Captain Charles Duncan of the *Princess Royal* saw it in 1788. At one time, the river was called Simpson's River, after Hudson's Bay Company fur trader Captain Aemilius Simpson. (Prince Rupert is 55 kilometres south of the site of the HBC's old Fort Simpson, which was also named after the captain.) The Skeena was also once known as the Babine River, a name that now belongs to one of the Skeena's tributaries.

The Skeena's moniker dates from an 1867 map. Skeena is a derivation of the Tsimshian First Nation name for the river, which has been variously spelled 'Xsan, K-Shian and

K'shian and means "water out of the clouds" or "river of mists."

SKIDEGATE (2006: pop. 781) This Haida First Nation village on Graham Island was named after its principal chief, who greeted the first non-Aboriginal fur traders to visit here in 1787. His name was recorded as Skit-ei-get. The location was variously spelled Skitekat, Skittegate, Skitgiss, Skittagates and Skettegats before the British Admiralty adopted the spelling used by Captain Daniel Pender when he referred to the nearby channel and inlet during his survey of the area in 1866. Many sources incorrectly interpret the Haida word to mean "red paint stone." Actually, the original Haida name was Sgiidagids, which means "child of red chiton." The community was officially known by government authorities as Skidegate Mission from 1946 to 1998, when "Mission" was dropped to reflect long-time local usage. Coincidentally, three kilometres to the west was a much smaller community called Skidegate Landing, which, from 1946 until 1992, was offically called Skidegate. Its name was changed to Skidgate Landing to reflect common usage, and it was amalgamated into the village of Queen Charlotte in 2005.

SLOCAN Three communities (Slocan, Slocan Park and South Slocan), a lake, two rivers (the Slocan and the Little Slocan) and a valley share this name. Slocan Lake (69 km²) and the Slocan River in the Selkirk Mountains were first seen by non-Aboriginals when Hudson's Bay Company employee William Kittson stumbled upon them in 1824. The valley was first explored by the Palliser Expedition in 1859. The current name was quickly applied to the lake, the valley and the Slocan River but was variously spelled as Schlocan, Shlocan and Sloghan. It is not known when the present spelling was first used. The Little Slocan River, which flows northwest of Nelson into the Slocan River, has been labelled as such on maps as far back as 1893.

S

The village of Slocan (2006: pop. 314), located at the south end of Slocan Lake, was established in the 1890s as a service and transportation centre for the local lead and silver mines. It was called Slocan City when a post office opened there in 1896, but the moniker was shortened the following year.

Slocan Park is 20 kilometres south of Slocan, and was established before a post office opened there in 1903. The community was originally called Gutelius, after Frederick Passmore Gutelius, the general manager of the Columbia and Western Railway, who had earlier been the CPR's construction superintendent in the Rossland-Trail area in the 1890s. The moniker was changed in 1912, when a petition was circulated among its residents to have the community renamed after a local park. About eight kilometres south of Slocan Park is South Slocan, which also dates from the 1890s.

The name Slocan is from a Syilx'tsn (Okanagan) First Nation word that translates into "pierce or strike on the head." The moniker refers to the Okanagans' practice of harpooning or spearing salmon.

SMITH INLET / SMITH SOUND In 1786, Captain James Hanna, the commanding officer of the *Sea Otter*, named this inlet and sound, which are located south of Calvert Island. Unfortunately, he left us no clues as to who Smith was.

SMITHERS (2006: pop. 5217) This town had its beginnings in 1913, when the Grand Trunk Pacific Railway established a divisional point there and called it Smithers. The name honours Sir Alfred Waldron Smithers, a British financier and the head of the GTP at the time. Smithers is on the Bulkley River, halfway between Hazelton and Houston.

SODA CREEK This small community was named after a nearby creek. The town acquired the moniker in 1863 when the Royal Engineers surveyed the townsite. It is uncertain when the creek got its name. "Soda" refers to the fact that the water in the creek flows through a formation of calcium carbonate and bubbles like soda water. Both the community and the creek are located 33 kilometres north of Williams Lake. And, of course, for those who enjoy a whiskey and soda, Whiskey Creek is less than five kilometres away.

SOMASS RIVER This 10-kilometre-long river flows south into Alberni Inlet just west of Port Alberni. Its current name dates back to British Admiralty charts from 1863. Somass is a derivation of the Nuu-chah-nulth (Nootka) First Nation name for the river, Tsu-ma-uss. Non-Aboriginal sources have interpreted the word to mean "flowing down," "current in water" or "river of many tributaries washing the earth," but Nuu-chah-nulth elders have translated it as "washing." Explorer Robert Brown listed Klistachnit, which means "creek by a hillside," as another First Nations name for the river.

SOMERVILLE ISLAND (54 km²) Captain Daniel Pender named this island at the entrance of Observatory Inlet in 1868 for Mary (née Somerville) Cunningham. Nearby Cunningham Passage was named at about the same time by Pender for Mary's son, Robert. Both Robert and his brother John settled on the north British Columbia coast in 1862 (John in Metlakatla and Robert in Port Simpson) and were prominent residents in that part of the province. It is not known if Mary ever visited BC.

SONORA ISLAND (166 km²) This island is located at the north end of Georgia Strait near Campbell River. It, along with Maurelle and Quadra islands, was originally thought by early surveyors to be part of one large island known as Valdes Island. Sonora Island acquired its current name in 1903, when the Geographic Board of Canada christened it after the Spanish Navy schooner, *Sonora*. The ship was commanded by Lieutenant Commander Juan Francisco

S

de la Bodega y Quadra when he visited the British Columbia coast in 1775.

SOOKE A district municipality, as well a basin, a bay, a harbour, an inlet, a lake and a river share this name. All are located about 25 kilometres west of Victoria. The basin, harbour and inlet were collectively christened Puerto de Revillagigedo in 1790 by Spanish Navy Sub-Lieutenant Manual Quimper. That name honours Juan Vicente de Güemes Padilla Horcasitas y Aguayo, the 2nd Count of Revillagigedo and the newly installed viceroy of New Spain (i.e., Mexico). The moniker, however, did not stick, and the inlet was renamed by Captain Henry Kellett, commanding officer of the HMS *Herald*, when he surveyed the southern part of Vancouver Island in 1846.

The other geological features with the name Sooke were probably renamed at the same time or shortly thereafter. The community of Sooke (2006: pop. 9704), founded in 1849, was christened after the inlet and the river. Its early residents, at least until the 1860s, spelled its name as Soke or Soake. The current spelling was adopted when a post office was built there in 1864. Sooke is a derivation of the name of the T'Sou-ke First Nation people, who still live in the area. Early records also spell their name Sâ'ok, Sock, Sok, Sokes and Tsohke. T'Sou-ke is the people's name for the stickleback fish that are found in Sooke Basin.

SORRENTO (2006: pop. 1360) This community was founded and named in the early 1880s by real estate promoter James Kinghorn. The capitalist mistakenly believed that the Canadian Pacific Railway would be rerouted along the southern shore of Shuswap Lake, so he laid out a townsite there. Kinghorn had spent his honeymoon in Sorrento, Italy, and the view from this piece of land overlooking Shuswap Lake reminded him of the sight of the Isle of Capri from the Italian city. The CPR never arrived, but the town grew nevertheless.

SOUTH HAZELTON *See* Hazelton.

SOUTH PENDER ISLAND *See* Pender Islands.

SOUTHGATE The 44-kilometre-long Southgate River flows southwest and west into Bute Inlet. It was named in 1862 by Captain George Richards for James Johnson Southgate, a Victoria general merchant and local politician who did a lot of business with the Royal Navy in the early 1860s. Nearby is Southgate Peak (2042 m), the supposed site of a lost gold mine from the late 19th century. There is also a collection of islands known as the Southgate Group in Haida Gwaii (Queen Charlotte Islands). Captain Daniel Pender named these islands for Southgate in 1864. Southgate Island is part of the group.

SPALLUMCHEEN (2006: pop. 4960) This district municipality is 20 kilometres north of Vernon and entirely surrounds the city of Armstrong. The first settlers arrived in the area in the 1860s and named the community after nearby Shuswap River, which, at the time, was also known variously as the Spellmacheen, the Spillemeechene or the Spallymsheen. The community's moniker was spelled Spallamucheen when a post office opened there in 1881, but it was changed 11 years later to reflect the spelling in the municipality's letters of incorporation that were filed with the provincial government in 1891. Spallumcheen is a derivation of the name of the Splats'in First Nation people. The Splats'in are a branch of the Secwepemc (Shuswap) First Nation, an Interior Salish people. Sources vary as to the meaning of Splats'in. One says that it is a Secwepemc word meaning "flat area along edge." Another authority suggests that Splats'in is an Interior Salish place name meaning "beautiful place" or "beautiful valley."

SPANISH BANK It was along this southwest coastline of Burrard Inlet that Captain George Vancouver found two

Spanish vessels anchored, the brig *Sutil* and the schooner *Mexicana*, when he met with their captains, the explorers Dionisio Alcalá-Galiano and Cayetano Valdés y Flores, in 1792. Ironically, the bank is shown, but not named, in the Spaniards' charts and is not mentioned at all on Vancouver's chart. Captain George Richards named the location when he was surveying Burrard Inlet in 1859.

SPARWOOD (2006: pop. 3618) This district municipality is 28 kilometres north of Fernie. The community was settled in the 1890s and took its name from a local railway station, which, in turn, was christened during the construction of the Crows Nest Southern Railway. According to Sparwood's postmaster in 1905, "the engineers remarked that the size and quality of the trees here were such as were required for spars: hence the name 'Sparwood.'" (Spars are used in the building of ocean vessels.) In 1966, the village of Sparwood was merged with the communities of Michel and Natal and re-incorporated as a district municipality.

SPENCES BRIDGE (also informally known as Spence's Bridge) (estimated pop. 450) This community is located 37 kilometres north of Lytton, where the Nicola and Thompson rivers meet. It was originally called Cook's Ferry, after Mortimer Cook, who operated a ferry across the Thompson River from 1862 to 1865. In 1865, with a government contract in hand, Thomas Spence built a toll bridge at this spot—the first bridge across the Thompson—that eventually replaced the ferry. The place was known as Spence's Bridge by 1868; the apostrophe was officially dropped in 1930.

SPILLER A sea channel, a passage, a mountain range and a river are all named after Corporal Richard Spiller of the Royal Marines. Spiller served on the *Beaver* from 1863 to 1870, while it was under the command of the British Navy's Captain Daniel Pender. Spiller was also Pender's personal attendant. Pender named the channel, located north of Bella Bella, and the passage, at the northeast end of Queen Charlotte Sound, after Spiller in 1865–66. He also christened the mountain range and the river, both on Porcher Island, in 1867.

SPILLIMACHEEN A community, as well as a mountain and a river share this name. All are located about 60 kilometres southeast of Golden. The settlement dates from at least 1864 and was named after the river. However, when a post office opened there in 1889, it (and, hence, the town) was named Galena, after the lead sulphide ore that was mined in the area. It's believed that the new name was adopted to avoid confusion with Spallamacheen (near Vernon), whose post office opened eight years earlier. The Canadian Pacific Railway, however, ignored the postal authorities and christened its station Spillimacheen. The name of the local post office was changed in 1946 to reflect the moniker of the CPR station. It's not known when the river was first called by this name. However, a 1901 letter to the Geographic Board of Canada states: "Spillimachene has been used in the official Reports for some time— previously, it was Spillemcheen, but the former represents the pronunciation best. I would suggest that Spillimacheen be adopted as conforming with terminations of Similkameen, Tulameen, etc."

Early records provide a number of different spellings of both the community's and the river's name, including Speylumacheen and Spillomochene. The mountain (2865 m) was called Spallumcheen Mountain in 1883 and Spillemcheen Mountain seven years later. The mountain's current name was formally adopted in 1951. Spillimacheen is a derivation of the Syilx'tsn (Okanagan) First Nation word *spelemtsin*, which means "flat area along the edge."

SPROAT A community, a lake, a mountain, a river and a waterfall share this name, and all are located just north-west of Port Alberni. Sproat Lake (38 km^2), as well as the river and the falls, were named by Robert Brown in 1863 after Gilbert Malcolm Sproat, the manager of a large sawmill at the head of Alberni Inlet, where Port Alberni now sits. Brown had just arrived on Vancouver Island to head a three-year expedition to collect seeds, roots and plants for the British Columbia Botanical Association of Edinburgh and met Sproat only the day before he stumbled across the lake. Although Brown claimed in his journal that the lake was "not found on the map," Sproat Lake was previously called Kleecoot Lake by loggers and others around the inlet. Kleecoot was an anglicized version of the Nootka First Nation name Klee-coot, which means "wide open." Before loggers and other non-Aboriginals came to the area, the Nootka called Sproat River Tu-quootlth, which means "jumping area for fish." The community of Sproat Lake (2006: pop. 1837), on the east end of the lake, had been established by 1892 and is just north of the community of Kleecoot. Nearby Mount Sproat (2439 m) was also named after the lake by 1898.

SPUZZUM This small community 18 kilometres north of Yale in the Fraser Canyon was a Nlaka'pamux (Thompson Salish) First Nation village when Simon Fraser spent the night there while travelling down the Fraser River in 1808. Its name was changed to Simon's House, when a depot for the Hudson's Bay Company brigades was built in 1848, but the original name had been revived by 1897. The moniker is the anglicized spelling of the Nlaka'pamux word *spôzm* or *spôzem*, which means "a little flat" or "little flat (lands)." The name refers to the small stretch of flat land on either side of nearby Spuzzum Creek. One source erroneously states that the name is a local variant of the Chinook Jargon word *spatsum*, which refers to a reed used in basketry.

SQUAMISH / SQUAMISH RIVER The site of the district municipality of Squamish (2006: pop. 14,949), located at the head of Howe Sound, was originally occupied by the people of the Squamish First Nation, who now live along Howe Sound and the north shore of Burrard Inlet. The Squamish River flows south from the Coast Mountains through the city into Howe Sound. The river was labelled as the Squawmisht River on an 1863 British Admiralty chart and officially received its current name in 1911. Non-Aboriginals started to arrive in the area in the 1880s, and they immediately adopted the name (with the modern spelling) for their community. Squamish is an anglicization of the Squamish people's name for themselves, the Skwxwú7mesh. In Skwxwú7mesh Snichim (the Squamish language), the word means "mother of the wind" and might refer to the steady wind that blows off Howe Sound into the city.

Squamish was rechristened Newport in 1912, because local land promoters thought a more "civilized" name would attract more customers. The new name, however, was not popular with the locals, so the Pacific Great Eastern Railway held a contest in 1914 for school children to pick another name for the railway's Howe Sound terminal. The name Newport won, thus defeating the purpose of the contest, but D'Arcy Tate, the vice-president of the PGE, overruled the kids and brought back the name Squamish.

ST. ELIAS MOUNTAINS The name of this mountain range in the northwest corner of British Columbia was officially adopted in 1918. It was named after nearby St. Elias Island (in Alaska) and Mount St. Elias (located in Alaska and Yukon), both of which were christened in 1741 by Danish explorer Vitus Bering on St. Elias' Day, July 16.

ST. NICHOLAS PEAK (2938 m) Mountaineer Arthur O. Wheeler gave this mountain its name in 1908, because he thought one side of it bore a striking resemblance to Jolly Old Saint Nick. The original Santa Claus, Saint Nicholas, the fourth-century bishop of Myra, is also the patron saint of climbers. St. Nicholas Peak sits on the Alberta border at the north end of Yoho National Park.

STANLEY PARK (4.05 km²) The second largest urban park in Canada (only Calgary's Nose Hill Park is bigger), this site in Vancouver was initially called Coal Peninsula because of the coal deposits found there. It was a military reserve for some years before the federal government handed it over to the city in 1887 to be used as a park. The park opened the following year and was named after Frederick Stanley, the 1st Baron Stanley of Preston (better known as Lord Stanley), who had just become Canada's new Governor General.

STAVE LAKE / STAVE RIVER It is not known exactly when the Stave River got its name, but the why is clear—the Hudson's Bay Company cut wood from the river's banks as far back as 1829 to use as staves in the construction of barrels at Fort Langley. Stave Lake (59 km²) was created when a hydroelectric dam was built across the river in 1908–21. The lake and river are both north of Mission.

STEPHENS ISLAND (67 km²) This island was named in 1793 by Captain George Vancouver for Sir Philip Stephens, member of the British House of Commons and secretary to the British Admiralty. Stephens Island is in Chatham Sound, about 40 kilometres west of Prince Rupert.

STEVESTON This Richmond neighbourhood, fishing village and popular tourist attraction was named for Manoah Steves, who settled there in 1877 to begin a dairy farm. Originally called Steves, the name was changed to Steveston in 1889 shortly after Victoria's *Daily Colonist* wrote that "the little village now clustered at Steves will soon grow into a thriving business centre."

STEWART (2006: pop. 496) This district municipality was named after brothers John and Robert Stewart, two

S

prospectors who were the first to settle in the area in 1902. Robert became the community's first postmaster in 1905 and, therefore, had the task of officially naming the town. Stewart is at the head of the Portland Canal on the Alaska border.

STIKINE The 640-kilometre-long Stikine River (589 kilometres in British Columbia, the rest in Alaska) was given its name in 1799 by Captain James Rowan of the American whaling ship *Eliza*. An 1848 Russian map called it Ryka Stakhin (Stakhin River). The region surrounding the river was known as the Stickeen Territories when the area came under British control in 1862 and was made a part of British Columbia the following year. The Americans called it the St. Francis River when they purchased Alaska from the Russians in 1867. It was also once called Pelly's River. During the 19th century, the name Stikine was spelled more than a dozen different ways, including Shikene, Stahkin, Stakhinski, Stickeen and Stickienes, until Captain Rowan's original name was adopted by the American government in 1869. The Geographic Board of Canada did not approve the final spelling until 1898.

Stikine is a derivation of the Tlingit First Nation name for the river, Shtax'héen or Shtax' Héen, which as been variously translated as "the great river," "cloudy river" and "bitter waters." The community of Stikine is located on the west side of the river, near the Alaska border. Originally called Boundary, its name was changed to reflect that of the river in 1964. Canada's longest canyon, known as the Grand Canyon of the Stikine since at least 1929, stretches about 72 kilometres upstream, beginning at a point near Telegraph Creek.

STRAIT OF GEORGIA (also known as Georgia Strait) Spanish naval explorer Francisco de Eliza y Reventa originally named this strait Gran Canal de Nuestra Señora del Rosario la Marinera in 1791, and for years the name

S

was abbreviated as Canal del Rosario on Spanish charts. However, on June 4, 1792, the birthday of King George III, Captain George Vancouver claimed the strait and all of its islands and shorelines for his monarch and called it the Gulphe of Georgia in His Majesty's honour. The spelling was modernized to the Gulf of Georgia in 1800, before the strait itself was renamed the Strait of Georgia in 1865 by Captain George Richards, who had recently been appointed the Royal Navy's new chief hydrographer. The strait separates southern Vancouver Island from the British Columbia mainland and extends 220 kilometres from the San Juan Islands to Campbell River.

STRATHCONA PROVINCIAL PARK (2538 km^2) Located in the middle of Vancouver Island, British Columbia's oldest provincial park was established in 1911 and named after Donald Smith, the 1st Baron Strathcona and Mount Royal, who was at the time Canada's High Commissioner to the United Kingdom. Earlier in his career, Smith had been an official of the Hudson's Bay Company, the president of the Bank of Montreal, the financial backer of the Canadian Pacific Railway, a noted philanthropist and a member of the House of Commons. It was Smith who drove the last iron spike into the CPR rail line at Craigellachie in 1885, linking the Atlantic and Pacific oceans.

S

STUART ISLAND An island and a community share this name. The island lies at the mouth of Bute Inlet and was, like the inlet, named in 1792 by Captain George Vancouver for John Stuart, the 3rd Earl of Bute, a former British prime minister and a good friend of King George III. Stuart's grandson, Charles Stuart, was that year a midshipman on Vancouver's ship, the HMS *Discovery*. The community, which was settled in the early 1900s, is located on the island. It was called Bruce's Landing for a brief time in the 1920s, after George Bruce, the local postmaster and general store owner.

STUART LAKE / STUART RIVER There are four Stuart Lakes in British Columbia, but the largest of these (356 km²) is the one directly northwest of Fort St. James. It was named by North West Company explorer Simon Fraser when he spent the winter of 1806–07 there. The name honours Fraser's fellow NWCer, John Stuart, who accompanied Fraser on his three-year expedition through the British Columbia Interior. Stuart River, which starts at the southern tip of the lake, was also named for John Stuart. The traditional Dakelh (Carrier) First Nation name for the lake is Nak'al Bun.

SUMAS This name once belonged to an extensive lake near Abbotsford, which was drained in the 1920s. The resulting lowlands, now used for agriculture, are known as Sumas Prairie. There was also a district municipality of Sumas, located south of Abbotsford, that was incorporated in 1924 but merged with Abbotsford in 1972. A nearby river that flows from Washington State into the Fraser River, as well as a small mountain range northeast of Abbotsford, collectively known as Sumas Mountain, still have the name. During the mid-19th century, Sumas was frequently spelled Smess and is a derivation of the name of the Sum-Aht First Nation, a branch of the Stó:lô First Nation that used to live around Sumas Lake. The Stó:lô First Nation is an alliance of a number of Halq'eméylem (also known as Halkomelem) communities, and Sum-Aht is a Halq'eméylem name that has been variously translated as "big opening," "big, flat opening," "a big, level opening" and "flat, level."

S

SUMMERLAND (2006: pop. 10,828) This district municipality was named by land developer John Moore Robinson when he founded the community in 1902. He picked the name because of the climate. Summerland is located on the west side of Okanagan Lake.

SUNDERLAND CHANNEL It is not certain who christened this sea passage or when, but it was probably named by either Captain George Richards or Captain Daniel Pender in the early 1860s. In any case, the channel, located east of Johnstone Strait and north of Hardwicke Island, was named in honour of Captain John Wellbore Sunderland Spencer, the commanding officer of the HMS *Topaze*, while that ship sailed in British Columbia waters from 1859 to 1863. Spencer was the sixth son of Francis Spencer, the 1st Baron Churchill and the grandson of George Spencer, the 4th Duke of Marlborough. He was a distant relative of British Prime Minister Sir Winston Churchill.

SUNSHINE COAST This strip of coastline northwest of Vancouver from Howe Sound to Desolation Sound got its name from a 1925 Union Steamship Company promotion brochure that promised "Sunshine and Sea-charm along Holiday Shores on the Gulf Coast." Providing daily leisure excursions to the Sunshine Coast and elsewhere for passengers was an important part of the company's business from 1920, when the shipping line purchased a resort on Bowen Island, until the line was sold in 1959. The name fits. Depending on the location, this area gets between 1400 and 2400 hours of sunshine every year, which means the coast gets a lot more sunny days than cloudy or wet ones.

S

SURREY (2006: pop. 394,976) When Surrey was incorporated in 1879, most of its less than 1000 residents were British immigrants, and a number of them claimed credit for naming this city. Most said they did so because they were originally from the county of Surrey in England, and they either liked the name or their new home reminded them of their old one. Some sources also say that a possible reason for the moniker is the coincidence that Surrey, England, is located south across the Thames River from Westminster (a part of London), and

British Columbia's Surrey is south across the Fraser River from New Westminster.

SWARTZ BAY Some say that this bay on the north end of the Saanich Peninsula was named after John Aaron Swart, who bought land there in 1876 (or 1879). Others argue that it was christened after an American squatter, Lansing O. Swart, who lived there. According to one source, the two were brothers from New York who came to British Columbia by way of the California gold fields. In any case, Swart's Bay (a name that is still used by some) became Swartz Bay when the latter spelling was adopted by the Canadian Hydrographic Service in 1934. The bay is the site of a major ferry terminal, and an attempt to restore the original name in 1968 was rejected by BC Ferries because of the costs involved and the confusion it would create among travellers.

SWINDLE ISLAND (289 km^2) One of the largest islands off British Columbia's coast, the origin of this isle's name is lost to history. The moniker first appears on an 1867 British Admiralty chart, but to what or whom it refers is no longer known. The island is located between Price and Princess Royal islands.

S

T

TAGHUM (2006: pop. 211) This community was founded in 1888 by a prospector from Minnesota, M. Monaghan, and was christened Williams Siding when a post office opened there in 1905. The settlement was renamed Taghum in 1924. Taghum is the anglicized spelling of the Chinook Jargon word *táxem,* which means "six." The name is appropriate because Taghum is six miles (10 kilometres) west of Nelson.

TAGISH LAKE (212 km² in British Columbia) This lake lies in northwest British Columbia and the Yukon. American cavalry lieutenant Frederick Schwatka christened it Lake Bove in 1883, in honour of an Italian Navy lieutenant (probably the Italian explorer Giacomo Bove). Surveyor George Dawson renamed it Tagish Lake four years later, after the people of the local Tagish First Nation. The Tagish call themselves the Ta:gizi Dene ("Tagish people"). The word *tagish* is a derivation of the Tagish place name Ta:gizi, which means "it (the spring ice) is breaking up."

TAHSIS A village, an inlet, a river, a sea passage and a mountain all share this name. Tahsis Inlet separates Nootka Island from Vancouver Island. Both the community and the river are at the head of the inlet. The Tahsis Narrows are north of Nootka Island and west of Tahsis Inlet. Tahsis Mountain (1325 m) is east of the inlet.

The community of Tahsis (2006: pop. 366) was already a Mowachaht First Nation (part of the Nuu-chah-nulth First Nation) village when Spanish naval explorer Lieutenant Commander Juan Francisco de la Bodega y Quadra and Captain George Vancouver visited it in 1792. The Spanish called the settlement Tasis,

Vancouver labelled it Tahsheis on his charts, and John Jewitt spelled it Tashees in 1803. When a post office opened there in 1938, it (and, hence, the village) was named Tahsis. It was renamed Port Tahsis by the end of the year, but the postal authorities reverted to Tahsis in 1945.

Quadra christened Tahsis Inlet with the name Canal de Tasis, and the Tahsis Narrows as Canal de Buena Esperanza (Good Hope Canal) in 1792. The British Admiralty anglicized the inlet's name in 1849 and called it Tasis Canal. People kept adding an *h* to the spelling of the inlet as far back as the 1860s, and the name was officially changed to Tahsis Canal in 1938. It went from a canal to an inlet in 1947. For some reason, the British Admiralty did not retain the Spanish name for the narrows but went along with Captain George Richards, when he called them the Tasis Narrows sometime between 1859 and 1862. The *h* was also added to its name in 1938. It is not clear when Tahsis Mountain was named.

Tahsis is a derivation of the Mowachaht place name, Tahsheesh (often misspelled Tahsees), which means "crossing," "gateway," "passage" or "road." It has also been translated as "trail at beach" or "where the water travel stops and they have to walk." The latter translation refers to the fact that Tahsis Inlet and Tahsis River were part of a First Nations trail that led to the east side of Vancouver Island.

TAKHINI RIVER This river flows northwest into the Yukon. The people of the Southern Tutchone First Nation called it Näkhu chù, which means "crossing with a raft." Takhini comes from a Tlingit First Nation word meaning "king salmon." In the 1800s, there was a large Tlingit salmon fishing camp west of the river, just across the Yukon border.

TAKU MOUNTAIN / TAKU RIVER The Taku River begins south of Atlin Lake and flows southwest across the Alaska border and into Taku Inlet, from which it takes its name. The inlet was first christened Taco Gulf by Hudson's Bay Company governor Sir George Simpson during his last visit to British Columbia in 1841. (The Russians had earlier called the inlet Rukav Ledyanoy or "icy arm.") Different spellings include Tacou and Tahko. The current spelling dates from at least 1906, when the Americans officially adopted Taku River as the name of the waterway. Canadian authorities did not get around to approving the moniker until 1933.

There are actually two Taku Mountains. One (1790 m) is 21 kilometres northwest of Atlin and received its name in 1951. The other Taku Mountain (566 m) is in Alaska, 32 kilometres southeast of Juneau. It was named in 1888. A glacier, a harbour, a lake and several other geological locations in Alaska share this name.

The name Taku was taken from the name of the T'aaku band of the Tlingit First Nation. One source says that T'aaku is a derivation of the Tlingit place name Tah-wakh-tha-ku. Everyone agrees that T'aaku (or Tah-wakh-tha-ku) means "the place where the geese sit down" or "place where geese gather." Another source says that Taku is a contraction of the Tlingit words *t'aawak* ("Canadian geese"), *la* (a classifier) and *ku* ("flood tide"), which together mean "geese brought in on the tide."

TAPPEN / MOUNT TAPPEN The unincorporated community of Tappen (2006: pop. 773) began when a sawmill was built on the site in about 1883. An 1891 map identifies the settlement as Tappen Station; the post office that opened the following year was called Tappen Siding. The moniker was changed to Brightwater in 1908 but changed back to simply Tappen in 1911. The community was christened in honour of Herbert Tappan (note the misspelling), a Harvard-educated Canadian Pacific Railway construction subcontractor and a cousin of Andrew Onderdonk, the chief CPR construction contractor in British Columbia in the 1880s. Tappan camped nearby in 1884 while laying track for the CPR. The community of Tappen is 10 kilometres north of Salmon Arm. Nearby is Mount Tappen. It was originally called Tappen Mountain in 1922 after the community and then renamed in 1963.

TAYLOR (2006: pop. 1384) This district municipality is 18 kilometres south of Fort St. John. It was originally named Taylor Flats after its first residents, Donald Herbert and Charlotte Taylor, who arrived here with their children in 1912. "Herbie" was a Hudson's Bay Company fur trader, farmer and ferry operator. However, another early settler, Robert "Bob" Barker, had other ideas about the moniker, so whenever Taylor went out of town to tend to his traplines, Barker replaced the sign saying "Taylor Flats" with another identifying the community as "Barker Flats." Coincidentally, Taylor would do the same to Barker's sign whenever Barker was away. The matter was finally settled when a post office called Taylor opened in the community in 1923.

TELEGRAPH CREEK Both a small community (estimated pop. 400) and a creek share this name. The town is the only settlement on the Stikine River in northwest British Columbia. The first settlers arrived in the area in 1861, and the community was later named after the creek. The creek, in turn, was christened in 1866 by a survey crew for the Collins Overland Telegraph Company. It was the company's intent, which was later abandoned, to create a communications link between San Francisco and Russia by running a telegraph line through BC and Alaska and across the Bering Strait.

TELKWA / TELKWA RIVER The village of Telkwa (2006: pop. 1295), just southeast of Smithers, is located where the Bulkley and Telkwa rivers meet. Another community, Aldermere, was staked out on the bluff above Telkwa in 1904, but three years later, many businesses and residents moved down the hill and established the present-day village on the shores of the Telkwa River to be closer to the anticipated Grand Trunk Pacific Railway (GTP) tracks. Those tracks were originally to be laid just across the Bulkley River at Hubert, but land speculators tried to make a profit off the GTP, and the railway went to present-day Smithers instead. Both Aldermere and Hubert are now ghost towns, but Telkwa has survived.

It is not clear when the Telkwa River was christened, but its name dates from at least 1905. Most say that Telkwa means "where the rivers meet" in the Witsuwit'en language of the local Wet'suwet'en First Nation. However, it may also be a derivation of the Witsuwit'en place name Dehilkwa, which means "where the rivers flow west." One source also indicates that Telkwa is the Dakelh (Carrier) First Nation word for "frog." (The Dakelh are neighbours of the Wet'suwet'en.)

TERRACE (2006: pop. 11,320) This city on the Skeena River is 140 kilometres east of Prince Rupert. It was first called Eby, after a married couple who built a store there, and was renamed Littleton shortly afterward for one of its first settlers, George Little, who arrived in 1905. Little himself gave the community its present name in 1911. When the Grand Trunk Pacific Railway decided to place its tracks on his land, Little not only acquiesced but offered free land for a railway station, provided the GTR named the station after him. The railway company agreed, and Little laid out a townsite adjacent to the station that was to be called Littleton. The federal postal authorities, however, rejected the name because another community in New Brunswick had the same moniker. Little then noticed four layers of level land above the Skeena River. Called "benches" or "terraces," they were formed during the last ice age and inspired Little to rename the place Terrace.

TESLIN LAKE / TESLIN RIVER Teslin Lake (317 km², only 104 km² in British Columbia) straddles the Yukon-BC border. Teslin River flows northwest from British Columbia through the lake and into the Yukon River in the Yukon. The current name of both the lake and river were adopted by the Geographic Board of Canada in 1898, the same year that the Hudson's Bay Company established a trading post on the lake. The people of the Tagish First Nation called the river Nasathane, which means "no salmon." The river is also called Délin Chú in the Northern Tutchone First Nation language, which is spoken north of Teslin Lake in the Yukon. That name means "water running out from the lake." Surveyor Michael Byrne (of Burns Lake fame) was told in 1881 by the local First Nations people that the river was called Hootalinkwa, a derivation of the Northern Tutchone word *hudinlin*, which means "running against the mountain." In 1883, American explorer Frederick Schwatka christened the waterway Newberry River after an American educator, John Newberry of New York, but the name did not stick. Surveyor George Dawson, in 1887, was the first to call the body of water Teslin Lake. Teslin is a derivation of the Tlingit First Nation place name Tes-lin-too, which means "long, narrow lake." It is also the name of the Teslin Tlingit First Nation and of a community in the Yukon. According to one source, the Tlingit originally used the name to refer to the Nałasìn (Nisutlin) River in the Yukon and not to either Teslin Lake or Teslin River.

TÊTE JAUNE CACHE This small community (estimated pop. 500) at the west end of Yellowhead Pass, northwest of Valemount, was established in 1911 when the Grand Trunk Pacific Railway laid its tracks there. The name is French for "Yellow Head's hiding place" and refers to the yellow-haired Pierre Bostonais (who was also known as Pierre Bostonnais and Pierre Hatsination). Bostonais was an Iroquois Métis trapper and fur trader who worked as a guide for the North West Company and the Hudson's Bay Company from 1816 to 1827. He guided the first HBC party across the Rocky Mountains in 1820. Yellowhead Pass, as well as a nearby lake and a mountain, are also named after him. *See* Yellowhead.

TEXADA ISLAND (302 km²) Located on the east side of Georgia Strait south of Powell River, Texada Island is the largest of the Gulf Islands. José María Narváez, the commanding officer of the Spanish vessel *Santa Saturnina*, named it Isla de Texada in 1791, in honour of Spanish Rear Admiral Félix Ignacio de Tejada y Suárez de Lara. The name had been anglicized by the British Admiralty by 1862.

TEZZERON LAKE (64 km²) The name of this body of water, north of Stuart Lake, is a derivation of Chuzghun, the original Dakelh (Carrier) First Nation name for the lake. Several similar meanings have been suggested for the word. Some translate it as "down feathers place," in reference to the lake being the nesting place for waterfowl. Another possible interpretation is "snowflake lake." The prefix *chuz* typically translates as "snowflakes," but others argue that when used in Chuzghun, it alludes to the moulting process that waterfowl undergo after nesting. (Think of the resemblance of bird down in water to snowflakes.) Another linguist believes that the correct name is the similarly pronounced Ts'uzghun, which means "moulting lake." The prefix *ts'uz* means "down feather," and the suffix *ghun* means "a lake located by or along a ridge." Some Dakelh, however, dispute these inter-pretations and say that *chuz* means "soft wood," *ghun* means "area" and the name Chuzghun means "a body of water surrounded by trees," referring to the old, hollow trees along the lake's shores. Interestingly, the trees that grow along the lake are black cottonwoods, and their cottony fluff floats in the air like snowflakes. It is not known when, or by whom, the current spelling was first applied.

THETIS ISLAND (10.35 km²) This name is shared by an island near Chemainus and the community (2006: pop. 372) on it. Captain George Richards christened the island in about 1859 after the HM frigate *Thetis*, a 36-gun vessel that sailed British Columbia waters from 1851 to 1853. (Nearby Kuper Island was named at the same time for Augustus Kuper, the captain of the *Thetis*.) The first settlers arrived on the island in 1875.

THOMPSON RIVER North West Company explorer Simon Fraser named this river in 1808 for fellow NWC'er David Thompson. Thompson himself never saw the river. The Thompson begins with two branches. The North Thompson flows 365 kilometres from the Cariboo Mountains to Kamloops. The South Thompson meets it there after flowing 169 kilometres from Shuswap Lake. Once combined into one river, the Thompson runs another 169 kilometres before it converges with the Fraser River at Lytton.

THURLOW ISLANDS When Captain George Vancouver came across these isles in 1792, he thought they were a single body of land, which he named Thurlow Island. They've since been discovered to be two separate islands, which are now called East Thurlow Island (105 km²) and West Thurlow Island (82 km²). The two were christened after Edward Thurlow, the 1st Baron Thurlow, an English politician and the Lord Chancellor of Great Britain. The islands are on the north side of Johnstone Strait, between Bute and Knight inlets.

TINTAGEL This small community, located 12 kilometres east of Burns Lake, was first settled in about 1915 and named after the famous Tintagel Castle of Arthurian legend in Cornwall, England. In 1967, the town received a 45-kilogram stone from the castle as a gift from the British government to British Columbia to commemorate Canada's centennial.

TLELL (2006: pop. 187) This community on the east side of Graham Island dates from 1901 (or 1904, depending on the source), when William Thomas "Mexican Tom" Hodges established a ranch on the banks of the Tlell River. Tlell is a very old Haida name for this location. One source says that word defies translation, whereas another says that it is of uncertain meaning. Others claim that the name means either "place of big surf" or "land of berries."

TOBA An inlet, a mountain and a river share this name. Toba Inlet, located at the north end of Georgia Strait, was discovered in 1792 by Spanish explorers Dionisio Alcalá-Galiano and Cayetano Valdés y Flores. They called it Canal de la Tabla because of a wooden plank they found there carved with First Nation hieroglyphics. (*Tabla* is Spanish for table.) A 1793 Spanish chart labels the inlet "Bo. [Brazo] de las Tablas," but another Spanish map only two years later calls it "Brazo de Toba." There are two theories as to why the spelling was changed. One blames a Spanish chart engraver, who erroneously turned *Tabla* into *Toba*. The other is that the inlet was renamed to honour Antonio Tova (or Toba) y Arredondo, a Spanish naval officer who was with Galiano and Valdés on Alexandro Malaspina's visit to the British Columbia coast in 1791. Supposedly, Tova was the only one of Malaspina's officers who did not yet have a British Columbia place named after him. (In Spanish, the sounds of the letters *b* and *v* are barely distinquishable.) The name Toba Inlet was officially adopted in 1924 but was already in use long before then. Nearby Toba Mountain (895 m) was labelled Mount Toba on British Admiralty charts from 1867, and the current name dates from 1930. The river is also named after the inlet.

TOFINO / TOFINO INLET The district municipality of Tofino (2006: pop. 1655) dates from 1875, when a trading post was established on Clayoquot Island, just across Tofino Inlet from the site of the present-day community. Over time, Tofino's residents moved from the island to Tofino's current location. The settlement was named after the inlet, which, in turn, was named in 1792 by the Spanish explorers Dionisio Alcalá-Galiano and Cayetano Valdés y Flores for Vicente Tofiño de San Miguel, a hydrographer and a rear admiral in the Spanish Navy.

TOLMIE CHANNEL This channel, which separates Princess Royal Island from the British Columbia mainland, was named for Dr. William Fraser Tolmie in about 1845 by the Hudson's Bay Company. The good doctor worked for the HBC as a surgeon, clerk and fur trader. In 1843, he was sent to the HBC's Fort Nisqually on Puget Sound to take charge of its trade and farming operations. Tolmie later moved to Victoria and entered colonial and provincial politics. His son, Simon Fraser Tolmie, was premier of British Columbia from 1928 to 1933. Jane Island, in nearby Finlayson Channel, is named after Tolmie's wife, Jane.

TOWER OF LONDON RANGE This mountain range in northeast British Columbia was named in 1960 by five members of the City of London Regiment of the Royal Fusiliers (who guard the famous Tower of London). The soldiers came to BC that year on a mountaineering expedition and named the peaks after the fortress' towers (Beauchamp Peak, Devereux Peak and The White Tower) and for individuals connected with the Tower (Constable Peak, Lord Mayor Peak and Merchant Taylors Peak).

TRAIL (2006: pop. 7237) This city began in 1891 as a steamboat landing established by Frank Hanna and Eugene Topping. The site was along the route used to ship ore from the nearby mines at present-day Rossland to the smelter at Butte, Montana. That same year, Topping had a townsite surveyed on the land. It was initially called Trail Creek Landing because Trail Creek flows into the Columbia River there. The creek, in turn, got its name because the old Dewdney Trail (constructed in 1860–65) followed it to the Columbia River. The settlement was renamed Trail Creek when a post office opened there on Dominion Day (now Canada Day) in 1891, and the moniker was shortened again in 1897. Trail is on the Columbia River, 18 kilometres north of the American border.

TRANQUILLE A small community 10 kilometres northwest of Kamloops shares this name with a nearby lake and river. The moniker was first applied to the river on an 1827 map. Chief Pacamoos was the leader of the local band of the Secwepemc (Shuswap) First Nation at that time, but his friendly, quiet, patient and easy-going manner led the fur traders at Fort Kamloops to call him Chief Tranquil (also spelled Sanquil). The current spelling of Tranquille was not used until 1871. It has been suggested by one source that the river's moniker was originally meant to describe its quiet flow and that the chief acquired his nickname from it. The lake was labelled with this name in 1916, but the moniker was probably in common usage long before then. The community was founded in 1868.

TREMBLEUR LAKE (115 km^2) This lake, located northwest of Stuart Lake, was originally called Cross Lake and then Traverse Lake, because it runs perpendicular to the other lakes in the region. The current name dates from 1930 and was chosen because winds constantly keep the surface of its water from being still. The traditional Dakelh (Carrier) First Nation name for the lake is Dzindlat Bun.

TRUTCH Mount Trutch (3246 m), located 31 kilometres northeast of Donald, was named in 1920 for Joseph

Trutch, British Columbia's first lieutenant-governor from 1871 to 1876. Originally christened Trutch Mountain, the peak was given its current moniker 37 years later. The small community of Trutch, located 210 kilometres northwest of Fort St. John on the Alaska Highway, and Trutch Island (59 km²), southeast of Banks Island, were also named after the civil engineer and politician.

TSAR MOUNTAIN (3417 m) This mountain was named in 1920 by Arthur O. Wheeler while he was surveying the British Columbia–Alberta border. Seven years later, Wheeler wrote: "When I saw it, so strikingly dominating its surroundings in isolated majesty, I named it 'Czar' but later, when recording it, the spelling with 'T's' seemed more appropriate." Tsar Mountain is located east of Cummins Lakes Provincial Park.

TSAWWASSEN (2006: pop. 20,933) This neighbourhood in Delta is home to a large BC Ferries terminal. The area's first non-Aboriginal settlers arrived in the 1870s, but the name was in use as far back as 1857, when it was called Cheahwassen in an international boundary report. There have been nearly a dozen other spellings since then, including Cheewasson, Chewassen, Chewassin, Pswwassan, Sewathen, Tsawassen, Tsawwassan, Tscwwassan, Tshe-wass-an, Tschewsassen and Tsswassen. The current spelling dates from a 1916 report by the Royal Commission on Indian Affairs and was adopted by the Geographic Board of Canada in 1953. The name refers to the people of the Tsawwassen First Nation who live in the area and speak the Halq'em-ylem (Halkomelem) language. Tsawwassen is a derivation of the Halq'em-ylem place name Scəwaθn, which means "land facing the sea." The correct pronunciation of the moniker is *sa-WOSSen*, though many incorrectly say *TA-wossen*.

TSIMPSEAN PENINSULA This peninsula northwest of Prince Rupert takes its name from the people of the local Tsimshian First Nation. The Geographic Board of Canada officially adopted the moniker in 1927, but it dates from at least 1881. It has also gone through several spellings over the years, including Chimsain, Chimsyan Timshian, Tsimpsian and Tsimp-Sheean. The Tsimshian who live on the peninsula speak the Coast Tsimshian, or Sm'algax, language, and the name Tsimshian is a derivation of the Sm'algax word *ts'msyan*, which means "inside the Skeena River."

TUCKER BAY *See* Jedediah Island.

TUMBLER RIDGE (2006: pop. 2454) The British Columbia government built this district municipality in the early 1980s as a company town for Teck Corporation employees who worked at the nearby Bullmoose and Quintette open-pit coal mines. The name refers to the frequent rockslides on a geological formation just north of the community.

TURNAGAIN RIVER This river in north-central British Columbia was named by Hudson's Bay Company explorer John Black. This was as far as Black travelled before turning around to head home during his expedition of 1824. Black called it Turn-Again River; the name had been shortened by 1897. The traditional Kaska First Nation name for this river is Gacho.

TURNOUR ISLAND (54 km^2) This island, located at the mouth of Knight Inlet, was named by Captain Daniel Pender in about 1866 for Captain Nicholas Edward Brooke Turnour. Captain Turnour was the commanding officer of the HM steam corvette *Clio*, which sailed off the British Columbia coast from 1864 to 1868.

TUSK PEAK (3362 m) This mountain was named in 1920 by the surveyors of the Interprovincial Boundary Survey as they were demarcating the border between British Columbia and Alberta. The peak is so named because its summit resembles a tusk. Tusk Peak is located northwest of Golden, between Hamber Lake and Cummins Lake provincial parks.

TWEEDSMUIR PROVINCIAL PARK (9742 km²) Located in north-central British Columbia, this is the largest provincial park in BC. It was established in 1938 and named after John Buchan, the 1st Baron Tweedsmuir of Elsfield. The noted author and Governor General of Canada travelled extensively throughout the site of the future park by float plane and on horseback in 1937.

TZOUHALEM / MOUNT TZOUHALEM Both this small community and the nearby mountain (502 m) are located just east of Duncan. The residential settlement was named after the peak, which, in turn, was named after Tzouhalem, a fierce Cowichan First Nation chief who led an attack on Fort Victoria in 1844. He was feared as much by his fellow Cowichan and other First Nations peoples as he was by non-Aboriginals; some even say that he was demented. He had at least 14 wives (and possibly many more) and had a habit of acquiring them by killing their husbands. Tzouhalem was eventually banished from his own band because of the many murders he committed, and he was forced to live in a cave on the mountain that bears his name. Tzouhalem was killed in 1854 on Kuper Island. It might have been one of his wives who did him in, though others say that he died at the hands of the husband of a woman Tzouhalem wanted to add to his harem. In any case, Tzouhalem's head was cut off and used as a football by the people of the Lamalcha First Nation who live on the island. Fur trader

Roderick Finlayson, who was in charge at Fort Victoria from 1843 to 1849, referred to the chief as Tsoughelam.

Mount Tzouhalem was called Tzohailim Hill on an 1855 map and Tzohailin Hill on an 1864 British Admiralty chart. It was officially christened Tzuhalem Mountain in 1911 and renamed Mount Tzuhalem in 1950. The current moniker was adopted in 2000, after somebody finally checked with the Cowichan First Nation about the correct spelling. The settlement dates from at least 1903 and was named after the mountain. Originally, its moniker was correctly spelled as Tzouhalem, but the postal authorities respelled it Tzuhalem in 1911. The correct spelling was restored in 2000.

T

U

UCLUELET / UCLUELET INLET The district municipality of Ucluelet (2006: pop. 1487) dates from 1860, when the first non-Aboriginal settler, Captain Charles Stuart, opened a store near Ucluelet Inlet. The inlet itself was named Ucluelet Arm (because it is an arm of Barkley Sound) in 1861 by Captain George Richards of the HMS *Hecate*; it acquired its current name in 1934. Both the settlement and the inlet took their name from the people of the nearby Yuu-tluth-aht (Ucluelet) First Nation, which is a branch of the Nuu-Chah-Nulth First Nation. *Yuu-tl* is a Nuu-Chah-Nulth word meaning "a good landing place for canoes," and the name Yuu-tluth-aht translates into "the people with the safe landing place for canoes."

UNION BAY Both a bay and a community (2006: pop. 1066) share this name. The bay was named after British Columbia industrialist Robert Dunsmuir's Union Colliery Company, which built a large, deep-sea loading dock there in 1889 to serve as the coal port for his local mines. At one time, the bay had the largest wharf in the province and the village was soon established nearby.

UPPER ARROW LAKE *See* Arrow Lakes.

V

VALEMOUNT (2006: pop. 1018) This village dates from about 1909, about when the first settlers arrived. At roughly the same time, a roadhouse was built to accommodate the anticipated travellers who would use the proposed Canadian Northern Railway line that was to be built through the area. A railway station was built on the site in 1912 or 1913; a post office was opened in 1913. It (and, hence, the settlement) was called Cranberry Lake, after a nearby 2.8-square-kilometre, shallow body of water created by a beaver dam; in the lake was an island where cranberries grew wild. Swift Creek drained the lake into the McLennan River.

The name of the post office (and the town) was changed to Swift Creek in 1918. In 1927, the CN decided to move its railway station about two kilometres west and asked the local residents to christen the new location. Valemount was CN's suggestion; the alternative was Burgoyne, after Jim Burgoyne, who had worked in the area for many years. The post office at Swift Creek changed its moniker to Valemount in 1928, to match the name of the new CN station. The name Valemount comes from the fact that the village is in a valley between steep mountains. One source says the name is short for the phrase "vale amid the mountains." Valemount is 25 kilometres west of Mount Robson Provincial Park.

VALHALLA MOUNTAIN / VALHALLA RANGES The Valhalla Ranges are a series of mountain ranges between Lower Arrow Lake and Slocan Lake. The range was originally named the Valhalla Mountains by geologist Reginald Brock in 1875, after the hall of immortality of

Norse mythology. Renamed the Valhalla Range in 1955, the area became the Valhalla Ranges five years later. In 1889, surveyor George Dawson named Mount Odin and Mount Thor, both within the ranges, after two Norse gods. Hundreds of kilometres away, 10 kilometres west of the Stikine River, is Valhalla Mountain (2437 m). Its moniker was officially adopted in 1935, but it was a well-established name with local residents long before then.

VAN ANDA (2006: pop. 324). This community on the northeast side of Texada Island was founded in 1897 and was named after the Van Anda Copper and Gold Mining Company, which opened the nearby famous Copper Queen mine earlier that same year. The mining company was named by its owner, Seattle capitalist Edward Blewitt, after his friend, *New York Sun* journalist Carl Vattel van Anda. However, when the post office opened in Van Anda in 1897, the moniker was incorrectly spelled as one word, Vananda. That remained the town's official name until the mistake was corrected to reflect public usage in 1992.

VANCOUVER (2006: pop. 578,041) British Columbia's largest city was named after Captain George Vancouver. Between 1792 and 1794, while in command of the HMS *Discovery*, Vancouver extensively explored and sur- veyed the Pacific Coast between Puget Sound and Alaska, including Burrard Inlet, on whose southern shore the city now stands. In 1884, the Canadian Pacific Railway decided to locate its western terminus at a harbour on Burrard Inlet near present-day Gastown. Already in existence at the site was the small settlement of Granville. A townsite was laid out along the harbour by the CPR in 1885, and the new city of Vancouver, which included Granville, was incorporated the following year. The name was chosen by William van Horne, the general manager of the CPR. Van Horne felt that, unlike the other two suggested monikers, Granville and Liverpool, the name of Vancouver was (thanks to Vancouver Island)

already firmly associated in the world's mind with Canada's west coast.

VANCOUVER ISLAND (31,764 km²) Like the city of Vancouver, British Columbia's largest island is named after Captain George Vancouver. The building of a fort by the Spanish at Friendly Cove in 1789 almost led to a war between Britain and Spain, but a treaty was signed the next year to resolve the situation. The two countries sent commissioners to Nootka Island in 1792 to implement the agreement. To celebrate their meeting, the two delegates, Captain Vancouver and Juan Francisco de la Bodega y Quadra, named nearby Vancouver Island after themselves. For decades, it was known as Quadra and Vancouver's Island, but Hudson's Bay Company traders had shortened it to Vancouver's Island by 1824. The present name (without the apostrophe and *s*) came into common usage in about 1860.

VANDERHOOF (2006: pop. 4064) This district municipality was laid out in 1914 by Chicago publicity agent Herbert Vanderhoof and named after him by the Grand Trunk Pacific Railway, who owned the land occupied by the townsite. The promoter had been hired by the GTP, the Canadian Northern Railway, the Canadian Pacific Railway and the Canadian government to use his magazine, *Canada West*, and various farm journals to attract American settlers to western Canada. In Dutch, *vanderhoof* means "on the farm." Vanderhoof is 97 kilometres west of Prince George.

VENN PASSAGE This sea passage just west of Prince Rupert was named by Anglican missionary William Duncan after the Reverend Henry Venn, the leader of the Church Mission Society in London, England, from 1841 to 1873. It was the CMS that sent Duncan to British Columbia in 1857. The name Venn was later adopted by Captain George Richards when Richards surveyed the area in 1862. The passage was known as Venn Creek until 1911; "creek" is an old nautical word for a small inlet.

VERNON (2006: pop. 35,944) This city began as Priest's Valley in 1862, when Father Paul Durieu built a cabin there as an out-station for the priests at the Okanagan Mission. The settlement might (or might not—sources vary) have once been called Forge Valley because of a local blacksmith's shop. It might also have been known at one point as Centreville. In any case, the community acquired its current moniker in 1887, when it was named after Forbes George Vernon and possibly also for his brother, Charles. The Vernons arrived in 1863 and developed a ranch at nearby Coldstream. Charles sold his share to Forbes and left for Victoria in 1883. Forbes stayed behind, became a member of the provincial legislature and was, in 1887, British Columbia's Chief Commissioner of Lands and Works. Vernon is near the northeast end of Okanagan Lake.

THE VICE PRESIDENT *See* The President.

VICTORIA (2006: pop. 78,057) This city and provincial capital on the southeast tip of Vancouver Island dates back to the construction of a Hudson's Bay Company trading post in 1843. It was initially called Fort Camosun, after the local First Nations name for the harbour. HBC chief trader Charles Ross, who built the post, then changed the name to Fort Albert, after Queen Victoria's husband, Prince Albert. The HBC's Northern Department had other plans and called it Fort Victoria. That summer, supply ships referred to it by all three names. Finally, some clarification was sought from the HBC's headquarters in London, England, and a terse reply confirmed that the trading post was to be named after the monarch herself. The post was given the moniker Fort Victoria in a formal ceremony in December 1843.

V

A settlement slowly grew around the fort, and a townsite was formally laid out in 1851–52, which was officially christened Victoria in 1852.

VIEW ROYAL (2006: pop. 8768) This town was first settled in the 1850s by Dr. John Helmcken, Hudson's Bay Company physician and colonial politician. It was named about 100 years later because of its view of Royal Roads and was finally incorporated in 1988. View Royal is six kilometres west of Victoria.

V

W

W.A.C. BENNETT DAM It took five years, from 1962 to 1967, to build this 183-metre-high, two-kilometre-long, power-generating dam on the Peace River, 24 kilometres west of Hudson's Hope. Behind the dam is Williston Reservoir (1761 km²), the largest body of fresh water in British Columbia. The dam was named after W.A.C. (William Andrew Cecil) Bennett, the longest-serving premier (in office from 1952 until 1972) in BC history.

WADDINGTON CHANNEL / WADDINGTON HARBOUR Both the natural harbour at the head of Bute Inlet and the sea passage between East and West Redonda islands were named in 1862 by Captain George Richard for Alfred Waddington. Waddington was a wealthy Victoria businessman who unsuccessfully tried to build a wagon road in the 1860s from the head of Bute Inlet up the Homathko River, through the Coast Mountains and on to Fort Alexandria. In 1858, he also wrote the first book (aside from government publications) to be published in British Columbia. *See* Mount Waddington.

WALES ISLAND / WALES POINT Wales Point, which is located on Wales Island (92 km²), was named in 1793 by Captain George Vancouver for astronomer and mathematician William Wales. Wales was the mathematical master at Christ's Hospital in London, England, from 1775 to 1798, where he taught nautical astronomy and navigation. Wales earlier served as the astronomer on Captain James Cook's second Pacific voyage (1772–75), during which he shared his knowledge with Vancouver and Cook's other junior officers. The British Hydrographic

Office named the island after Wales in 1871. Both the island and the point are located in Observatory Inlet.

WARDNER This small community was founded and christened in 1896 by James F. Wardner, a mining and railway promoter from Bellingham, Washington, who established a number of townsites in Canada and the United States. Wardner is 26 kilometres southeast of Cranbrook.

WARFIELD (2006: pop. 1729) Located between Rossland and Trail, this village was established in the early 20th century by the Consolidated Mining and Smelting Company for its employees. The CMS also owned the smelter in Trail, which was built in 1895 by American industrialist Frederick Heinze; the company named Warfield after Heinze's close friend and business associate, Carlos Warfield.

WASA (2006: pop. 222) This community was named by its first settler, Nils Hanson. Hanson arrived in 1885 and established a 260-hectare ranch, which he called Wasa. Most sources say he named the location after his hometown of Vaasa, on the west coast of Finland. However, one biographer points out that Hanson was actually from Skole in southern Sweden and contends that he named his ranch after an early Scandinavian king known for hospitality and kindness. This might have been King Gustav Vasa of Sweden, the founder of the Vasa Dynasty, which ruled Sweden from 1523 to 1654. In any case, a village was established near Hanson's ranch. When a post office was opened in 1902, Hanson was the first postmaster, and he named it (and, hence, the town) after the ranch. Just north of the community is Wasa Lake. It was called Hanson Lake, after Nils Hanson, at least as far back as back as 1915, but the name was changed in 1964 to reflect local usage.

WEBSTERS CORNERS This neighbourhood in Maple Ridge is named after James Murray Webster, a Scotsman who came to British Columbia in 1883. A former sea captain, Webster settled in the area, first working as a farmer, then becoming the local postmaster in 1891. He named the post office (and, hence, the town) after himself.

WELLINGTON Once its own separate township, this suburb of Nanaimo was founded in the early 1870s by industrialist and politician Robert Dunsmuir and was the site of one of his coal mines. Dunsmuir named the community after Arthur Wellesley, the 1st Duke of Wellington, who defeated Napoleon at the Battle of Waterloo and later became the prime minister of Britain. Wellington is eight kilometres northwest of downtown Nanaimo.

WELLS (2006: pop. 236) This district municipality was initially a company town. It was built in 1933 and maintained by Fred M. Wells' Cariboo Gold Quartz Mining Company, after Wells discovered gold in the area, starting a small gold rush. Wells is just northwest of Barkerville.

WELLS GRAY PROVINCIAL PARK Established in 1939, this park (5297 km²) was named after Arthur Wellesley "Wells" Gray, the former mayor of New Westminster and, from 1933 to 1944, the provincial Minister of Lands. The park is in central British Columbia, between Canim and Quesnel lakes and the North Thompson River.

WEST BAY *See* Gambier Island.

WEST KELOWNA *See* Kelowna.

WEST VANCOUVER (2006: pop. 42,131) This district municipality is located on the western end of the north shore of Burrard Inlet. The community began in the 1880s, when wealthy Vancouverites began building summer cottages in the area, and was part of the District of North Vancouver until 1912. The moniker dates from at least 1910, when the West Vancouver Transportation Company ferried passengers across the Burrard Inlet from Vancouver.

WESTBANK (2006: pop. 3930) This neighbourhood in West Kelowna is so named because it sits on the west bank of Okanagan Lake. The name was suggested in 1902 by John Davidson, who had settled in the area 10 years earlier.

WESTHOLME This small community is now part of North Cowichan. It was called Hall's Crossing when the Esquimalt and Nanaimo Railway laid its tracks there in 1886. A local resident, retired naval captain Charles Edward Barkley (grandson of Charles William Barkley of Barkley Sound fame), gave his mail to the mail clerk whenever the train stopped at the local station. Soon, his neighbours asked Barkley to hand in their mail, too, and before he knew it, Barkley was the local postmaster, running the post office out of his home. Barkley called the post office Westholme, because his house was his "home in the west." One story has it that Barkley picked the name, because his home was the westerly one of the two farms that he owned, but family members dispute that tale. The moniker was applied to the entire community by 1892.

WESTWOLD The area in which this small community is located was known as Grand Prairie as far back as 1826. Walter Homfray built a hotel on the site in 1895 and called it the Adelphi. Five years later, when a post office opened there, Homfray managed to have it, and hence the town, named after the hotel. This angered his neighbours, who favoured the old moniker. The name was eventually changed in 1926, but by that time a community called Grand Prairie had already been established in Alberta, and the postal authorities would not allow another. That's when local resident L.R. Pearse, an immigrant from England, suggested Westwold. *Wold* is an Old English word meaning "high, open plain." It's said that old-time residents didn't care for this name, either. Westwold is about halfway between Kamloops and Vernon.

WHISTLER / WHISTLER MOUNTAIN Whistler is British Columbia's only resort municipality (2006: pop. 9248). Located southwest of Pemberton, it was incorporated in 1975 and named after nearby Whistler Mountain (2181 m). The mountain, in turn, was named for the high-pitched, piercing sound of the marmots that live in large colonies on the mountain's upper slopes. The peak's moniker was officially adopted in 1965, though it had been in local usage since the beginning of the 20th century. The mountain's first name was London Mountain. Some say it was named by a Pacific Great Eastern Railway crew member who worked in the area—the heavy fog and rain on the mountain reminded him of his native London, England. Others say the name referred to the nearby London mineral claim, which was staked in 1903. However, the promoters of the ski resort at Whistler didn't think London Mountain was a marketable name, and they successfully petitioned the government to have the name changed.

WHITE ROCK (2006: pop. 18,755) This city on the southwest corner of the Lower Mainland was named for a giant, 437-tonne boulder that sits on the shore of Semiahmoo Bay. Large enough to be a navigational aid to passing boats, the rock was left by an ancient glacier and coloured white by centuries of bird guano. Today, it is painted four times a year to give it a pristine, white look. There are many First Nations traditions about the origin of the rock. One says that it marks the spot where emissaries of the Creator passed. Another holds that the rock was hurled across the Strait of Georgia by the son of a sea god—a First Nations version of Hercules—to mark the spot where he and his mortal bride would live together.

WHITING RIVER This river in the northwest corner of British Columbia flows southwest into Gilbert Bay in

Alaska. United States Navy Lieutenant Commander Charles M. Thomas named it in 1888 for Robert Whiting, the assistant surgeon in his survey party.

WHONNOCK This community is now part of Maple Ridge. The first non-Aboriginal settler arrived in the area in 1860, and the village that was established took its name from the local Ooanuck Band of the Kwantlen First Nation. (The Ooanuck are now part of the Fort Langley Band.) The moniker has gone through a variety of spellings. When the Canadian Pacific Railway built a station there, the station and the town were called Wharnock. When a post office later opened in 1885, the spelling was changed to Whonnock, even though the local First Nations Reserve used only one *n* at that time (it now uses two). The federal government changed the spelling to Whonock in 1939, but a petition signed by more than four-fifths of the community caused Ottawa to reverse the decision 30 years later. Ooanuck is a Halkomelem First Nation name that means "place where there are always humpback salmon" and refers to the only species of salmon found in the creek that flows through the community.

WHYTECLIFF *See* Horseshoe Bay.

WILLIAMS LAKE A community and a lake share this name. The city (2006: pop. 10,744), located between 100 Mile House and Quesnel, was christened in 1861 after the nearby lake, which, in turn, was named at about the same time for Chief William, a local Secwepemc (Shuswap) First Nation leader who helped keep the peace between the local First Nations people and the miners during the Cariboo Gold Rush. The body of water had previously been called Columetza Lake and Lac de Colum-en-eet-sa.

WILLISTON RESERVOIR (1773 km²) Located in north-central British Columbia at the headwaters of the Peace

River, this is the largest body of fresh water in the province. The reservoir was created in 1968 with the construction of the W.A.C. Bennett Dam near Hudson's Hope. It was named after Ray Williston, the provincial Minister of Lands and Forests from 1956 to 1972.

WILMER (2006: pop. 253) This community just north of Invermere was established in the late 1890s. It was called Peterborough when the local post office opened in 1900, but postal authorities rejected the name to avoid confusion with the much larger Peterborough in Ontario. The town was renamed in 1902 after its first non-Aboriginal resident, rancher and lumberman Wilmer Cleveland Wells.

WINDERMERE / WINDERMERE LAKE The community of Windermere (2006: pop. 1259), located southeast of Invermere, was established in the 1880s and named after the lake. Windermere Lake was previously known as Kootenae Lake and Lower Columbia Lake before it was christened in 1883 by Gilbert Sproat, who was surveying the Columbia Valley (where this body of water is found) for the provincial government. Sproat, a Scotsman, thought the lake resembled Lake Windermere in northwest England's Lake District.

WINFIELD This small community is located 30 kilometres south of Vernon. It was named Alvaston by its first postmaster in 1909, after a place in England, but had been rechristened by 1930 after Winfield Lodge, the home of the community's first settler, Thomas Wood. Sources vary as to whether Wood, a rancher, arrived there in the 1860s or in 1871.

WINTER HARBOUR A harbour and a community that overlooks it share this name. The harbour, located on the northwest side of Quatsino Sound, was named in 1864 by Captain George Richards because of the protection it provided ships from violent winter storms. The small fishing village (estimated pop. 20) began when a clam cannery was built there in 1904. The settlement was originally called Queenstown but was renamed in 1935. The harbour itself was rechristened Leeson Harbour in 1930, after local resident Jobe Leeson, to avoid confusion with another harbour by the same name (now called Winter Inlet) on Pearse Island. At the request of local residents, the harbour's moniker was changed back in 1947 to reflect the name of the community.

WRECK BEACH The name of this famous clothing-optional site on the western tip of Vancouver dates back to 1928, when three log barges and a floating grain container (the *Biscayne,* the *Bingamon,* the *Black Wolf* and the *Blatchford*) were sunk off its shores by their owner, the Pacific Tug and Barge Company, to create a breakwater for a large log-storage ground. The moniker became official in 1982. Until then, the beach was also known as University Beach because of its proximity to the University of British Columbia, as well as Acadia Beach, Point Grey Beach, Tower Beach and Ulksen Beach.

WYCLIFFE (2006: pop. 189) This community, 12 kilometres northwest of Cranbrook, was settled in about 1900. It was originally known as Bayard, but the name was changed in 1906 to honour John Wycliffe, the famous 14th-century English churchman and translator of the Bible.

WYNNDEL (2006: pop. 597) This community near the south end of Kootenay Lake was settled in the 1890s. There is a dispute as to whom it was named after. Fruit growing has always been a major local industry, and most sources say the settlement was christened after one of the first successful fruit growers in the area. Others contend that the moniker honours a North-West Mounted Police officer named Wynn, who came to British Columbia with Sam Steele in 1885 and later served with distinction in the Boer War. It is also believed by some that Wynndel was not the town fathers' first choice, but that their initial pick, Duck Creek, was rejected by federal postal authorities because a town with a similar name already existed elsewhere in Canada.

W

X

XENIA LAKE This small body of water (0.13 km²) is located northwest of Christina Lake, near Grand Forks. The name appears on a 1923 map but is probably much older. It has been suggested that the moniker is a reference to *xenia*, the Greek concept of generosity. Long-time area residents point out, however, that the lake was once called Little Christina Lake (after the nearby body of water) and that fur trappers used Xina and Xenia as abbreviations. Others say that it is taken from the botanical term by the same name. (*Xenia* is the influence that pollen has upon the fruit or seeds after pollination has occurred. For example, the kernels of a head of corn may be a variety of colours depending upon what strain of corn the pollen came from.)

X

Y

YAHK A community, a mountain and a river all share this name. The town of Yahk (2006: pop. 127) is located on the Moyie River, 25 kilometres east of Creston; the Yahk River is 22 kilometres east of the village. Yahk Mountain (2186 m) is at the head of the river, 35 kilometres northeast of the town.

The Canadian Pacific Railway placed its tracks through present-day Yahk in 1898. A railway station was built shortly afterward and, by 1905, a thriving town existed that was named after the peak. Although not officially adopted until 1924, the name was applied long before then to the mountain and the river. The current spelling dates from the 1860s, when colonial governor Frederick Seymour changed the names of the Yaak and other rivers to distinguish British Columbia's waterways from those in the United States. *Yaak* is a Ktunaxa (Kootenay) First Nation word. Some believe that it means "bow" (as in bow and arrow) and that it refers to the large south-west-north bend in the nearby Kootenay River as well as to the territory inside the "bow," where Yahk is located. It has also been suggested that *yaak* means "a place where the river bends" and "a place where life necessities are plentiful." Some believe it means "female caribou." Finally, others think that Yahk is a derivation of the Ktunaxa word *a'k*, which means "arrow" and that it describes the river's arrow-like intersection with the Kootenay River's "bow."

YAKOUN RIVER The largest river on Haida Gwaii (Queen Charlotte Islands), the Yakoun flows north through the centre of Graham Island to Masset Inlet. There's also a Yakoun Bay and a Yakoun Lake on Graham Island. The name is very old and is a Haida First Nation word that has been given many interpretations, including "straight point," "in the middle" and "on the east."

YALE (2006: pop. 186) This community began in 1847 as a Hudson's Bay Company trading outpost called Fort Yale. It was named after James Murray Yale, the HBC chief trader in charge of Fort Langley. The settlement of Yale sprang up around the outpost virtually overnight during the 1858 gold rush. Yale is on the Fraser River, 32 kilometres north of Hope.

YARROW Now within Chilliwack's municipal borders, Yarrow was once a separate community. Located 18 kilometres west of downtown Chilliwack, it was originally settled in the 1890s and was first called Majuba Hill, after a battle in the South African (Boer) War of 1899–1902. The British Columbia Electric Railway Company (BCER) built a depot there in 1910, which it called Yarrow Station, but the community continued to be called Majuba Hill for at least three more years.

There are two explanations behind the name Yarrow. First, when the BCER was building railway stations for its new Fraser Valley line, company executive Michael Urwin drew up a list of "our oldest important shareholders," including someone named Yarrow, that the stations should be christened after. The other story is that the community was named after the bitter local wildflower, as a symbol of a bitter dispute between the BCER and a local resident who, at gunpoint, held up for several hours the laying of track over a private cemetery he owned.

YELLOWHEAD A lake, a mountain and a mountain pass all share this name, as well as a highway that links Prince Rupert and Hope and then heads eastward through the pass and on to Winnipeg. Yellowhead is the English translation of the French nickname, Tête Jaune, which was

Y

given by voyageurs to the yellow-haired Pierre Bostonais (also known as Pierre Bostonnais and Pierre Hatsination), an Iroquois Métis fur trapper and trader who worked as a guide for the North West Company and the Hudson's Bay Company from 1816 to 1827. He guided the first HBC party across the Rocky Mountains in 1820. Bostonnais used Yellowhead Pass, located on the Alberta border, west of Jasper National Park, to take his furs to Jasper. The pass was also known by a number of other names in the 19th century, including Cowdung Pass, Jasper Pass, Leather Pass and Tête Jaune Pass. Yellowhead Mountain, known by its current name by 1921, is actually a mountain ridge west of the pass with a number of peaks on it. Yellowhead Lake, located just south of the pass, was called Cow Dung Lake and Buffalo Dung Lake on maps from the mid-19th century. The lake was known by its current name by 1898. Some have argued that fur traders François Decoigne or Jasper Hawes were Tête Jaune, but Parks Canada historians have proven them wrong. *See* Tête Jaune Cache.

YENNADON This community is now part of Maple Ridge. Its first non-Aboriginal settler arrived in 1875, and the area was initially called South Lillooet because it sits on the banks of the Alouette River (then known as the south branch of the Lillooet River). The moniker was changed when the local post office opened in 1911. The government asked the town's first postmaster, E.W. Prowse, to rename the place because there was already a post office at Lillooet, and it was felt that another town with a similar name would be too confusing. Prowse chose to christen the site after his grandfather's home, Yennadon Manor, in Devonshire, England.

YEO ISLAND / YEO ISLANDS Yeo Island (92 km²), located between Spiller and Bullock channels, was named in 1866 by Captain Daniel Pender. The Yeo Islands, on the west side of Ballenas Channel, were christened about six years earlier by Captain George Richards in honour

Y

of Doctor Gerald Yeo, the surgeon on Rear Admiral Robert Baynes' flagship, the HMS *Ganges*, while the ship was sailing in British Columbia's waters from 1857 to 1860.

YMIR / YMIR MOUNTAIN The community of Ymir (2006: pop. 233) is 28 kilometres north of Nelson. There are two stories behind its name. In one, the village was laid out in 1897 by the Nelson and Fort Shepherd Railway and was named by the company's president, Daniel Corbin, for the nearby Ymir Range. The range, in turn, was named in about 1885 by geologist George Dawson for the ancient Norse god Ymir, the father of Odin and the giants. In the other tale, Ymir was originally called Quartz Creek because its first post office was located at the point where Quartz Creek emptied into the Salmo River. The community was then renamed Ymier by three local residents, including Joe Petrie, who said the moniker came from a range of mountains in his home country of France. However, the railway dropped the *e* when they built a station there. The name of Ymir no longer applies to the local mountain range but only to a single peak, Ymir Mountain (2398 m).

YOHO A national park, a glacier, a lake, two rivers (Yoho and Little Yoho), a valley, a mountain pass and two mountains all share this name. The national park is located on the Alberta border, east of Golden, and was established in 1886. Most of the other sites are within or near the park, including Yoho Peak (2773 m). However, hundreds of kilometres away, 45 kilometres southeast of Tumbler Ridge, is Yoho Mountain (1349 m). *Yoho* is a Cree First Nation expression indicating astonishment, awe and wonder, as when one is amazed by the park's spectacular stone walls, waterfalls and mountain peaks.

YOUBOU (2006: pop. 734) This community began in 1913 with the construction of a sawmill owned by the Empire

Lumber Company. Originally called Cottonwood, the town was renamed in 1926 when its first post office opened. The postal authorities refused to accept Cottonwood because another community with that name already existed elsewhere in Canada. The current moniker is a combination of the first three letters of the surnames of Empire Lumber's general manager, C.C. Yount, and its president, G.B. Bouten. Youbou is located on the north side of Cowichan Lake.

YUQUOT This community's estimated population is currently fewer than 20 people, but archaeological evidence indicates that this summer village has been inhabited for at least 4200 years, making it one of the longest continuously occupied sites in British Columbia. Located at the southeast end of Nootka Island, it is a village of the Mowachaht / Muchalaht First Nation, one of the Nuu-chah-nulth (Nootka) First Nations. Yuquot is a Nootka name that means "where the winds blow from many directions." The community had also been known for more than two centuries as Friendly Cove because of the hospitable reception that Captain James Cook received when he stopped there in 1778, but that name now officially refers only to the local cove itself and not to the village.

Y

Z

ZEBALLOS The village of Zeballos (2006: pop. 189) was named in 1937 after the Zeballos Inlet, which, in turn, was named in 1791 by Spanish Navy Captain Alexandro Malaspina for Lieutenant Ciriaco Cevallos. (Zeballos is an alternate spelling for Cevallos. In Spanish, the letter z is pronounced like a c, and the letter v is pronounced like the letter b.) Cevallos was an officer in Malaspina's expedition that year along the Pacific Northwest Coast. The inlet is north of Nootka Island. Malaspina originally called it Zeballos Arm because he considered it a branch, or arm, of Esperanza Inlet. The village is at the head of the inlet and was established during a local gold rush in 1935–36.

Zeballos Peak (1578 m) is located 14 kilometres northwest of the community. It was christened Zeballos Mountain in 1934, but the moniker was changed in 1982. Nearby Zeballos Lake and Zeballos River were also named after the inlet.

ZUCIARTE CHANNEL It is not known who first named this channel, but it was listed on the oldest British Admiralty chart, dated 1841, of Nootka Sound. The name is a derivation of Ze-sa-at, which is the name of a band of the Muchalat First Nation. Zuciarte Channel separates Bligh Island from Nootka Island.

Z

APPENDIX

Notes on Non-English Names and Words and Names of British Columbia First Nations

Many British Columbia place names have their origins in non-English words and names. Following modern rules of grammar, those words, when mentioned, are italicized, whereas place names are not. For instance, the name of Anyox Creek is taken from the Nisga'a First Nation word *anyoose*, while the name of the Alsek River is a derivation of the Southern Tutchone First Nation place name A?séxh' and Anahim Lake was christened after the Tsilhqot'in leader Chief Anaham.

Also, many of BC's First Nations now use their traditional names and spellings of those names to identify themselves rather than the names and spellings that were attached to them decades ago by European fur traders, explorers, and settlers. Whenever this has occurred, an effort has been made to include both names. For example, the Secwepemc First Nation, which used to be called the Shuswap First Nation, is identified throughout this book as the Secwepemc (Shuswap) First Nation.

NOTES ON SOURCES

Interviews

Unpublished interviews by Sylvia Bramhill, Fort Nelson, BC historian and assistant librarian at the Fort Nelson (BC) Public Library, of George Behn, former Chief of the Fort Nelson First Nation (a Slavey First Nation), 4 September 2009; of Fort Nelson First Nation band elders Mary Behn, 4 September 2009, and Mimi Needlay, 5 September 2009; and of Norman McCarthy, Fort Nelson First Nation band member, 9 October 2009.

Unpublished interview by Dorothy Wright, clerk at the Williams Lake (BC) Branch of the Cariboo Regional District Library, of Arnold Jenner, GIS (Geographic Information Systems) Technician, Cariboo Regional District, Williams Lake, BC, 18 February 2010.

Books

Akrigg, G.P.V., and Helen B. Akrigg. *British Columbia Place Names*. Victoria: Sono Nis, 1986.

Athalmer: The Sunny City of British Columbia. Vancouver: British Canadian Securities, ca. 1912.

Bancroft, Hubert Howe. *History of the Northwest Coast. Vol. I: 1543–1800 in The Works of Hubert Howe Bancroft*. Vol. XXVII. San Francisco: The History Company, 1886.

Basque, Garnet. *British Columbia Ghost Town Atlas*. Langley, BC: Sunfire, 1982.

Bilsland, W.W., and W.E. Ireland. *Atlin, 1898–1910: The Story of a Gold Boom, with Pictorial Supplement*. Atlin, BC: Atlin Centennial Committee, 1971.

Bonner, Virginia. *The Hamlet with an Attitude: 1886–1945, The Story of Cobble Hill Village*. Duncan, BC: Firgrove, 2001.

Brooks, Carellin. *Wreck Beach*. Vancouver: New Star, 2007.

Brown, Robert. *Robert Brown and the Vancouver Island Exploring Expedition*. John Hayman, ed. Vancouver: UBC Press, 1989.

Campbell, Ken. *Fort Simpson: Fur Fort at Laxlqu'alaams*. Suwilaay'msga na_ ga'niiyatgm / Teachings of Our Grandfathers Series, No. 4. Prince Rupert, BC: Tsimshian Chiefs, n.d. [ca. 1992].

The Canadian Encyclopedia. 3 vols. Edmonton: Hurtig, 1985.

Canadian Permanent Committee on Geographical Names. *Gazetteer of Canada. British Columbia*. 3rd ed. Ottawa: Geographical Surveys Division, Surveys and Mapping Branch, Energy, Mines and Resources Canada, 1985.

Cassidy, Maureen. *The Gathering Place: A History of the Wet'uwet'en Village of Tse-kya*. Hagwilget, BC: Hagwilget Band Council, 1987.

Chisholm, Barbara, and Andrea Gutsche. *Superior: Under the Shadow of the Gods*. Russell Floren, project producer. Toronto: Lynx Images, 1998.

Christensen, Bev. *Prince George: Railways, Rivers, and Timber*. Burlington, ON: Windsor Publications, 1989.

Colquhoun, Alan. *Modern Architecture*. New York: Oxford University Press, 2002.

Curtis, Edward S. *The Salishan Tribes of the Coast. The Chimakum and the Quilliute. The Willapa*. Vol. 9 of *The North American Indian*. Seattle: E.S. Curtis, 1913.

Decker, Francis, Margaret Fougberg, and Mary Ronayne. *Pemberton: The History of a Settlement*. Gordon R. Elliott, ed. Pemberton, BC: Pemberton Pioneer Women, 1977.

Denig, Edwin Thompson, and J.N.B. Hewitt. *The Assiniboine.* Norman: University of Oklahoma Press, 2000.

Dickinson, Christine Frances, and Diane Solie Smith. *Atlin: The Story of British Columbia's Last Gold Rush*. Atlin, BC: Atlin Historical Society, 1995.

Douglas, R., compiler. *Meaning of Canadian City Names*. "Reprinted from the 17th Report of the Geographic Board [of Canada]." Ottawa: F.A. Acland, 1922.

Eilers, Marlene A. *Queen Victoria's Descendants*. New York: Atlantic International, 1987.

Elliott, Gordon. *Memories of the Chemainus Valley: A History of a People*. Chemainus, BC: Chemainus Valley Historical Society, 1978.

Encyclopedia Canadiana: The Encyclopedia of Canada. Vol. 10. Toronto: Grolier, 1970.

Fiske, Jo-Anne, and Betty Patrick. *Cis Dideen Kat=When the Plumes Rise: The Way of the Lake Babine Nation.* Vancouver: University of British Columbia Press, n.d. [ca. 2000]

Ford, Helen, Gene Joyce, and Dorrit MacLeod, eds. *Place Names of the Alberni Valley.* Port Alberni, BC: Alberni District Museum and Historical Society, n.d.

Francis, Daniel, ed. *Encyclopedia of British Columbia.* Madeira Park: Harbour, 2000.

Francis, R. Douglas, Richard Jones, and Donald B. Smith. *Origins: Canadian History to Confederation.* 4th ed. Toronto: Harcourt Canada, 2000.

Geological Survey of Canada. *Reports of Exploration and Surveys, 1877–8: Report of Progress for 1877–78.* Montreal: Dawson Brothers, 1879.

Gibbs, George. *Dictionary of the Chinook Jargon, or Trade Language of Oregon.* New York: Cramoisy, 1863. Reprinted as vol. 12 of the Shea's Library of American Linguistics series, New York: AMS Press, 1970.

Gibson, Alice L. *Green Branches and Fallen Leaves: The Story of a Community, Shawnigan Lake, 1887–1967.* Shawnigan Lake, BC: Shawnigan Lake Confederation Centennial Celebrations Committee of 1966–67, printed by the Cowichan Leader, n.d. [ca. 1966].

Godman, Josephine. *Pioneer Days of Port Renfrew.* T.W. Paterson, ed. Victoria: Solitaire, n.d. [ca. 1973].

Gough, Barry. *Gunboat Frontier: British Maritime Authority and Northwest Coast Indians, 1846–1890.* Vancouver: UBC Press, 1984.

Hancock, Ian F. *A List of Place Names in the Pacific North-west Derived from the Chinook Jargon, With a Word-list of the Language.* Vancouver: Vancouver Public Library, 1972.

Helgesen, Marion I., compiler and ed. *Footprints: Pioneer Families of the Metchosin District, Southern Vancouver Island, 1851–1900.* Victoria: Metchosin School Museum Society, 1983.

Hines, H.K. *An Illustrated History of the State of Washington.* Chicago: Lewis, 1893.

Hitz, Charles W. *Through the Rapids: The History of Princess Louisa Inlet.* Kirkland, WA: Sitka 2 Publishing, 2003.

Horetzky, Charles. *Canada on the Pacific.* Montreal: Dawson Brothers, 1874.

Hughes, Ben. *History of the Comox Valley.* Nanaimo, BC: Evergreen Press, n.d.

Klassen, Agatha E., ed. *Yarrow: A Portrait in Mosaic.* Yarrow, BC: self-published, 1976.

Kuipers, A.H. *A report on Shuswap, with a Squamish lexical appendix.* Paris: Peeters/SELAF, 1989.

Laforet, Andrea, and Annie York. *Spuzzum: Fraser Canyon Histories, 1808–1939.* Vancouver: UBC Press in association with the Canadian Museum of Civilization, 1988.

Lee, Sidney. *King Edward VII: A Biography. Vol. 2. The Reign, 22nd January, 1901 to 6th May 1910.* New York: Macmillan, 1927.

Little, C.H. *18th-Century Maritime Influences on History and Place Names of British Columbia.* Madrid: Editorial Naval, 1991.

Luxton, Eleanor G. *Banff: Canada's First National Park.* Banff: Summerthought, n.d.

Mackie, Richard Somerset. *Trading Beyond the Mountains: The British Fur Trade on the Pacific, 1793–1843*. Vancouver, UBC Press, 1997.

Mitcham, Allison. *Atlin: The Last Utopia*. Hantsport, NS: Lancelot Press, 1989.

Morris, Richard, ed. *Encyclopedia of American History*. New York: Harper and Row, 1970.

Nakayama, Toshihide. *Nuuchahnulth (Nootka) Morphosyntax*. University of California Publications in Linguistics Series, vol. 134. Berkeley and Los Angeles: University of California Press, 2001.

Nicholson, George. *Vancouver Island's West Coast, 1762–1962*. Victoria: self-published, 1970.

Nicolay, C.G. *The Oregon Territory: Geographical and Physical Account of That Country And Its Inhabitants With Outlines of Its History And Discovery*. London: Hodson, 1860.

Paterson, T.W. *A Place Called Cowichan: Historically Significant Place Names of the Cowichan Valley*. Duncan, BC: Firgrove, 2005.

Paterson, T.W. *Lower Mainland*. British Columbia Ghost Town Series: 2. Langley, BC: Sunfire, 1984.

Patillo, Roger. *The Canadian Rockies: Pioneers, Legends and True Tales*. Aldergrove, BC: Amberlea Press, and Victoria: Trafford Publishing, 2005.

Phillilps, Terrence. *Harvesting the Fraser: A History of Early Delta*. Alex Gabriel and Laura Cheadle, eds. Delta, BC: Delta Museum and Archives, 2003.

Pryce, Paula. *"Keeping the Lakes' Way": Reburial and the Re-creation of a Moral World Among an Invisible People*. Toronto: University of Toronto Press, n.d.

Pritzker, Barry. *A Native American Encyclopedia: History, Culture, and Peoples*. Oxford: Oxford University Press, 2000.

Rayburn, Alan. *Dictionary of Canadian Place Names*. Don Mills, ON: Oxford University Press, 1999.

Rayburn, Alan. *Naming Canada: Stories About Canadian Place Names*. Toronto: University of Toronto Press, 2001.

Rice, Keren. *Fort Nelson Dene Topical Dictionary*. Unpublished manuscript. 1983.

Roberts, John E. *A Discovery Journal of George Vancouver's First Survey Season on the Coasts of Washington and British Columbia 1792 Including the Work with the Spanish Explorers Galiano and Valdes*. Victoria: Monk Office Supply, 1997.

Rose, Alex. *Land Facing the Sea: Tsawwassen First Nation, A Fact Book*. Delta, BC: Tsawwassen First Nation, n.d.

Scott, Andrew. *The Encyclopedia of Raincoast Place Names: A Complete Reference to Coastal British Columbia*. Madeira Park, BC: Harbour, 2009.

Selters, Andy. *Ways to the Sky: A Historical Guide to North American Mountaineering*. American Alpine Book Series. Golden, CO: American Alpine Club, 2004.

Snyders, Tom, and Jennifer O'Rourke. *Namely Vancouver: A Hidden History of Vancouver Place Names*. Vancouver: Arsenal Pulp, 2001.

Steele, Peter. *Atlin's Gold*. Prince George, BC: Caitlin, 1995.

Taylor, Harry, ed. *Powell River's First 50 Years*. Powell River, BC: Powell River News, 1960.

Waite, Donald E. *The Langley Story Illustrated: An Early History of the Municipality of Langley*. Maple Ridge, BC: self-published, 1977.

Walbran, John T. *British Columbia Coast Names, 1592–1906: Their Origin and History with Map and Illustrations*. Ottawa: Government Printing Bureau, 1909. (Republished for the Vancouver Public Library by J.J. Douglas, West Vancouver, 1971.)

Weibull, Jörgen. *Swedish History in Outline*. Trans. by Paul Britten Austin. Stockholm: Swedish Institute, 1993.

Wilkinson, Glayda, and Marjorie Fitzpatrick. *A Century of Life in Elko: 1899–1999*. Elko, BC: Elko Parks and Recreation, 1999.

Journal, Magazine and Newspaper Articles

Bell, Sarah J. "Internal C Reduplication in Shuswap." *Linguistic Inquiry* (Vol. 14, No. 2). Spring 1983, 332–38.

"Broker L.J. Field Sued for $705,000; Carlos Warfield, F.A. Heinze's Friend, Trying to Recover on a Missing Collateral Transaction." *New York Times,* 25 April 1910.

Doe, Nick A. "The Table of Toba Inlet." *SHALE* (No. 11). May 2005, 22–36.

Elliott, Marie. "Murder on the North Trail: Jewish Merchant in the Cariboo, 1862." *The Scribe* (Vol. 14, No. 1). January 1994, 10–12.

Hunter, Mike. "New 'Glory Hole' Claim: Veteran Prospector Laughed at Legendary Curse in His 30-Year Search for Mine." *The Province*. 1 October 1989.

Lucas, Harry. "Names of Nuu-chah-nulth Nations and Their Meanings." *Ha-Shilth-Sa* (Port Alberni, BC) (Vol. 30, No. 1. 16). January 2003.

McKinnon, Kaitlin. "Sir Charles Hibbert Tupper, K.C." *The Advocate* (Vol. 68). Janaury 2010, 94–96.

Nesteroff, Greg. "Edward Mahon and the Naming of Castlegar." *BC Historical News* (Vol. 36, No. 1). Winter 2002–03, pp. 24–25.

Schwatka, Frederick. "Exploration of the Yukon River in 1883." *American Geographical Society Journal,* 1884, 345–82.

Smedman, Lisa. "Quite a Town." *The Vancouver Courier*. 2 February 2007.

White, Derryll. "Basin Biography: Nils Hanson." *The Basin Record*. (Newsletter of the Columbia Basin Institute of Regional History, Vol. 2, No. 5). n.d., 3.

"White Rock Looks South to Solve Identity Crisis" *Vancouver Sun*. 18 June 2008.

Harris v. Lindeborg, [1931] S.C.R. 235. Supreme Court of Canada, 13 December 1930.

Websites

ABC Bookworld. "Juan Perez." www.abcbookworld.com/view_author. php?id=3261 (accessed 27 August 2009).

All About Roberts Creek, British Columbia. "History of Roberts Creek." www. bigpacific.com/robertscreek/history.html (accessed 4 September 2009).

All Nations Stamp and Coin. "Newsletter #152, September 18, 2008. Things to do in the Neighbourhood: Kerrisdale Village." www.allnationsstampandcoin. com/newsletters/news152.html (accessed 26 February 2010).

Bamberton Historical Society. "Bamberton Memories." www. bambertonhistoricalsociety.org/ (accessed 5 July 2009).

BC Treaty Commission. www.bctreaty.net (accessed 31 August 2009).

Beacon Hill Park. "History." www.beaconhillpark.com/history.html (accessed 5 July 2009).

Birrell, Dave. "PeakFinder." www.peakfinder.com/ (accessed 3 November 2009).

Braches, Fred. "Whonnock History." www.whonnock.ca/whonnock-history/index.html (accessed 26 February 2010).

Brissenden, Constance, and Larry Loyie. "The History of Metropolitan Vancouver: Hall of Fame." www.vancouverhistory.ca/whoswho_A.htm (accessed 4 September 2009).

Britannia Beach. britanniabeach.com/ (accessed 16 October 2009).

BritishColumbia.com. www.britishcolumbia.com/Regions (accessed 3 November 2009).

British Columbia Ministry of Agriculture and Lands. "Integrated Land Management Bureau. GeoBC. Crown Registry and Geographic Base Branch. BC Geographical Names Information System." archive.ilmb.gov.bc.ca/bcnames/ (accessed 3 November 2009).

British Columbia Ministry of Agriculture and Lands. "Socio-Economic Profile. The Quatsino First Nation: History and Continuity." archive.ilmb.gov.bc.ca/slrp/marine/north_island/quatsino/docs/dec03/socioeconomic_profile.pdf (accessed 21 February 2010).

British Columbia Ministry of the Environment. "BC Parks: Kokanee Creek Provincial Park." www.env.gov.bc.ca/bcparks/explore/parkpgs/kokanee_crk/ (accessed 5 September 2009).

Brown, Chester, and Elmer Wiens. "Yarrow, British Columbia. Yarrow Pioneers: Vedder River Flats and Majuba Hill." In website of Pat [Gillis] and Elmer [Wiens]. Album. www.elmerwiens.ca/home/album3_4.html (accessed 11 September 2009).

Brown, Chester, and Elmer Wiens. "Yarrow's Pioneers and Settlers: Vedder River Flats." 1 August 2009. www.yarrowbc.ca/pioneers/vedderflats.html (accessed 9 October 2009).

Caleb Pike Heritage Park. www.calebpikeheritagepark.org/ (accessed 29 September 2009).

Cameron, Laura Jean. "Openings to a Lake: Historical Approaches to Sumas Lake, British Columbia." Vancouver: University of British Columbia. MA Thesis, 1994. circle.ubc.ca/bitstream/2429/5322/1/ubc_1994-0431.pdf (accessed 9 October 2009).

Canada, Government of. "Canadian History Military Gateway." www.phmc.gc.ca/html/br-ex/search-eng.asp?No=20&N=100097+20001&Ne=40000 (accessed 11 September 2009).

Canada, Government of. "Parks Canada: Gwaii Haanas National Park Reserve and Haida Heritage Site." www.pc.gc.ca/eng/pn-np/bc/gwaiihaanas/index.aspx (accessed 28 August 2009).

Canada, Government of. "Parks Canada: Rogers Pass National Historic Site of Canada." www.pc.gc.ca/eng/lhn-nhs/bc/rogers/edu/edu4.aspx (accessed 3 July 2009).

Canada, Government of. "Statistics Canada: 2006 Community Profiles." www12.statcan.ca/census-recensement/2006/dp-pd/prof/92-591/index.cfm?Lang=E (accessed 3 November 2009).

Canadian Mountain Encyclopedia. www.bivouac.com (accessed 3 November 2009).

Canal Flats, Village of. canalflats.com/index.php?option=com_content&task=vie w&id=30&Itemid=40 (accessed 19 August 2009).

Canim Lake Band. "The Tsq'escenemc: The People of the Broken Rock." www.canimlakeband.com/aboutus.htm (accessed 26 February 2010).

"The Cariboo Community of Likely, British Columbia" www.likely-bc.ca/ (accessed 5 July 2009).

CaribooLINKS Web Publishing. "Canim Lake Band 'Tsqescen." www.cariboolinks.com/ctc/canim/ (accessed 19 August 2009).

Carpenter, Jennifer. "The Heiltsuk Cultural Education Centre." www.hcec.ca/ bellabella.html (accessed 6 September 2009).

Casselman, William Gordon. "Bill Casselman's Canadian Word of the Day and Words of the World." www.billcasselman.com/place_names_of_the_world/ kitsilano_bc.htm (accessed 10 July 2009).

Cedar and Canvas Adventures. "Yukon Canoe Trips." www.cedarcanvas.com/ rivertrips.asp (accessed 20 October 2009).

Chandonnet, Ann. "Native Place Names: Offering Clues to Juneau's Past." *The Juneau Empire* (Juneau, AK). 3 March 2002. JuneauEmpire.com. www.juneauempire.com/stories/030302/Ins_names.shtml (accessed 22 October 2009).

Chemainus Chamber of Commerce Visitor Information Centre. "Chemainus World Famous Murals." www.chemainus.bc.ca (accessed 5 October 2009).

The Children of Fort Langley. www.fortlangley.ca/ (accessed 19 July 2009).

City of Parksville. "History of Parksville." www.city.parksville.bc.ca/cms. asp?wpID=191 (accessed 14 August 2009).

City of Richmond. "City Hall: Archives." www.richmond.ca/cityhall/archives/ about/about.htm (accessed 4 September 2009).

Cleveland Dam and Capilano Regional Park, North Vancouver, British Columbia, Canada. www.greatervancouverparks.com/ClevelandDam01.html (accessed 22 September 2009).

CMHC [Canada Mortgage and Housing Corporation] "Welcome to Granville Island: Island Heritage." www.granvilleisland.com/discover-island/island-heritage (accessed 22 February 2010).

Cochlan, Dave. "LandQuest Realty Corp. Sandspit: Queen Charlotte Islands." www.landquest.com/MNCOAST/Sandspit07002/SandspitWeb.pdf (accessed 6 September 2009).

Community Webpages. "Information About Your Comm-unity." vancouver.ca/ community_profiles/communityList.htm (accessed 5 October 2009).

Craig Heritage Park Museum and Archives. "A Chrono-logical History of Parksville." www.parksvillemuseum.ca/Parksville.htm (accessed 14 August 2009).

Deep Cove Heritage Society. www.deepcovebc.com/deepcovebcheritage.html (accessed 21 August 2009).

Dictionary of Canadian Biography Online. www.biographi.ca/index-e.html. (accessed 3 November 2009).

District of Houston. www.houston.ca/siteengine/activepage.asp?PageID=11 (accessed 15 July 2009).

District of Kent, Agassiz. www.district.kent.bc.ca (accessed 5 October 2009).

District of Sicamous. www.district.sicamous.bc.ca/siteengine/activepage.asp (accessed 24 September 2009).

Ditidaht First Nation. www.ditidaht.ca/history.htm (accessed 2 September 2009).

Doukhobor Genealogy Website. www.doukhobor.org/pn-details.html?rec=392 (accessed 3 August 2009).

Ecole Secondaire Hugh McRoberts Secondary School. "Student Handbook, 2005–2006." www2.sd38.bc.ca/mcroberts-web/agenda.pdf (accessed 4 September 2009).

ECONOMICexpert.com "Wrangell, Alaska." www.economicexpert.com/a/ Wrangell:Alaska.html (accessed 29 September 2009).

Esquimalt, Township of. "Esquimalt History: From Early First Nations Presence to Today." www.esquimalt.ca/files/PDF/Business_and_Development/history_ overview.pdf (accessed 24 August 2009).

First Nation Community of Lax Kw'alaams. www.laxkwalaams.ca/ (accessed 17 August 2009).

Fraser, Alistar B. "Kootenay Lake: Toponymy." kootenay-lake.ca/geography/toponymy/ (accessed 5 September 2009).

Friends of Geographical Names of Alberta. "Peace River." www.placenamesofalberta.ca/300_names_definitions/peaceriver.html (accessed 19 October 2009).

Galleria: Stories of the BC Co-op Movement. "Co-operative Fruit Growers Association of Wynndel." bcics.uvic.ca/galleria/bc.php?group=19&tourtype= 2&story=15 (accessed 18 October 2009).

Gambier Island Community. www.gambierisland.org (accessed 26 February 2010).

G.E. Bridges and Associates, Inc., and Robinson Consulting and Associates. "Northwest BC Mining Projects: Socio-Economic Impact Assessment. July 2005." www.llbc.leg.bc.ca/public/pubdocs/bcdocs/379509/ socio_econ_impact_asses.pdf (accessed 21 February 2010).

Gold Country Community Society. "Adventures in Gold Country: Communities & Map." www.exploregoldcountry.com/communities.php (accessed 5 February 2010).

Great Unsolved Mysteries in Canadian History. "Klatsassin and the Chilcotin War: Tsilhqot[in Culture." www.canadianmysteries.ca/sites/klatsassin/context/ tsilhqotinculture/indexen.html (accessed 28 September 2009).

Greater Vernon Museum and Archives. www.vernonmuseum.ca/search.php#photos (accessed 15 July 2009).

Harrison Heritage House. "101 Things to do in Harrison Hot Springs: Learn Harrison Hot Springs History." www.harrison-hot-springs.com/learn.shtml (accessed 2 October 2009).

Harvey, Athelstan George. "'Jock' Lynn of Lynn Creek." Unpublished manuscript. n.d. [ca. 1945]. Text located in BC Archives, MS1925, Box 26, File 5.) The Royal Engineers in Her Britannic Majesty's Colonies of Vancouver's Island and British Columbia. "Sapper John Linn." www.royalengineers.ca/Linn.html (accessed 12 July 2009).

Heikkila, Karen Ann. "Teaching Through Toponymy: Using Indigenous Place-Names in Outdoor Science Camps." MA thesis. University of British Columbia, 2007. cura.unbc.ca/library/heikkila_thesis_FINAL_protected.pdf (accessed 16 October 2009).

Heritage BC Stops. "K-Shian: The Skeena." www.heritagebcstops.com/ north-by-northwest-tour/k-shian-the-skeena (accessed 29 September 2009).

Heritage Community Foundation and Friends of Geographical Names of Alberta. "Cree Place Names." www.albertasource.ca/Placenames/programs/ cree/names.html (accessed 19 October 2009).

Heritage Community Foundation and Friends of Geographical Names of Alberta "Place Names of Alberta: Shoshone, Kootenay and Crow." www.albertasource. ca/placenames/programs/other/crow.html (accessed 9 September 2009).

Hill's Native Art. "Artists' Bios: Sid Lamarche." www.hillsnativeart.com/artists/ biosdetail.php?recordIDArtistsDetail=0163 (accessed 10 July 2009).

Hul'qumi'num Treaty Group. "Hul'qumi'num People." www.hulquminum.bc.ca/ hulquminum_people/ (accessed 20 August 2009).

Historical Map Society of British Columbia. 137.82.96.56/browse/map/id_2589/ (accessed 29 September 2009).

Hudson's Bay Company. www.hbc.com/hbcheritage/ (accessed 13 August 2009).

Humphreys, Danda. "Who Put The 'Pat' in Pat Bay?" Excerpted from *On The Street Where You Live: Pioneer Pathways of Early Victoria*. Surrey: Heritage House, 1999. www.vancouverisland.com/guestwriters/?id=30 (accessed 14 July 2009).

Info Vancouver. "The Sights and Sounds of Vancouver: Kitsilano." www. infovancouver.com/things-to-see-and-do/greater-vancouver/kitsilano (accessed 15 July 2009).

I-Hos Gallery. www.ihosgallery.com/history.html (accessed 26 February 2010).

Ka:'yu:'k't'h/Che: k:tle7et'h' (Kyuquot/Checleseht). www.kyuquot.ca/people.html (accessed 20 July 2009).

Kaska Dene Council. www.kaskadenacouncil.com (accessed 22 September 2009).

Keremeos: The Fruit Stand Capital of Canada. keremeos.net/history.html (accessed 21 February 2010).

Kidfish. "First Nations Perspective: The Carrier Dene People of North Central BC." www.kidfish.bc.ca/first_nations/names.htm (accessed 27 August 2009).

Kitsilano.net. "My Neighbourhood." www.kitsilano.net/kits.htm. (accessed 15 July 2009).

Kitsilano 4th Avenue Business Associaton. www.kitsilano4thavenue.com/History (accessed 4 July 2009).

K'ómoks First Nation. www.comoxband.ca/ (accessed 22 September 2009).

Koop, Will. "Red Fish Up the River: A Report on the Former Coquitlam Salmon Migrations and the Hydro-Electric Developments at Coquitlam Lake, British Columbia, Pre-1914." www.bchydro.com/bcrp/reports/docs/ RedFishUpTheRiver.pdf (accessed 11 September 2009).

Kootenay Lake. www.kootenay-lake.ca (accessed 23 October 2009).

Kootenay Lake. "Kootenay, Kootenai: A Note About Names." www. greatcanadianlakes.com/british_columbia/kootenay/culture-home.html (accessed 3 August 2009).

Kwikwetlem First Nation. www.kwikwetlem.com/home (accessed 11 September 2009).

Lake Babine Nation. "Member Bands." www.lakebabine.com/nation/382/member+bands (accessed 5 July 2009).

Lake Country Museum. "Our History: Historical Map, 1850–2005." www.lakecountrymuseum.com/history-map.php (accessed 18 July 2009).

Lake Lubbers. "Lake Osoyoos." www.lakelubbers.com/lake-osoyoos-913/ (accessed 13 October 2009).

Lambert Lake Inn. www.lambertlakeinn.ca/history.html (accessed 24 September 2009).

Lions Bay, The Municipality of the Village of. www.lionsbay.ca/page/page/508347.htm (accessed 20 July 2009).

Logan, Don. "Pioneers and Early Settlers: Savona's Ferry." Gold Country GeoTourism Program. www.geotourismcanada.com/doc_download. aspx?document_id=249 (accessed 15 February 2010).

Lone Wolf Law Enforcement Memorabilia. "History of Canada Customs." members.shaw.ca/customs/History/BCPorts/ (accessed 4 September 2009).

Lundberg, Murray. "The History of Fort St. John, British Columbia." explorenorth.com/library/communities/canada/bl-ftstjohnhistory.htm (accessed 26 February 2010).

Lundy, Darryl. ThePeerage.com: A Genealogical Survey of the Peerage of Britain as Well as the Royal Families of Europe. www.thepeerage.com/ (accessed 9 July 2009).

Maple Ridge, British Columbia. www.mapleridge.ca/EN/main/ municipal/728/4605/4783/Heritage_Resources_booklet.html (accessed 26 August 2009).

McKay, Alice (Chief of the Matsqui First Nation), correspondence to Brian Murphy (Project Assessment Director, ILM Project, Environmental Assessment Office, Province of British Columbia), 23 January 2009. a100. gov.bc.ca/appsdata/epic/documents/p290/1233255786112_1e456ef13441 2e3201c3f0558895f4db4930ba1c89afee761cb2b65ae1ffae88.pdf (accessed 30 September 2009).

Malahat First Nation. www.malahatnation.ca/ (accessed 6 July 2009).

Maple Ridge Museum and Community Archives. www.mapleridgemuseum. org/08_community/08_neighbourhood.html (accessed 26 August 2009).

Masset, The Village of. www.massetbc.com/html/history.html (accessed 14 July 2009).

Miller, Ilana D. "…I Danced With a Man Who Danced With a Girl Who Danced With the Prince of Wales… or 'Bertie's Long Vacation.'" European Royal History Journal (April, 2001). www.directarticle.org/Bertie.pdf (accessed 5 September 2009).

Mission District Historical Society. "Heritage Places: Dewdney Community." www.missiondhs.com/heritageplaces/initiatives/profiles/DewdneyComm. html (accessed 21 August 2009).

Montemurro, Loretta. "Sparwood." www.travel-british-columbia.com/ kootenay_rockies/sparwood.aspx (accessed 9 October 2009).

Montrose, The Village of. www.montrose.ca/community/history.php (accessed 15 July 2009).

Mowachaht/Muchalaht First Nation. "Yuquot." www.yuquot.ca/yuquot.html (accessed 26 August 2009).

MSA Museum Society. "Origin of the Name 'Abbotsford.'" www.msamuseum.ca/index.php/general-information/general-abbotsford-history/50-origin-of-the-name-qabbotsfordq (accessed 5 July 2009).

Murray, John. "Early Australian Adventures: 4.3 The Lady Nelson Under Lt. J. Murray: 'Log Book' Review of Two Bays." www.earlyaustralianadventures.com.au/index.php?page=4-3-the-lady-nelson-under-lt-john-murray-log-book-review-of-two-bays (accessed 24 February 2010).

Nanoose First Nation. www.nanoose.org (accessed 12 July 2009).

National Museum of the American Indian. "The Kwakwaka'wakw: A Study of a North Pacific Coast People and the Potlatch." www.nmai.si.edu/education/files/Kwak_Poster_TG.pdf (accessed 28 August 2009).

Nisga'a Lismis Government. "About Nisga'a Lismis Government." www.nisgaalisims.ca/about-nisgaa-lisims-government (accessed 18 July 2009).

Nootka Sound Service, Ltd. "Early Exploration." www.mvuchuck.com/early-bc-exploration.php (accessed 24 July 2009).

North Vancouver, District of. "District History." www.dnv.org/article.asp?c=465 (accessed 15 July 2009).

Ocean Falls Economic Development Committee. www.traveloceanfalls.com (accessed 9 July 2009).

Olalla, British Columbia, Canada. keremeos.net/olalla/ (accessed 16 July 2009).

Okanagan Archive Trust Society: Oldphotos.ca. www.oldphotos.ca/how_naramata_got_its_name.php (accessed 21 February 2010).

Peeohpeeoh. www.fortlangley.ca/Peopeoh.html (accessed 26 August 2009).

Pemberton, Village of. www.pemberton.ca/index.php?option=com_content&task=view&id=66&Itemid=338 (accessed 14 August 2009).

Poser, William J. "The Names of the First Nations Languages of British Columbia." www.billposer.org/Papers/bclgnames.pdf (accessed 6 September 2009).

Purdy, Reg. "Mexican Tom and The Kid." 1985. Transcribed by Bernice Frizzle. The Stillwater Woods Blog, posted 7 April 2009. stillwoods.blogspot.com/2009_04_01_archive.html (accessed 18 February 2010).

Reed, Michael P. "The Intrepid Mrs. Sally James Farnham: An American Sculptor Rediscovered." Aristos website. www.aristos.org/aris-07/farnham.htm (accessed 21 February 2010).

Revelstoke Museum and Archives. www.revelstokemuseum.ca/history.html (accessed 4 September 2009).

Ringuette, Janis. "Beacon Hill Park History, 1842–2008." Beacon Hill Park History website. www.beaconhillparkhistory.org/ (accessed 8 July 2009).

Riondel, British Columbia. www.riondel.ca/pagefour.htm (accessed 4 September 2009).

Rochon, Lisa. "The Stones of Banff." Alpine Club of Canada website. www.alpineclubofcanada.ca/facility/abbot-article.html (accessed 26 February 2010).

Russell, Michael. "British Columbia: The Story of Canal Flats." www.gb.ro/index.php?action=showam&id=273677 (accessed 19 August 2009).

shíshálh first nation: Sechelt First Nation. www.secheltnation.ca/ (accessed 13 July 2009).

Sicamous and District Chamber of Commerce. www.sicamouschamber.bc.ca/html/history.html (accessed 24 September 2009).

Silverton, British Columbia. www.silverton.ca/ (accessed 12 July 2009).

Skidegate Band Council. "Visiting Skidegate." www.skidegate.ca/Pages/VisitingSkg.html (accessed 27 September 2009).

Steveston Museum. "Steveston Recollections: The History of a Village. Miss Lulu Sweet." www.virtualmuseum.ca/pm.php?id=record_detail&fl=&lg=English&ex=00000127&rd=63041 (accessed 12 July 2009).

Stewart, John. "Sport Fishing in the Kamloops Region." www.city.kamloops.bc.ca/museum/archives/pdfs/N280%20-%20Sport%20Fishing%20in%20the%20Kamloops%20Region.pdf (accessed 8 July 2009).

Swanson, James L. "Spiral Road: Place Names in the Canadian Rockies." www.spiralroad.com/sr/pn/ (accessed 3 November 2009).

Syilx: Okanagan Nation Alliance. www.syilx.org/history-history.php (accessed 9 October 2009).

Sydenham, Michael J., and Jean A. Sydenham. "Sir Evan Nepean." Nepean Museum website. nepeanmuseum.ca/collection/sir_evan_nepean.php (accessed 1 September 2009).

Tahsis, Village of. www.villageoftahsis.com (accessed 5 September 2009).

Taylor, District of. www.districtoftaylor.com/history.shtml (accessed 7 October 2009).

Telkwa, Village of. www.telkwa.com/html/history.htm (accessed 7 October 2009).

Thom, Brian. "Ethnographic Overview of Stó:lo People and the Traditional Use of the Hudson's Bay Company Brigade Trail Area." home.istar.ca/~bthom/trail-hbc.htm (accessed 27 September 2009).

Til, Heather. "Sechelt History." Bigpacific.com website. www.bigpacific.com/sechelt/history.html (accessed 18 July 2009).

Thompson-Nicola Regional District. "Discover Thompson-Nicola: Clearwater Community Profile." www.discoverthompson-nicola.com/communityProfiles/clearwaterProfile.pdf (accessed 20 August 2009).

Tofino Internet Services Ltd. "Tofino Guide." www.tofino-bc.com/about/tofino-history.php (accessed 8 October 2009).

TourismBC. "Regions and Cities." www.hellobc.com/en-CA/RegionsCities/BritishColumbia.htm (accessed 3 November 2009).

Tourism Bowen. www.bowenisland.org (accessed 29 September 2009).

Tourism Chilliwack. www.tourismchilliwack.com/content.php?pageID=27 (accessed 10 September 2009).

Tourism Kamloops. "The Geography of Kamloops." www.tourismkamloops.com/home_showSection_ID_608.html (accessed 27 August 2009).

Tourism Yukon. "Teslin: Teslin Tlingit Council." travelyukon.com/aboutyukonterritory/yukoncommunities/teslin/teslinfirstnations/ (accessed 20 October 2009).

Travel British Columbia. "Bowser." www.travel-british-columbia.com/vancouver_island_and_the_gulf_islands/bowser.aspx (accessed 5 September 2009).

T'Sou-ke Nation. www.tsoukenation.com/ (accessed 9 October 2009).

United States Geographical Service. "United States Board on Geographic Names." geonames.usgs.gov/ (accessed 3 November 2009).

VancouverIsland.com. www.vancouverisland.com/Regions/ (accessed 3 November 2009).

Virtual Crowsnest Highway. www.crowsnest-highway.ca/index.htm (accessed 15 September 2009).

Virtual Museum of Canada. "Valemount & Area Museum, Valemount, British Columbia." www.virtualmuseum.ca/pm_v2.php?id=story_line_index&fl=0&lg=English&ex=00000321&pos=1 (accessed 2 September 2009).

Virtual Tourist. "Whitehorse–Skagway Highway Scenes" a Skagway Travel Page by jamiesno." members.virtualtourist.com/m/tt/4f284/ (accessed 7 September 2009).

Wasden, William, Jr. "Kwakwaka'wakw Dances and Dancing: Why We Dance." www.native-dance.ca/index.php/Kwakwaka'wakw/Why_We_Dance?tp=z&bg=5&ln=e&gfx=h&wd=2 (accessed 3 September 2009).

Wells Historical Society and Wells Museum. "Mining the Motherlode: Introduction to Cariboo's Second Gold Rush." wellsmuseum.ca/town.htm (accessed 26 August 2009).

West Chilcotin Tourism Association. www.visitthewestchilcotin.com/Chilcotin-History.html (accessed 11 September 2009).

Wonder, Karen. "First Nations Land Rights and Environmentalism in British Columbia: Fisheries. Kwakwaka'wakw. www.firstnations.eu/fisheries/kwakwakawakw.htm (accessed 3 September 2009).

Wonder, Karen. First Nations Land Rights and Environmentalism in British Columbia: Development. St'át'imc. www.firstnations.de/development/statimc.htm (accessed 6 September 2009).

Wynton, Angela. "Pioneers and Early Settlers: Logan Lake Pioneers." Gold Country GeoTourism Program. www.geotourismcanada.com/doc_download.aspx?document_id=235 (accessed 26 February 2010).

Yahk-Kingsgate Recreation Society. "History of Yahk." yahkkingsgate.homestead.com/current.html#anchor_29 (accessed 25 August 2009).

Yahk Kingsgate Newsletters. yahkkingsgate.homestead.com/Newsletter-1.html (accessed 25 August 2009).

Yinka Déné Language Institute. "The Chilcotin Language." www.ydli.org/langs/chilcotin.htm (accessed 28 September 2009).

Yinka Déné Language Institute. "The Coast Tsimshian Language." www.ydli.org/langs/coastsim.htm (accessed 9 October 2009).

Yukon Tourism and Culture. "Sights and Sites: Yukon Point of Interest Signage." www.yukonheritage.com/Sign/ (accessed 20 October 2009).

Mark Thorburn loves history and is the author of the bestselling *Bathroom Book of British Columbia History*. He has contributed to and edited several history textbooks and references and has written for newspapers all across North America. Mark has lived life as a lawyer and college instructor, as well as a historian and writer. He has a broad educational background, with a BA in political science, a law degree and two MA degrees in Canadian and American history. In his free time, Mark reads great books, goes to the theatre, watches classic movies and listens to Celtic music. He also likes hanging out at some of Vancouver's well-known spots, including Gastown, Granville Island, Robson Street and Stanley Park.